The Watcher's Guide

MILLIONS VANISHED

BRIAN PAUL LAKINS

All Scripture quotations contain the
OLD AND NEW TESTAMENTS
of the
AUTHORIZED OR KING JAMES VERSION TEXT
Always read next to an open Bible (Acts 17:11; 1 Thess. 5:21; 2 Tim. 2:15)

Copyright © 2016 Brian Lakins

All rights reserved. No part of this publication may be reproduced, distributed, or transmitted in any form or by any means, including photocopying, recording, or other electronic or mechanical methods, without the prior written permission of the publisher, except in the case of brief quotations embodied in reviews and certain other non-commercial uses permitted by copyright law.

www.MillionsVanished.com
For more information, please email: ***1thes4.16@gmail.com***

Cover Design and Interior Layout *&* Design by
Quest Publications
Website: ***www.questpub.questforgod.org***
Email: ***questpublications@outlook.com***

Published By:
Quest Publications
6-176 Henry Street
Brantford, ON, N3S 5C8
Canada

ISBN-13: 978-1-988439-05-1

DEDICATION

Years of faithful watching for the coming of our Lord is both exciting and and depressing. Any watcher understands this to be true. There's been moments in time when all signs pointed to the immediate rapture of the saints. Utter despair follows utter joy when the hope you have has not been exchanged for a crown. Enduring another year is agonizing when you believe you're about to see heaven's door open. This book is dedicated to all the watchers of old whose oil has not run out. He is coming soon!

Contents

Chapter 1—WHY WE WATCH 1

Chapter 2—ARE YOU CHASING THE STAR? 5

Chapter 3—FEASTS OF THE LORD / APPOINTED TIMES 18
    Appointed Times with God 25
    Future Fulfillment's For The Feasts 30
    Rapture On The Feast Of Trumpets 31
    Second Coming On The Day Of Atonement 37
    Millennial Reign Begins
    On The feast Of Tabernacles 41

Chapter 4—UNDERSTANDING THE RAPTURE / TRIBULATION GAP 46

Chapter 5—BOOK 2's COVER UNVEILED 50

Chapter 6—THE DOCTRINE OF IMMINENCY 57

Chapter 7—AM I DATE-SETTING? 63

Chapter 8—THAT DAY AND HOUR KNOWETH NO MAN 68
    Does Jesus Not Know the Rapture Day 75
    The dead church is not watchful 84
    The lukewarm church is not watching 85

Chapter 9—EVENTS PEOPLE ARE WAITING ON BEFORE THE RAPTURE 86
    1. The Day of the Saints 87
    2. Sudden Destruction 98
    3. A Great Revival 100
    4. A United Church 101
    5. The Wealth Of The Wicked 103
    6. The Fullness Of The Gentiles 108

Chapter 10—FOUNDATIONS FOR BUILDING A BIBLICAL TIME-LINE 112
    1. Names and Time Frames for the 7 Year Tribulation .. 113
    2. 1,260; 1,290; 1,335 Days of Daniel 12 122
    3. 2,300 Days of Daniel 8:14 123
    4. Will The Days Be Shortened? 125
    5. Understanding the Order of the Book of Revelation 129
    6. End-Times 136
    7. War Of Gog And Magog 138
    8. Two Witnesses 144
    9. Sun-Clothed Woman 156
    10. 144,000 161
    11. Babylon 163
    12. The Day of the Lord 165

Chapter 11—PUTTING TOGETHER THE BIBLICAL TIME-LINE 170
    I. 2016 – 2023 Timeline 170

Chapter 12—WHEN IS THE RAPTURE? 180
    Shemitah 188
    Jubilee Years (a year of restoration) 196

Chapter 13—HOW TO BE READY 199
    1. Basic Salvation Knowledge 200
    2. Can The Left Behind Still Be Saved? 202
    3. Suicide 204
    4. Qualifications for Partakers in the Rapture 211
    5. Reasons For Being Left Behind 212

INTRODUCTION

The gospel is good news. It's about a relationship, not a list of dos and do nots." This is what we hear from the pulpit. This is what the multitudes proclaim on Christian forums and Christian circles. It's true that the gospel means good news, and it surely is what it proclaims of itself.

There are those that would reduce the gospel to John 1:1 – John 3:16, and then onto the crucifixion, burial, resurrection, and ascension (Isa. 52:14; 53:1-12; Jn. 19:17-37; Acts 1:10-11; 1 Cor. 15:3-8; Rev. 1:7, 18). This gives us the beginning of Christ in the ageless past, His deity (Rev. 1:8, 11; 21:6; 22:13), and that He will come back just as easily as He left (Jn. 1:1; Rev. 1:7, 17; Acts 1:10-11 19:11-16). According to modern teachings, the epistles really tell Christians nothing else that they need to know. At least, that's what is implied.

Warnings to the righteous are reduced to warnings to the non-believers. Anything and everything that brings a negative connotation is shot down as bad news and offensive, therefore not gospel, because the gospel means good news. The gospel's commandments are seen as desires, not something God requires. There are 1,050 commands in the New Testament alone, yet modern Christendom has downplayed them to the point of accusing those of us who teach them to be preaching the Mosaic Law. This is not so. I am no Pharisee, nor are we legalistic.

Out of all these commands given to us that make up our covenant made by the blood of Christ (Mat. 26:28), there is one that is unknown to most the Christian world. This command is to watch. Followers of Christ are told to be watchers (Mk. 13:34-37; Lk. 21:36). The command is two-fold. We must watch for the return of the Lord, whether it be the coming for the saints in the air (Jn. 14:1-3; Lk. 21:34-36; 1 Cor. 15:23,51-54; Eph. 5:27; Phil. 3:21; 1

Thess. 4:13-18; 5:1-11; 2 Thess. 2:7-8; Col. 3:4; Jas. 5:7-8; 1 Jn. 3:1-3), or with the saints to the earth (Zech. 14:5; Mt. 24:29-31; 2 Thess. 1:7-10; Jude 14-15; Rev. 19:11-21).

Ignorantly, people bring doubt to true watching and seek to bring mockery and disgrace to the watchers by proclaiming their common arguments. They are not the enemy. They are needing someone to be the town clown for them so some may have the devil's blindfold taken off their eyes. If we are worried about our image, then some will not believe, because we were not teaching. Today's clowns will be eternity's champions. We are at war.

When you're accused of chasing the rapture instead of chasing Jesus, or looking for the Antichrist instead of looking for Jesus, just tell them you are searching for the King. Isn't that what the magi did? The magi are known as the "three" wise men, though their number is not truly known. There are multiple scriptures on every subject in the Bible, and all end-time subjects have their place, lest the Holy Spirit inspired men to give future generations useless information.

"Looking for that blessed hope, and the glorious appearing of the great God and our Saviour Jesus Christ" (Tit. 2:13). People looked for the rapture in that day, proving there is no definite time element in Scripture for this event as pertaining to the year (Tit. 2:12; Phil. 3:20). It seems that looking for the rapture is a righteous act (Mark 13:34-37) and not separate from preaching righteousness (Titus 2:11-12).

> For the grace of God that bringeth salvation hath appeared to all men, Teaching us that, denying ungodliness and worldly lusts, we should live soberly, righteously, and godly, in this present world; Looking for that blessed hope, and the glorious appearing of the great God and our Saviour Jesus Christ; Looking for that blessed hope, and the glorious appearing of the great God and our Saviour Jesus Christ (Tit. 2:11-13).

We may not know the exact day or year, but you'll be surprised at what you don't know that you don't know that you can know! Hindsight is 50/50. Jesus fulfilled the first few feasts of the Lord as given in Leviticus 23. The last three feasts have not been fulfilled, but hindsight reveals that they will be. Prophecy is simple history told before it happens. We don't know the day or the year, but we can know the day of the unknown year. This will become clear.

People get discouraged with the encouraging. By proclaiming the biblical truth that Jesus is coming back soon, people say, "Yeah, but I've heard that my whole life. People even believed that in the 1st century." For me, that is even more encouraging (1 Thess. 4:18). If it's been so long a time from those written words, then how close are we now? Maybe even at the door. Jesus gave us the command to watch (Mk. 13:34-37), but few understand how to go about watching for the nearness of the return of the Lord, both in the air for the saints, and to the earth with the saints. This book will teach you how to watch for Jesus, just as we are told to do.

CHAPTER 1

WHY WE WATCH

There are 1,050 commands in the New Testament. One of the most simple of them all is the one word directive from Jesus. That word is watch. Though uncomplicated in concept, the application falls to the way side. No one really understands what Jesus means by this command. The majority of people believe it's wrong to even look for the rapture or the Second Coming, because no one knows the day or hour. So then, why are we told to watch?

Watching is verb. It expresses action on our part. To obey this command means we must be alert, watchful, spiritually awake and not asleep. Though simple, staying awake is neither easy nor common. The command has been given to us all, yet few have the desire that burns in the watcher; yet is ridiculed by most the Christian communities, making even a watcher feel like an outcast among a people of outcasts (Christians). Nevertheless, the truth is still speaking!

> Take ye heed, watch and pray: for ye know not when the time is. For the Son of man is as a man taking a far journey, who left his house, and gave authority to his servants, and to every man his work, and commanded the porter to watch. Watch ye therefore: for ye know not when the master of the house cometh, at even, or at midnight, or at the cockcrowing, or in the morning: Lest coming suddenly he find you sleeping. And what I say unto you I say unto all, Watch (Mk. 13:33-37).

But, what do we watch? It is the signs of the master's coming spoken to us as clear as day by men inspired by the Holy Spirit (2 Tim. 3:16-17; 2 Pt. 1:19-21). Where do we look for these signs? They are foretold and sprinkled throughout all of the Scriptures and they will be evident, both in the heavens and on the earth. How we watch is to be awake to the signs by remaining steadfast in the teachings of the entire Bible. We must remain vigilant and ever seeking God in heart, soul, mind, and strength. Always abounding more and more in wisdom, knowledge, and understanding.

As Gary Stearman wrote in his Prophecy In The News magazine, "Indeed, there is even a special blessing for those who diligently attempt to unravel the timing enigmas of Christ's coming for the church. As Paul wrote in 2 Timothy 4:8, 'Henceforth there is laid up for me a crown of righteousness, which the Lord, the righteous judge, shall give me at that day: and not to me only, but unto all them also that love his appearing.' Not everyone loves His appearing with such zeal that they are deeply motivated to study prophecy. Some, however, take Scripture at face value, and find it natural to follow a line of thinking that leads to discernment of the times and seasons. This is not a bad thing. Quite the contrary, the Bible urges watchfulness."

> Therefore be on the alert, for you do not know which day your Lord is coming. But be sure of this, that if the head of the house had known at what time of the night the thief was coming, he would have been on the alert and would not have allowed his house to be broken into. For this reason you also must be ready; for the Son of Man is coming at an hour when you do not think He will (Mat. 24:42-44).

> There will be great earthquakes, famines and pestilences in various places, and fearful events and great signs from heaven (Lk. 21:11).

Why We Watch

What are these great signs we're to look for in the heavens? .... We'll get into that later. There are many exciting and dreadful things coming that have been and are all being highly talked about among prophecy watchers, but we must first lay many other foundations. Some of these subjects I'm bringing will demand hours of teaching, for there are days upon days of information about them, but time is scarce. I've done my best to compile some of the richest knowledge of each subject for this book while leaving out the extra filler when at all possible.

Ladies and gentlemen, you are about to review the finest teaching of the end-times you've ever read before. What I'm going to be giving you in this teaching is a very specific time period to be watching for, as all the signs are pointing there. Take heart and take notice that I will not give a Harold Camping rapture day. I am merely presenting the possibility and probability that the rapture, the end of the church age and the beginning of Daniel's 70th Week, which is the 7 Year Tribulation, is right at the door.

When we see the conditions of a great storm coming, we issue a tornado watch, in that it is not an absolute, but the conditions and signs are all there. A tornado warning means that it is an absolute that a tornado has formed. I'm issuing evidence from many biblical subjects and clues that all deserve the call of the watchman that says, "We have a major rapture watch in full affect!"

Read attentively and discern for yourselves. Be a good Berean (Acts 17:11). Don't take my word for it. Search these things out to see if they are true. There are many, many subjects to discuss, but my secret ambition for this is not to tell you when the rapture is, but to make you aware that it is much, much sooner than you think. And above all things, whether the end of this age is today or many years from now, I want to make sure you are ready. Jesus is coming back for the glorious church, not the sleeping church (Eph. 5:27).

Jesus will only catch the ones off guard (He will only come as a thief) to those who are sleeping, dead, in sin, lukewarm, not sober, not enduring on the narrow path that's not paved with sin, not continuing in holiness, not abiding in sound doctrine, not remaining in righteousness and truth, not watching. These are the ones who will be caught off guard when the Master comes. In their hearts they have said their Master has delayed His coming. They are not fighting the desires of their flesh (Gal. 5:16-26; Jas. 1:13-16). They are not resisting the devil so he will flee (Jas. 4:7; 1 Pt. 5:6-9). They are not taking their thoughts captive and following the Holy Spirit (2 Cor. 10:5; Rom. 8:1-16). They believe they have time to repent later. I'm happy to see you faithfully watching for the coming of our Master, just as we have been commanded to do so.

> The lord of that servant shall come in a day when he looketh not for him, and in an hour that he is not aware of, And shall cut him in pieces, and appoint him his portion with the hypocrites: there shall be weeping and gnashing of teeth (Mat. 24:50; Lk. 12:46).

There is another application to watchfulness found in Scripture. Watching is two-fold. Take heed to yourselves, or be on guard! We are exhorted to be in a high state of spiritual alertness. The church is asleep in most places. Believers were commanded by Paul to awake to righteousness and stop sinning (1 Cor. 15:33-34). They did not literally go to sleep, it was a spiritual slumber. If language in Scripture is metaphoric, symbolic, or figurative, then find the literal truth conveyed. Here is what "sleep" indicates when pertaining to believers who have never died. They became desensitized or deadened to their relationship with Jesus. They are not overcomers of sin (Rev. 2:7, 11, 17, 26; 3:5, 12, 21), not enduring to be saved (Mat. 10:22; 1 Cor. 9:24-27; 2 Tim. 4:8; Heb. 12:1-8; Jas. 1:1-16), not living righteous (Rom. 8:1-13; Gal. 5:16-26), and are workers of iniquity not doing the will of God (Mat. 7:21-23; Lk. 6:46; Jas. 1:22-25).

Chapter 2

ARE YOU CHASING THE STAR?

The wise men understood why they were chasing a star. It wasn't the star they wanted, it was the Redeemer, the Messiah, the Son of God in the flesh. These wise men of untold number were looking for the First Coming. Their diligence brought them to God. They received their reward.

You understand what it means to be chasing a star or you would not have chosen this book. Few people in the faith actually have the desire to study prophecy with the understanding and watchfulness the Holy Spirit inspired. You have no less wisdom than the wise men had if you are diligently seeking God, not just in His ways, but also in watching for His Second Coming. You will receive your reward. We aren't literally chasing a star, but we are figuratively chasing a star. We can learn much by the success of the wise men's watching. Read on...

> Cast not away therefore your confidence, which hath great recompence of reward. For ye have need of patience, that, after ye have done the will of God, ye might receive the promise. For yet a little while, and he that shall come will come, and will not tarry. Now the just shall live by faith: but if any man draw back, my soul shall have no pleasure in him. But we are not of them who draw back unto perdition; but of them that believe to the saving of the soul (Heb. 10:35-39).

Seven main dispensations of man have been revealed in Scripture from Adam until the end of the Millennial Reign, or the Dispensation of Divine Government. These come between the Dispensation of Angels, known as the Ante-Chaotic Age, and the Dispensation of Faithful Angels and the Redeemed Humans, which begins after the Great White Throne Judgment at the end of the Millennial Reign.

The Ante-Chaotic Age finds it's dispensation in the eternal past (Gen. 1:1; Job 38:4-7; Isa. 14:12-14; Ezek. 28:11-17). How long this age lasted is not known to man, nor do we have any idea of when it began. The Dispensation of Faithful Angels and Redeemed Man finds it's time in the eternal future (Rev. 21-22; Isa. 66:22-24; 2 Pt. 3:13). As far as we see from Scripture, this dispensation truly does have no end (Dan. 7:18).

Seven dispensations in human history have come between the eternal past and the eternal future; between the creation of man in the six days of Genesis 1-2 and the final restoration of man in the New Heavens and the New Earth of Revelation 21 – Revelation 22. The seven dispensations are now now listed and referenced: The Dispensation of Innocence (Gen. 2:15 – 3:21); The Dispensation of Conscience (Gen. 3:22 - 8:14). This age was from the fall of man and his banishment from the Garden of Eden to the Flood of Noah and lasted 1,656 years; The Dispensation of Human Government (Gen. 8:15 - 11:32). This age was from the Flood of Noah to the call of Abraham and lasted 427 years.

The Dispensation of Promise (Gen. 12:1 - Ex. 12:37). This age was from the call of Abraham to the exodus of Israel from Egypt under Moses and lasted 430 years; The Dispensation of Law (Ex. 12:38 - Mt. 2:23; 11:10-13; Lk. 16:16). This age was from the exodus of Israel from Egypt under Moses to the preaching of the kingdom of heaven by John the Baptist; or from Moses to the First Coming of Jesus Christ, a period of over 1,718 years; The Dispensation of Grace (Mt. 3:1 - Rev. 19:10). This age has already lasted nearly 2,000 years from the First Coming of Christ, and it will proceed until the Second Coming of Christ in the soon coming future. How much longer the will age last is what watchers search tirelessly for; The Dispensation of Divine Government, or the Millennium (Rev. 19:11 - 20:15). This age will cover the period from the Second Coming of Christ to the last rebellion of Satan, demons, fallen angels, man, and any other ungodly hybrids on the earth, a period of 1,000 years (Rev. 20:1-10).

Angels rejoiced when God created the earth and hung it on nothing (Job 38:4-7). They were there in the Ante-Chaotic Age, or Dispensation of Angels. For as long as there has been an earth, even an unknown amount of time before this, there have been ages and dispensations. The average person is only aware of natural times and seasons, but there are also definite times and seasons for preordained events in God's eternal plan. To the average person it may seem that everything is moving normal as it ever was, but they don't see the climax of our existence that's peaking it's head around the corner. Can you see it? You will!

The plan of God has definite appointed times. Jesus made five references to the end of the world, which should have been more accurately translated by the King James translators as the end of this age. [world] Greek: aion (GSN-<G165>), age; a period of time whether long or short. The earth and man will continue forever (Gen. 8:22; 9:12; Eccl. 1:4; Ps. 104:5; Isa. 9:6-7; Dan. 7:13-14; Rev. 11:15; 21:3 - 22:5). Jesus was referring to the end of the age, the Church Age, not the end of the world (Mat. 12:32; 13:39-40, 49; 24:3; 28:20). Are you ready to learn how to watch the signs given to man from God for our security, hope, and awareness?

The Age of Pisces is the shortest cycle and began around 26 AD, which is when Jesus began His earthly ministry if many scholars are correct in calculating His birth at 4 BC. God doesn't want us ignorant and blind, Satan does. Astronomy is of God and foretells His appointed times. We are beginning the astronomical Age of Aquarius, the next age. The enemy knows dispensations, ages, and prophecy

(Mat. 8:29; Rev. 12:12). The wise men knew by the times and a star when Christ's First Coming was (Mat. 2:1-10). There are three times more writings on the Second Coming than the First Coming. Jesus rebuked those who did not discern the signs of the time as well as they could discern the natural seasons (Mat. 16:1-3). Jesus knew the 7 feasts of the Lord found in Leviticus 23 were appointed times to be fulfilled by Him (Mat. 16:21; 26:2; Gen. 1:14; Col. 2:16-17). The feast of trumpets is the next feast to be fulfilled, ending the church age, beginning The Seven Year Tribulation shortly there after.

Just like a woman knows she must travail if she is with child but knows not the day or the hour, so it is with the coming of our Lord (Mt. 24:36, 39, 42-51; 25:13). A woman knows the season, about nine months. A watcher knows the season, and we've been watching for years. We know the day and the hour of the rapture, but not the year. In Colossians 2:16-17, we're reminded that the feasts and Sabbaths are a shadow of things to come. In Matthew 16:3, Jesus rebukes the Pharisees as hypocrites for not discerning signs of the times as prophesied in Scripture regarding His coming.

Were these Feasts of the Lord (Lev. 23) only meant to be sacrificial offerings of bulls & goats, or were they a foreshadow / typology of God's redemptive plan? Feasts… aka Solemn Appointed Times of the Lord that will be fulfilled (Lev. 23:1-4). The Hebrew word translated "Feasts" means "Appointed Times". According to Deuteronomy 16:16, God commands Israel to keep His Feasts and appear before the Lord with thanksgiving "forever" (Ex. 12:14). In Zechariah 14, it seems even the gentiles are to keep them. All of these great feast days find their fulfillment in the events of the First Coming to the events of the Second Coming (Gen. 1:14; Mat. 8:29; Acts 17:26). Many have said the rapture will happen on this or that date and they aren't date-setting, they are date finding. They spoke as watchers, but were unwise by speaking with an absolute.

> For the vision is yet for an appointed time, but at the end it shall speak, and not lie: though it tarry, wait for it; because it will surely come, it will not tarry (Hab. 2:3).

The vision referred to is speaking of the Second Coming. It is an appointed time, not an unknown time that will happen after the church has done it's part to enable Christ to come to earth again. No, not that! The church will not be unified, the wealth of the wicked will not come to righteous, nor will their be a great revival before the rapture can happen. People believe certain things must come to pass before the rapture can happen, and then the Second Coming will happen seven years later. By those implications, the Second Coming would not have an appointed day. More on this in chapter 9.

2014 - 2015 held the forth set of back to back blood-red moons on Passover (Lev. 23:4-5) and Tabernacles (Lev. 23:33-44) in more than 500 years. This is the 8th occurrence of this kind since 1 A.D. The last three of these occurrences were connected to the Jewish people: 1492 (The Spanish Inquisition), 1948 (Statehood for Israel and the War of Independence), and 1967 (The Six-Day War). All major prophecies have been fulfilled except the ones to be fulfilled in the last 7 years of this dispensation. As we know, God reveals His plans of the ages to his prophets and His people before He takes action.

> Surely the Lord GOD will do nothing, but he revealeth his secret unto his servants the prophets (Amos 3:7).

We don't have all the details of everything we can think to ask, but God's plans, His ways, His order, His dispensations have all been foretold in the Word. I'll give some examples of people knowing the time and ask you this, "Now wouldn't it stand to reason that the end-time events to come would be put more into focus the closer we are to them?" Of course we don't lean on our own understanding, so what has God said about it?

There has been more written about the Second Coming than of the First Coming, three times more. Enoch 1:9, quoted in Jude 14-15 speaks of the Second Coming before the First Coming and it is the oldest book we know of to date. The people of Christ's First Coming were rebuked for not being able to discern the times. They discerned the physical signs of the weather, but not spiritual signs.

> And he said also to the people, When ye see a cloud rise out of the west, straightway ye say, There cometh a shower; and so it is. And when ye see the south wind blow, ye say, There will be heat; and it cometh to pass. Ye hypocrites, ye can discern the face of the sky and of the earth; but how is it that ye do not discern this time (Lk. 12:54-56; cpl w/ Mat.16:1-3)?

Again, this was the First Coming and there is three times more written of concerning the Second Coming and the events surrounding it. We are supposed to be watching for these events (Lk. 21:34-36). This is a good time to bring to light that there are three sources of prophecy: God through the Holy Spirit (Acts 3:21; 2 Tim. 3:15-17; Heb. 1:1-2; 1 Pet. 1:10-13; 2 Pet. 1:21); Satan through demon inspiration (Gen. 3:4-5; 1 Sam. 28; 1 Ki. 22; 1 Chr. 10:13-14; Mt. 24:24; 2 Thess. 2:8-12; Rev. 13:11-18; 16:13-16; 19:20); and man's own personal spirit (Dt. 13:1-18; 18:20-21; Jer. 23:15-17, 25-40; 27:9-11, 14-18; 28:1-17; Ezek. 13:1-23; 22:23-31; 2 Cor. 14:29-33).

Fulfilled prophecy is generally accepted as being from God (Dt. 18:22), but even this test is not absolute. Deuteronomy 13:1-3 states that God may allow a sign from a false prophet to come to pass to see if His people will act contrary to His own Word. Therefore, the real test is if a prophecy is in harmony with the Word of God. Anything contrary to the Word is false, for God will never contradict Himself. All the ancient cultures point to 2012 from the knowledge given to them by their gods (fallen angels). These prophecies most likely will be close since they are a counterfeit, but the truth is not in them. Their gods are rebels against the only true God and bring deception entangled and intertwined with the truth. Jesus knew that the feasts were appointed times to be fulfilled and even knew the year as proven by His own words.

> Ye know that after two days is the feast of the Passover, and the Son of man is betrayed to be crucified (Mat. 26:2).

> From that time forth began Jesus to shew unto his disciples, how that he must go unto Jerusalem, and suffer many things of the elders and chief priests and scribes, and be killed, and be raised again the third day (Mat. 16:21).

> Saying, The Son of man must suffer many things, and be rejected of the elders and chief priests and scribes, and be slain, and be raised the third day (Lk. 9:22).

How did Jesus know He would fulfill Passover that year? There are no prophecies concerning the age the Messiah would be with He would be slain. What He did know was that Passover was a foreshadowing of what He must do as the spotless Lamb of God. Jesus also knew when He would die based on Daniel 9:24-27. We'll get to that soon.

The demons knew who Jesus was and knew this was too early for their punishment as seen by Matthew, "And, behold, they cried out, saying, What have we to do with thee, Jesus, thou Son of God? Art thou come hither to torment us before the time" (Mat. 8:29)? It stands to reason that they know the time frame of the appointed time since they knew it was not yet.

These kings, of unknown number, called the three wise men, also knew the timing of Christ's First Coming by way of the knowledge of the heavenly bodies and their knowledge of ancient prophecies from our Old Testament (Mat. 2:1-7). They were not told by angels as the shepherds were (Lk. 2:8-12). They weren't prophets, just researchers who put together the pieces God laid out for them. It's the devil that wants the church to be ignorant, not God.

The church accepts what the wise men did in finding the First Coming of Christ. Why then is it such a stretch for wise men today to look for the Second Coming of Christ by the same means? Our enemy wants us ignorant, NOT GOD!!! ... This is why Satan has the Antichrist try to change the times and laws (Dan. 7:25). I believe this is purposed to keep people ignorant concerning God's appointed times (Gen. 1:14; Lev. 23).

Noah knew the flood was coming, but didn't know when until the time was very close. Seven days before the flood came, Noah knew exacting when it would happen (Gen. 7:4). Lot knew destruction was coming on the cities he was living in and around. He knew it was immediate (Gen. 19:17-25). Moses knew 40 years would pass before they entered the Promised Land (Num. 14:25, 33, 42-45), and he had a vision of his death, knowing when this would happen (Num. 27:12-14; Dt. 3:23-29; Dt. 34:1-8). The two witnesses will know how long their ministry is and when they will die, when their resurrection and rapture will be, and even when there will be a great earthquake that is going to kill 7,000 men (Rev. 11:1-13). The 144,000 will know that they will be translated up just before the middle of the Tribulation period (Dan. 12:1-2; Rev. 12:5; 14:1-5).

Elijah already knew he would be translated that day. The chapter is introduced as if it were already a known fact. The sons of the prophets at Bethel knew Elijah was about to be raptured (2 Kings 2:3). Elisha knew it (2 Kings 2:3, 5). The sons of the prophets at Jericho knew it (2 Kings 2:5). Elijah knew it (2 Kings 2:9-10). Not only was it known that Elijah was to be taken to heaven that day, but it was also clear that it would be by a whirlwind (2 Kings 2:1), and that it wouldn't take place until they had passed Bethel and Jericho and crossed the Jordan river (2 Kings 2:2, 4, 6), for the Lord had sent him to all those places.

God has given us too many clues and warnings to bury your head in the lie that we are not supposed to know the day or the hour. This leads us to willful ignorance, or it means people are not even reading their Bible. If you are reading your Bible, make sure and study it as well (2 Tim. 2:15). Jesus never said we aren't supposed to know or that we can't know. This is a lie from our enemy to keep us blind and dumb. Jesus told us to watch! Jesus rebuked those who were not discerning during His First Coming.

Could Daniel 9:24-27 be one of the prophecies the wise men understood to know the King's birth would be in their own day? Before the prophecy in Daniel 9, no one could have had a good time frame of the Messiah's coming. But after that, any one who studied prophecy found in God's Word would have a general idea of when He would be born. Not knowing Jesus' age when He would die, they would not be able to narrow it down to the year.

However, knowing history of Daniel 9:25 would give you the year He would die.... "That from the going forth of the commandment to restore and to build Jerusalem unto the Messiah the Prince shall be seven weeks, and threescore and two weeks: the street shall be built again, and the wall, even in troublous times." This rebuilding officially began in 452 BC in the reign of Xerxes. An understanding of Isaiah 53 would have been helpful to know Jesus would have to die. Couple Isaiah with Daniel 9 and the wise men of that day would have known not only the year, but the very day of His death if they also understood the appointed times found in Leviticus 23 were only dress rehearsals that have actual fulfillments.

<u>Fulfilled</u> (1) **Feast of the Passover** (Lev. 23:4-5) - *Jesus' death*

<u>Fulfilled</u> (2) **Feast of unleaven bread** (Lev. 23:6-8) - *Jesus' burial*

<u>Fulfilled</u> (3) **Feast of first fruits** (Lev. 23:9-14) - *Jesus' resurrection*

<u>Fulfilled</u> (4) **Feast of Pentecost** (Lev. 23:15-22) - *Outpouring of the Holy Spirit*

<u>Will be fulfilled</u> (5) **Feast of trumpets** (Lev. 23:23-25) - *Rapture of the saints*

<u>Will be fulfilled</u> (6) **Feast of Atonement** (Lev. 23:26-32) - *The Second Coming*

<u>Will be fulfilled</u> (7) **Feast of tabernacles** (Lev. 23:33-44) - *Beginning of the Millennial Reign*

From Matthew 2:1-8, we see that not only these wise men knew of the coming Messiah, but also the "scribes" of King Herod. Matthew 2:2 refers to the King of the Jews. Tacitus and Sueronius testify that in the East at this time there was a general expectation of a king to be born in Judea who was to rule the whole world. Daniel predicted His coming and being "cut off" to be 483 years after the post-Babylonian captivity commandment to restore Jerusalem (Dan. 9:24-26). Jesus was born to rule and will do so forever after His Second Coming (Lk. 1:32-33; Jn. 18:37; Isa. 9:6-7; Rev. 11:15; 22:1-5).

The chief priests and scribes from Matthew 2:4 were asked by an evil king to tell him where the Messiah King should be born. Scribes were formerly secretaries to kings (2 Sam. 8:17; 20:25; 2 Ki. 12:10; 22:3-12). Later, they were copyists and interpreters of the Scriptures and laws of Israel, keepers of all records, and were the lawyers and schoolmasters in Israel (Ezra 7:6-21; Neh. 8:1-13; Mt. 23:2-34; Mk. 9:11; 14:43; 15:1; Lk. 5:17; 22:66; 23:10; Acts 4:5; 5:34; 1 Tim. 1:7). They believed in the coming of Christ, even looking for His coming. Many evil men from the past were greater watchers than most Christians are today. God forbid!

These scribes knew two things from Old Testament Scriptures. "And thou Bethlehem, in the land of Juda, art not the least among the princes of Juda: for out of thee shall come a Governor, that shall rule my people Israel" (Mt. 2:6; Mic. 5:2). They knew where the Messiah would be born, and they knew Christ will rule Israel (Isa. 9:6-7; Dan. 2:44-45; 7:13-14,27; Zech. 14; Lk. 1:32-33; Rev. 11:15; 20:1-15; 22:4-5). They just didn't seem to understand He would not only rule Israel, but all other nations from His Second Coming into eternity (Dan. 7:13-14, 18).

"There were two reasons all should have believed. First, the report itself (2 Tim. 3:15-17; 2 Pt. 1:19-21). God has spoken by the mouths of the prophets since the world began (Acts 3:21; Heb. 1:1-3; 1 Pet. 1:10-12). God Himself began the long list of prophecies of the coming Redeemer by promising that the Seed of the Woman would crush the serpent's head and restore man's dominion (Gen. 3:15-16). Abraham and Isaac spoke of Him coming through their seed (Gen. 12:1-3; 15:4-6; 17:4-8, 19-21; 21:12; 26:4). Jacob said He would come from Judah (Gen. 49:10). Moses predicted Him as a prophet like himself (Dt. 18:15-19). David referred to Him as coming from his seed (2 Sam. 7). Isaiah said He would be born of a virgin in Judah of the house of David (Isa. 7:14; 9:6-7), and pictured His rejection and sufferings (Isa. 52:13 - Isa. 53:12). Others also made reports of His coming, so Israel had no excuse for their unbelief when He did come.

Secondly, miracles confirming the report. The report was not only predicted and then literally fulfilled in Jesus of Nazareth, but there were also miracles confirming to Israel the fact that He was the true Messiah sent by God (Isa. 11:1-2; 42:1-6; 61:1-2; Mt. 11:1-6; Lk. 4:16-18; Acts 2:22; 10:38). The arm of the Lord is figurative of His power, which Isaiah predicted would be revealed along with the report (Jn. 5:20,36; 10:25-38; 12:38-40; 14:10-12; 15:24)." (Dake Annotated Reference Bible)

Any who had a clear understanding of Scripture living in the days of Jesus' earthly ministry would have been able to see that He was the Messiah and His death would be soon as Daniel 9:24-27 foretold. They would merely add 483 years (69 seven year periods) from the final command by Artaxerxes to rebuild Jerusalem and know the year the Messiah would have been cut off. A little history, which would have been widely known to the Jewish people concerning these things and a little knowledge of prophecy, which would also have been widely read.

"The 20th year of Artaxerxes was 92 years after the Babylonian captivity of 70 years. Darius the Mede, the Ahasuerus of Esther 1:1 and father of Cyrus, reigned 2 years after the fall of Babylon. Cyrus reigned 9 years; Cambyses 7; Darius I 35; Xerxes 21; and Artaxerxes 20 years before Nehemiah was sent back to Jerusalem to complete the walls (Neh. 1:1 – Neh. 7:4). Darius, Ahasuerus, or Artaxerxes are just titles, any or all of them could have been used by any of these kings. Artaxerxes just means "great king." To decide who is definitely referred to on the basis of such titles is impossible. We can only go by the time element in such passages." (Dake Annotated Reference Bible)

This is why Scripture indicates the year of their reign and how long they reigned. It is for the purpose of study, not merely reading through the Bible in a year to say you did. If we can understand this time element and historical fact almost 2,500 years after Jerusalem was built, then how much easier would people be able to understand this about 450 years after it happened? Historical facts are better understood when they are recent in time.

> In the first year of his reign I Daniel understood by books the number of the years, whereof the word of the LORD came to Jeremiah the prophet, that he would accomplish seventy years in the desolations of Jerusalem. And I set my face unto the Lord God, to seek by prayer and supplications, with fasting, and sackcloth, and ashes (Daniel 9:2-3).

The books Daniel was referring to in Daniel 9:2 was obviously the books of the prophet Jeremiah who foretold of the 70 years of captivity. It was now at the end of the 70 year period and Daniel was wondering if God had forgotten His promise. Sometimes its okay to remind God about His promises. By this we know that Daniel knew the year of the fulfillment by simple history, math, and Scripture. He knew the year, but not the day. He knew the time was upon him.

Simeon knew the time of the First Coming was upon him. Simeon, a Jew in Jerusalem who: was just and devout (Lk. 2:25), waited for the Messiah (Lk. 2:25), had the Holy Spirit (Lk. 2:25), received a revelation (Lk. 2:26), was led by the Spirit (Lk. 2:27), handled Jesus (Lk. 2:28; cp. 1 Jn. 1), prophesied (Lk. 2:28-35), and blessed Joseph and Mary (Lk. 2:34).

These faithful people of God watched for the Anointed One, the Savior of the world. They were chasing a star. We are also chasing the bright and morning star (Rev. 22:16). We will see Him in glory soon! This is why we watch and why we know it is good. Keep enduring, keep watching!

CHAPTER 3

FEASTS OF THE LORD / APPOINTED TIMES

"Most Christians are not familiar with the Hebraic concepts of the Bible, especially the seven appointed feasts and the yearly cycles ordained by God. Few Christians have heard about the new moon cycles and how Israel's calendar and prophetic future were hidden in the lunar cycles. Understanding the new moon unlocks deeper revelation of the seven main feasts. Three of these, the fall feasts, are introduced during the season of Teshuvah. This time is called the Days of Awe and Seasons of Joy."—Perry Stone and Bill Cloud

And God said, Let there be lights in the firmament of the heaven to divide the day from the night; and let them be for signs, and for seasons, and for days, and years (Gen. 1:14).

The "signs" is an easy one to figure out. The magi, we know them as "the 3 wise men," used the heavens as a means of not only finding the Messiah, but also as a way of knowing the First Coming was upon them. There will be blood red moons, a darkened sun, extremely large magnitude earthquakes, stars and fire falling from heaven in the days after the Rapture and at the Second Coming (Isa. 13:10; Ezek. 32:7-8; Joel 2:31; 3:15; Zech. 14:4-8; Acts 2:16-21; Mat. 24:29-31; Rev. 6:12-13; 8:5, 12; 9:2; 11:13, 19; 16:10, 18). The constellations actually told the gospel during the first 2,500 years after Adam (as theorized by some). This was the time before the written Word that Moses began in the Christian Bible and the Jewish Torah.

From Genesis 1, we learn absolutely every purpose God intended for the light from the sun and the moon. The seven-fold purpose of lights is to divide day and night, light and darkness (Gen. 1:14, 18), be for signs (Gen. 1:14), be for seasons (Gen. 1:14), be for days (Gen. 1:14), be for years (Gen. 1:14), give light on earth (Gen. 1:15, 17), and rule day and night eternally (Gen. 1:16, 18; 8:22).

Just a quick note of interest, since we are on the subject. The sun will shine for as long as the earth, Israel, and people remain. This will always be (Gen. 1:14-18; 8:22; Ps. 89:34-37; Jer. 31:35-37; 33:19-26). I was always told the sun would not be needed anymore when God physically comes to dwell on earth with man. They get this idea from Revelation 21:23.

> And the city had no need of the sun, neither of the moon, to shine in it: for the glory of God did lighten it, and the Lamb is the light thereof (Rev. 21:23).

The truth is that the sun and moon will be needed to give light to the earth for eternity. It will never burn out. God the Father is the one who gives light to the Holy City, not the earth. The truth from Scripture is that the moon will be as bright as the sun. The is the result from the sun becoming seven times brighter. Not only will the night be as bright as our current day, but the sun will light the earth for eternity, being seven times as bright. The sun will never burn out as many astronomers would tell us.

> Moreover the light of the moon shall be as the light of the sun, and the light of the sun shall be sevenfold, as the light of seven days, in the day that the LORD bindeth up the breach of his people, and healeth the stroke of their wound (Isa. 30:26).

Not only will this sunlight and moonlight be given while God is physically living on earth for all eternity (Rev. 21), but the sun becomes seven times brighter at the Second Coming, at least 1,000 years before God moves Himself and Jesus' bride (New Jerusalem) to earth (Rev. 21:2, 9-10). Isaiah 30:26 speaks of it happening "In the day." That day is when God blesses Israel and sets them free from all curses of the past and the great tribulation calamity of the future Antichrist who will seek to destroy all Jews (Dan. 9:27; 12:1-7; Ezek. 38-39; Zech. 12:10 - Zech. 14:21; Mt. 24:15-31).

The next verse says, "Behold, the name of the LORD cometh from far, burning with his anger, and the burden thereof is heavy: his lips are full of indignation, and his tongue as a devouring fire" (Isa. 30:27). The name of the Lord is sometimes put for the Lord Himself. Here it speaks of the coming of God from heaven to destroy Antichrist and the kings of the earth for their tribulation upon His people, Jews and saints (Isa. 63:1-5; Ezek. 38-39; Joel 2-3; Zech. 14; Mt. 25:31-46; Jude 1:14-15; Rev. 19). God the Father will accompany Jesus and His armies at Jesus' Second Coming, which will be the First Coming of God the Father in respect to doctrinal terminology.

The First Coming of God the Father will be at the Second Coming of Jesus Christ to the earth (Daniel 7:9, 13-14, 22; Zech. 14:5; Titus 2:13). At this time God will come to help Christ defeat and destroy the Antichrist kingdom (Dan. 7:1-22). He will then give the kingdom over to the Son (Dan. 7:13-14) and the saints (Dan. 7:18, 27). Christ will then be King over all the earth (Dan. 7:13-14, 27; Zech. 14:9; Mat. 25:31-46; Rev. 11:15; 20:1-10; 22:4-5). The Father will go back to heaven to remain for the first 1,000 years of the eternal reign of Christ and until Jesus has rid the earth of all rebellion (1 Cor. 15:24-28; Eph. 1:10).

The Second Coming of God the Father to the earth will be at the end of the Millennium when Christ has rid the earth of all rebels. God will then become "all in all" on earth as before rebellion was started by Lucifer and later by Adam (1 Cor. 15:24-28; Eph.

Feasts Of The Lord / Appointed Times

1:10). He will then move His capital city from the planet heaven to the planet earth to be among men forever (Gen. 1:1; Job 38:4-7) (Rev. 21:1-7, 9-10; Rev. 22:1-5). This is when the sun's light will not be needed in the current capital city of heaven when it is moved to earth.

The word "seasons" from Genesis 1:14 is our main focus. Let's examine these appointed times of the rapture and the Second Coming by the word "seasons" found in Genesis 1:14. The word that was translated "seasons" comes from the Hebrew word "mow'ed," which means an appointment, i.e. a fixed time or season; specifically, a festival; conventionally a year; by implication, an assembly (as convened for a definite purpose); technically the congregation; by extension, the place of meeting; also a signal (as appointed beforehand):--appointed (sign, time), (place of, solemn) assembly, congregation, (set, solemn) feast, (appointed, due) season, solemn(-ity), synogogue, (set) time (appointed).

So it is, Genesis 1:14 is telling us the sun and the moon have a purpose unacknowledged or untaught to the church. They are set in their ordered orbit in a way a clock-maker places the wheels of a clock. The sun and moon are prophetic time pieces showing us signs and appointed times. The same Hebrew word "mow'ed" is used in Leviticus 23, which has been translated "feasts."

These feasts have been proven by the First Coming events of Jesus to be appointed times. The feast of the Passover (Lev. 23:4-5) was fulfilled by Jesus' death (Mat. 26:2; Jn. 19:28-30; 1 Cor. 15:3). The feast of unleaven bread (Lev. 23:6-8) was fulfilled by Jesus' burial (Jn. 19:38-42; 1 Cor. 15:4). The feast of first fruits (Lev. 23:9-14) was fulfilled by Jesus' resurrection (Jn. 20:11-18; 1 Cor. 15:4, 20, 23). The feast of Pentecost (Lev. 23:15-22) was fulfilled by the outpouring of the Holy Spirit (Jn. 14:15-17, 26; 15:26-27; 16:8-11; Acts 2:1-4).

The Fall Feasts of the Lord give us a prophetic picture of future events that we will find ourselves participating in very soon.

The Feasts of the Lord are rehearsals for future events. The Jews were chosen to keep these feasts that foreshadowed future events, being prophetic pictures for sure. For example, the high priest would bound the Passover Lamb at 9 am every year. At 3 pm The lamb was slain and they would say, "It is finished." This was done as a dress rehearsal for about 1,700 years. The sacrificial lamb was to be spotless, which is what Jesus was as the Lamb slain (Heb. 4:15; 1 Pt. 1:19; 2:20-25).

The first four of seven feasts of the Lord were fulfilled in the order in which they were given (Lev. 23). These were fulfilled by the First Coming events of Christ. In retrospect, the last three feasts are also appointed times and could be called the seven appointed times of the Lord. Remember the Hebrew word "mow'ed" is translated seasons, feasts, and appointed times. They will be fulfilled in order by the events surrounding the Second Coming of Christ. We will clearly see that momentarily.

The recent eclipses on the Feasts of the Lord, as well as significant eclipses on other days significant to the Jewish people, are signs that are foretelling appointed times of the Lord. Eclipses are a certain way for God to use the sun and the moon to signify watchers of His coming events in His relation to His plan for man and dispensations. In retrospect, we can see Genesis 1:14 is telling us that the sun and moon are for signs and appointed times of the Lord (Lev. 23). We will study recent eclipses in an upcoming chapter. They are all recent and they are all many!

The New Testament does confirm what history has shown us. Paul understood the feasts of the Lord and knew the last three feasts would also be fulfilled. It seems these truths have been hidden to the church until these last few years. This truth is being taught more and realized by many, though it is still a mystery and unknown to the majority. Some say the ignorance here is due to Christians getting away from the Hebraic roots. Truth is there are many eternal truths we must know and keep from the Old Testament, but don't go too far and mix the Mosaic Law with grace (Gal. 1:6-8; 3:1-5; 4:19; 5:4).

Feasts Of The Lord / Appointed Times

There are many ways that were just given to a specific people for a specific time (Heb. 7:11-22; 8:5-6; 9:9-10; 10:1-18; Gal. 3:19-24).

Maybe these truths that the feasts of the Lord will all be fulfilled were lost in the dark ages. This is a period when common man was not entitled a Bible and the men in power had the Bible translated into Latin to hide the truths within. This is when the pre-tribulation rapture doctrine seems to have vanished. Both these facts were lost until the last times of the church age, but both were apparent from early church father writings, as well as plain Scripture.

> Let no man therefore judge you in meat, or in drink, or in respect of an holyday, or of the new moon, or of the sabbath days: Which are a shadow of things to come; but the body is of Christ (Col. 2:16-17).

I underlined the new moon appointed time because there is only one feast on a new moon. That new moon is on the fifth feast, called the feast of trumpets. It happens to be the next in line to be fulfilled. This is a correct translation of Colossians 2 according to A Hebrew and Chaldee Lexicon to the Old Testament by Furst of the Hebrew word BUA and the Hebrew WAW from The Lexicon In Veteris Testamenti Libros by Koehler and Baumgartner. "In respect of a festival or new moon or Sabbaths-which are a shadow FROM things to come- FOR the Body of Messiah" (Colossians 2:16-17). This may be true. We've already seen how Genesis 1:14 and Leviticus 23 could easily translate the Hebrew word mow'ed to be "appointed times."

In Colossians 2:16-17 we are reminded that the feasts and sabbaths are a shadow of things to come. In Matthew 16:3, Jesus rebukes the Pharisees as hypocrites for not discerning the signs of their time. Many scriptures were being fulfilled in front of their eyes, yet they ignored the Scripture regarding Jesus' coming. Were these "Feasts of the Lord" only meant to be sacrificial offerings of bulls and goats, or were they a foreshadow of God's redemptive plan? By now, I'm confident you understand the truth.

> And the LORD spake unto Moses, saying, Speak unto the children of Israel, and say unto them, Concerning the feasts of the LORD, which ye shall proclaim to be holy convocations, even these are my feasts. Six days shall work be done: but the seventh day is the sabbath of rest, an holy convocation; ye shall do no work therein: it is the sabbath of the LORD in all your dwellings. These are the feasts of the LORD, even holy convocations, which ye shall proclaim in their seasons (Lev. 23:1-4).

Feasts and Sabbaths are called "holy convocations." That is to say, they are intended to be times of meeting between God and man for holy purposes. These "Feasts / Holy Convocations," are also a combination of celebratory commemorations of God's providence fulfilled in the past, and the continued fulfillment of His remaining covenant promises for the future. The 7 Feasts of the Lord forming the foundations of all Prophecy and Eschatology Hermeneutics include: Typology and prophecy fulfilled of the 4 Feasts of Passover, Unleavened Bread, First Fruits, and Feast of Weeks (Pentecost), setting the stage for the last three feasts of Trumpets, Atonement and Tabernacles.

> Say not ye, There are yet four months, and then cometh harvest? behold, I say unto you, Lift up your eyes, and look on the fields; for they are white already to harvest. And he that reapeth receiveth wages, and gathereth fruit unto life eternal: that both he that soweth and he that reapeth may rejoice together. And herein is that saying true, One soweth, and another reapeth. I sent you to reap that whereon ye bestowed no labour: other men laboured, and ye are entered into their labours (Jn. 4:35-38).

Four months looks to be symbolic of the church age... the time in between the fulfillment of the spring feasts at the First Coming of Christ when the church age began, and when Jesus fulfills the fall feasts at His Second Coming and the church age has ended. The time for harvesting the souls is now, in this 2,000 +/- year time frame in between the First and the Second Coming, symbolized by the time in between the holy feasts of the Lord. This two thousand year period could be symbolized by the two days spoken of in Hosea. We will thoroughly discuss this later.

> After two days will he revive us: in the third day he will raise us up, and we shall live in his sight (Hos. 6:2).

For many, the Rapture is not an appointed time, for there are things that must happen in order for Jesus to come back. If that is true, then the same can be said for the Second Coming. Prominent teachers are teaching that there are things that will happen from the hands of the church before Jesus can return. That is a belief with some variable theories running side by side with it. We will get into those ideas, introducing their pillars, then examining them to see if they should be standing on good doctrinal foundation or not. That is chapter 9.

There are those who simply believe the end-time events are not set in stone. Some believe the rapture day will change if anyone guesses it's date. This is simply not the case. The fall feasts are every bit appointed for a specific time as the spring feasts were.

APPOINTED TIMES WITH GOD

These are the 7 eternal feasts of the Lord that have been fulfilled in the order in which God gave them. Feast of trumpets is next in line, also known as Rosh Hashanah. This will be fulfilled by the rapture. I can't give this list enough to refresh your minds to this fact. So here it is again:

Fulfilled (1) **Feast of the Passover** (Lev. 23:4-5) - *Jesus' death*

Fulfilled (2) **Feast of unleaven bread** (Lev. 23:6-8) - *Jesus' burial*

Fulfilled (3) **Feast of first fruits** (Lev. 23:9-14) - *Jesus' resurrection*

Fulfilled (4) **Feast of Pentecost** (Lev. 23:15-22) - *Outpouring of the Holy Spirit*

Will be fulfilled (5) **Feast of trumpets** (Lev. 23:23-25) - *Rapture of the saints*

Will be fulfilled (6) **Feast of Atonement** (Lev. 23:26-32) - *The Second Coming*

Will be fulfilled (7) **Feast of tabernacles** (Lev. 23:33-44) - *Beginning of the Millennial Reign*

Besides the above, I will give absolute proof that the rapture, Second Coming, and Millennial Reign are appointed to be fulfilled by fulfilling the fall feasts. First, let us look at simple language found throughout the Bible.

> For the vision is yet for an appointed time, but at the end it shall speak, and not lie: though it tarry, wait for it; because it will surely come, it will not tarry (Hab. 2:3).

The vision is set for an appointed time, this is clear, but what is the vision referring too? The verses before and after will help us understand clearly that the vision is speaking of the Second Coming of the Messiah.

> And the LORD answered me, and said, Write the vision, and make it plain upon tables, that he may run that readeth it. For the vision is yet for an appointed time, but at the end it shall

speak, and not lie: though it tarry, wait for it; because it will surely come, it will not tarry. Behold, his soul which is lifted up is not upright in him: but the just shall live by his faith (Hab. 2:2-4).

The vision is of the Second Coming of Christ (Heb. 9:28; Dan. 7:13-14; Zech. 14:1-5; Rev. 19:11-21), as proved in Hebrews 10:37-38, which has been quoted from Habakkuk 2:3-4.

For yet a little while, and he that shall come will come, and will not tarry. Now the just shall live by faith: but if any man draw back, my soul shall have no pleasure in him (Heb. 10:37-38).

The Second Coming is for an appointed time, but at the end it shall speak and not lie (Hab. 2:3). It will not lie, meaning it will surely happen just as the Lord God Almighty has foretold. Let no one mock until your sure foundation is shaken. Also, take note of the warning of those who draw back from their faith they should be living by. I would be remiss in my duties if I let that slide by. Faith is the beginning of justification (Rom. 5:1; Eph. 2:8-9), AND the continuation of justification (Heb. 10:38-39). The just shall live by faith, not put down their cross and live contrary to their covenant.

After two days will he revive us: in the third day he will raise us up, and we shall live in his sight. Then shall we know, if we follow on to know the LORD: his going forth is prepared as the morning; and he shall come unto us as the rain, as the latter and former rain unto the earth (Hos. 6:2-3).

Here again is a clue that the church age will only last for two days, or two thousand years, for a day is as a thousand years with God (2 Pt. 3:8). Another way to say this is that blindness on the part of Israel will last for two days, or two thousand years (Rom. 11:17-25). Spiritual blindness means you are dead in trespasses and sin. They are dead without Christ (2 Jn. 9). On the third day, when they see the

Lord and believe, then they will live again as a nation, and live again by the new birth (Eph. 2:1-10).

His going forth is prepared as the morning; and he shall come unto us as the rain" (Hos. 6:3). This refers to the definite preparation and time of the Second Coming of Christ in the plan of God. His coming is fixed as surely as the morning is eternally fixed to come at a certain time daily (Gen. 1:14-19; 8:22). His coming to save and bless Israel will be like refreshing rains after a long dry season - even as the latter and former rain upon the earth.

The former rain fell in October at the seed time. The latter or spring rain fell in March and April to cause the grain to mature and ripen. One came at the beginning and the other at the end (or harvest time) of good things. In the spiritual realm, God would come down upon Israel to make a complete harvest of the nation (Zech. 10:1; 12:10 - Zech. 13:1; Rom. 11:25-29). Now, a few verses later...

> Also, O Judah, he hath set an harvest for thee, when I returned the captivity of my people (Hos. 6:11).

The harvest is a reaping time of judgment. God is again proclaiming the truth that there are appointed times set for all future events. He says, "I have appointed a time to reap judgment for you also, O Judah!" But make no mistake, all Israel will be converted at the Second Coming of Christ (Zech. 12:10 - Zech. 13:1; Rom. 11:26; Isa. 66:8).

> So he came near where I stood: and when he came, I was afraid, and fell upon my face: but he said unto me, Understand, O son of man: for at the time of the end shall be the vision. Now as he was speaking with me, I was in a deep sleep on my face toward the ground: but he touched me, and set me upright. And he said, Behold, I will make thee know what shall be in the last end of the indignation: for at the time appointed the end shall be (Dan. 8:17-19).

The time of the end gives us the meaning of the vision. Like Habakkuk 2:2-4, the vision proves that the main object of the verse is to predict events at the end of this age in which we live, or just before the Second Coming of Christ and His eternal reign (cp. Dan. 8:19, 23-26; 2:40-45; 7:23-27; 9:27; 11:36-45; 12:7-13; Rev. 4:1 - Rev. 19:21). Daniel 8:9-25 will show you the indignation referred to from Daniel 8:19 is in fact speaking of the time right before the Second Coming.

The last end of the wrath of God upon the one (the little horn / Antichrist) that will cause the wrath of God to be poured out is as follows: Antichrist's wars (Dan. 8:9; 7:23-24; 9:24; 11:36-45; Rev. 19); His martyrdom of saints (Dan. 8:10-14, 24; 7:21; 9:27; 11:36-45; Rev. 13:11-18); His taking away the daily sacrifices in the future Jewish temple (Dan. 8:11-14; 9:27; 12:7-11; Mt. 24:15; Rev. 13); His placing the abomination of desolation in the temple (Dan. 8:11-14; 9:27; 11:45; 2 Thess. 2:4; Rev. 11:1-2; Rev. 13); His casting down the sanctuary or sacred place of sacrifice (Dan. 8:11-13).

He also causes many to rebel against God (Dan. 8:12; Rev. 13:11-18; 16:2, Rev. 10 - Rev. 11); His increasing sins among men (Dan. 8:12, 23; 2 Thess. 2:8-12; Rev. 13; 16:10-11); His casting down the truth to the ground (Dan. 8:12; 7:25; 2 Thess. 2:4, 8-12); His trampling the host under his feet (Dan. 8:13, 24-25; 7:21; 9:27; 11:40-45; Rev. 13); His fierceness against God and man (Dan. 8:23; Rev. 13); His yielding to the devil (Dan. 8:24; 11:36-39; 2 Thess. 2:8-12; Rev. 13); His ruthless destruction of life and property (Dan. 8:24; 11:36-46; Rev. 13); His deceptions (craftiness, Dan. 8:25; 2 Thess. 2:8-12; Rev. 13; 19:20); His self-exaltation (Dan. 8:25; 7:25; 11:36-45; 2 Thess. 2:4; Rev. 13); and His stubborn stand against Christ (Dan. 8:25; 2 Thess. 2:8; Rev. 19:19-21).

At the end of this age and at the Second Coming, the time for the fulfillment of the vision is appointed (Dan. 8:19, 23-25; 2:44-45; 7:23-27; 9:27; 11:36-45; Zech. 14; 2 Thess. 2:8-12; Rev. 19:11-21). The time of the end is stated in Daniel 8:25 as being when the little horn stands up against Christ. This is at the Second Coming, which has just been emphatically proven to be set forth as an appointed time. The whole plan of redemption was set forth by the Divine council of the Triune God. They planned this out before the foundation of this world was set (Eph. 1:4-5; 1 Pt. 1:20). The whole plan of redemption goes beyond the cross, even to the end of the thousand year reign of Christ and His saints (1 Cor. 15:24-28; Rev. 21:4; 22:3).

To clarify my beliefs as to the Sabbath, the 7th day rest of God is a foreshadowing of the day of rest God will have when the Millennial Reign is happening. One day is as 1,000 years with God and 1,000 years is as a day (2 Pt. 3:8). About 6,000 years has happened since God made Adam and 1,000 years will be as a rest for Him during His Son's Millennial Reign here on earth. Christians are not under command to be Sabbath keepers (Col. 2:14-17; Rom. 14:5-6; Gal. 3:9-10).

All ten commandments have been abolished in the Mosaic Covenant, often called the Old Covenant (2 Cor. 3:7-14; Eph. 2:14-15; Col. 2:14-17). All were re-established in our covenant except to keep the Sabbath (Rom. 14:5-6; Gal. 4:9-10; Col. 2:14-17), which was only in a covenant to Israel for a certain period of time (Dt. 4:7-8; 5:3; Isa. 1:13-15; Jere. 31:31-35; Hos. 2:11; Heb. 8:7). Christians today are only responsible for keeping commands found in our covenant, the New Covenant, or New Testament (Mt. 26:28; 2 Cor. 3:6-18; Heb. 8:6).

FUTURE FULFILLMENT'S FOR THE FEASTS

Rapture On The Feast Of Trumpets (Lev. 23:23-25)

Second Coming On The Day Of Atonement (Lev. 23:26-32)

Millennial Reign Begins On Feast Of Tabernacles (Lev. 23:33-44)

Rapture On The Feast Of Trumpets

There are many reasons why the feast of trumpets identifies the rapture. For me, there are two main reasons. First, the rapture is the next significant event in prophecy to happen and is in direct connect with a coming of Christ. Coincidentally, the next feast to be fulfilled is the feast of trumpets. Second, the rapture of the church will take place at the sounding of a trumpet, called the last trump (1 Cor. 15:52). Coincidentally, there is a literal trumpet blown at sunset in Jerusalem that is called the last trump.

This trumpet is a specific trumpet only blown once a year, ending the feast of trumpets at sunset. Paul understood this well when he gave us the revelation that the second phase of the first resurrection would be at the last trump. This is why he told the Thessalonians they were not in darkness concerning the times (1 Thess. 5:1, 4-5). 1 Thessalonians 5 is in view of 1 Thessalonians 4, which is a breathe before when Paul wrote about the trumpet of God (1 Thess. 4:16), which is what we hear when we "Come up Hither" (Rev. 4:1).

Here are some other reasons why Christians expect to see the rapture happen on the feast of trumpets, called Rosh Hashanah in Hebrew. There are seven days of awe in between the Feast of Trumpets and the Day of Atonement. These picture the seven years of tribulation. Atonement pictures Satan being defeated and cast away at the end of tribulation, as well as Israel being saved by their acceptance of the Messiah and having their sins taken away by the atonement of the sacrifice of Jesus. If you add the two day trumpets feast, and the day of atonement, the 7 days of awe are "ten days of tribulation" which might be referred to in Revelation 2:10. These are two I agree with. There are many more proof points you can find online, but I believe they are stretching for the sake of quantity. The proofs above are sufficient.

The rest of the "Rapture on the Feast of Trumpets" section is from: *http://watch.pair.com/rosh-hashana.html*

There are important parallels between Jewish feasts and the fulfillment of Christ. Jewish tradition holds that Rosh Hashanah celebrates the anniversary of the creation of the world, a day when "God takes stock of all of His Creation," which of course includes all of humanity. Translated from the Hebrew, Rosh Hashanah means "head of the year" – rosh means head, while hashanah means year. Jews believe that God's judgment on this day determines the course of the coming year.

God does not do things in vain, or without purpose. The Old Testament Holy Days were not just some sort of Divine make-work project to keep the Israelites busy while they were out wandering in the desert. All of the Old Testament Holy Days (Passover, Days of Unleavened Bread, The Feast of Weeks, The Feast of Trumpets, The Day of Atonement, The Festival of Tabernacles and the Last Day) were, and continue to be, living symbols of the stages of God's Plan of Salvation for all humanity.

> Behold, I shew you a mystery; We shall not all sleep, but we shall all be changed, In a moment, in the twinkling of an eye, at the last trump: for the trumpet shall sound, and the dead shall be raised incorruptible, and we shall be changed. For this corruptible must put on incorruption, and this mortal must put on immortality (1 Cor. 15:51-53).

> For this we say unto you by the word of the Lord, that we which are alive and remain unto the coming of the Lord shall not prevent them which are asleep. For the Lord himself shall descend from heaven with a shout, with the voice of the archangel, and with the trump of God: and the dead in Christ shall rise first: Then we which are alive and remain shall be caught up together with them in the clouds, to meet the Lord

in the air: and so shall we ever be with the Lord (1 Thess. 4:15-17).

A special season known as 'Teshuvah' which in Hebrew means "to return or repent", begins on the first day of the month of Elul and continues 40 days, ending with Yom Kippur. Thirty days into Teshuvah, on Tishrei 1, comes Rosh HaShanah. This begins a final ten-day period beginning on Rosh HaShanah and ending on Yom Kippur. These are known as the High Holy Days and as the Awesome Days. The sabbath that falls within this ten-day period is called 'Shabbat Shuvah', the Sabbath of Return. Five days after Yom Kippur is 'Sukkot', the Feast of Tabernacles. Teshuvah begins on Elul 1 and concludes on Tishrei 10, Yom Kippur. Each morning during the 30 days of the month of Elul, the trumpet (shofar) or ram's horn is blown to warn the people to repent and return to God.

Rosh HaShanah is also referred to as 'Yom Teruah', the Day of the Sounding of the Shofar, or the Day of the Awakening Blast. On the 30th of each month, the members of the High Court assembled in a courtyard in Jerusalem, where they waited to receive the testimony of two reliable witnesses. They then sanctified the new moon. The new moon is very difficult to see on the first day because it can be seen only about sunset, close to the sun, when the sun is traveling north. So, looking for a very slim faint crescent moon, which is very close to the sun, is a very difficult thing to do. If the moon's crescent was not seen on the 30th day, the new moon was automatically celebrated on the 31st day.

For this reason, Yom Teruah is always celebrated for two days. These two days are celebrated as though it is just one long day of forty-eight hours. The reason it is celebrated for two days is because if they waited to start the celebration until after the new moon had been sanctified, they would have missed half the celebration because the new moon can only be sanctified during daylight hours.

Yom Teruah, or the Feast of Trumpets, is the only feast that we do not know the day in which to keep it. Therefore, we have to be on the alert and watch for it. Teruah means "an awakening blast". A theme associated with Rosh HaShanah is the theme "to awake." Teruah is also translated as "shout." Whether it is by the blast of a shofar or the force of a supernatural shout, God's goal is to awaken us. "...Awake thou that sleepest, and arise from the dead, and Christ shall give thee light" (Eph. 5:14). * (my note) Notice how close that is written to an awesome rapture verse (Eph. 5:27).*

The theme of awakening from sleep is used throughout the Bible. It is found in John 11:11, Romans 13:11, Daniel 12:1-2 and Psalm 78:65. The shofar was also blown at the temple to begin the Sabbath each week. There are two types of trumpets used in the Bible: The silver trumpet; The shofar or ram's horn. Each sabbath, two men with silver trumpets and a man with a shofar made three trumpet blasts twice during the day. On Rosh HaShanah, it is different. The shofar is the primary trumpet. On Rosh HaShanah, a shofar delivers the first blast, a silver trumpet the second, and then a shofar the third. According to Leviticus 23:24 and Numbers 29:1, Rosh HaShanah is the day of the blowing of the trumpets.

> Speak unto the children of Israel, saying, in the seventh month, in the first day of the month, shall ye have a sabbath, a memorial of blowing of trumpets, an holy convocation (Leviticus 23:24).

> And in the seventh month, on the first day of the month, ye shall have an holy convocation; ye shall do no servile work: it is a day of blowing the trumpets unto you (Numbers 29:1).

The trumpet used for this purpose is the ram's horn, not trumpets made of metal as in Numbers 10. Another name for Rosh HaShanah is 'Yom HaDin,' the Day of Judgment. The righteous are separated and will be with God. This is known to us as the Rapture.

The wicked will face the wrath of God during the tribulation period. The shofar blown on Rosh HaShanah is known as the last trump, which the apostle Paul mentioned in 1 Thessalonians 4:16-17. At this time, the believers in Christ will escape the tribulation about to come upon earth and will be taken to heaven in the Rapture along with the righteous who had died before this time.

The gates of Heaven are opened on Rosh HaShanah so the righteous nation may enter (Isa. 26:2, Ps. 118:19-20). Because the gates of Heaven are understood to be open on Rosh HaShanah, this is further evidence that the Rapture of the followers of Christ will take place on Rosh HaShanah.

One of the reasons for blowing the shofar is to proclaim the resurrection of the dead. The resurrection of the dead will take place on Rosh HaShanah. In 1 Corinthians 15:52, the apostle Paul tells us that the resurrection of the dead will be "at the last trump." Earlier in 1 Corinthians 15:14, he wrote that without the Lord Jesus rising from the dead, our faith is in vain.

We cannot go to the Book of Revelation and say that the voice of the seventh angel (Revelation 11:15) is the last trump. In the first century, the last trump (shofar) meant a specific day in the year. In Judaism, there are three trumpets that have a name. They are the first trump, the last trump, and the great trump. Each one of these trumpets indicates a specific day in the Jewish year. The first trump is blown on the Feast of Pentecost (Exodus 19:19).

It proclaimed that God had betrothed Himself to Israel. The last trump is synonymous with Rosh HaShanah, according to Theodore Gaster in his book, Festivals of the Jewish Year, in his chapter on Rosh HaShanah. Herman Kieval also states the same thing in his book, The High Holy Days in the chapter on the shofar. The great trumpet is blown on Yom Kippur, which will herald the return of Jesus back to the earth (Matthew 24:31).

The first and last trump relate to the two horns of the ram, which according to Jewish tradition, was caught in the thicket on Mount Moriah when Abraham was ready to slay Isaac and offer him up as a burnt offering. This ram became the substitute for Isaac even as Jesus became the substitute for us and provided life for us through His death.

Rabbi Eliezer tells us in Pirkei Avot, that the left horn (first trump) was blown on Mount Sinai, and its right horn (the last trump) will be blown to herald the coming of the Lord for His Church. Isaiah 18:3 and 1 Thessalonians 4:13-18 speak of the resurrection of the dead. 1 Thessalonians 5 continues with the Day of the Lord and the birth-pangs. The festivals will, beyond a shadow of a doubt, tell you that the resurrection of the dead precedes the time of the Tribulation. 1 Thessalonians 4:16-17 says that the dead in Christ will rise first, and that the catching away of the believers will immediately follow.

The term 'rapture' comes from the Greek word 'harpazo', which means "to seize, catch away, catch up, pluck, pull, take by force" (1 Thess. 4:17). 2 Thessalonians 2:1 tells us, "Now we beseech you, brethren, by the coming of our Lord Jesus Christ, and by our gathering together unto Him." The phrase "gathering together" comes from the Greek word 'episunagoge', which means "an assembly." The feast of trumpets, through careful study depicts nothing less than the return of Jesus Christ for His church at the last trump, just before God pours His wrath and judgment on a sinful and Christ rejecting world.

To summarize: The Feast of Trumpets is when the "last trump" of the Rapture of 1 Corinthians 15 is blown. The Feast of Trumpets happens on the "new moon," which is 29.5 days after the last one, meaning it might occur on the 29th or 30th day, nobody knows for sure. The "Open Door" of the Rapture in Matthew 25; Revelation 3; Revelation 4:1 is a symbol of the Feast of Trumpets.

Feasts Of The Lord / Appointed Times

Thus says the Lord GOD: The gate of the inner court that faces east shall be shut on the six working days; but on the sabbath day it shall be opened and on the day of the new moon it shall be opened (Ezek 46:1).

We are told that the new moon and the Feasts of the Lord are a shadow of things to come in Colossians 2:16-17. Since the Feast of Trumpets is the only Feast of the Lord that falls on a new moon, we should take particular note. There are seven Days of Awe in between the Feast of Trumpets and the Day of Atonement. These picture the seven years of tribulation. Atonement pictures Satan being defeated and cast away at the end of tribulation. If you add the two-day Trumpets Feast, and the Day of Atonement, the 7 Days of Awe are "ten days of tribulation" which might be referred to in Revelation 2:10.

SECOND COMING ON THE DAY OF ATONEMENT

This is not proof of a 2016 Rapture or a 2023 Second Coming, but it will be helpful to those who don't know why The Feast Of The Great Day Of Atonement will be fulfilled by the Second Coming of Christ with His holy angels and saints. I need to use a specific timeframe of seven years for educational purposes. Note: Yom Kippur is Hebrew for The Day Of Atonement. Why does this feast day of the Lord fit the Second Coming of Christ? That's a great question and even if all the math, eschatology, and astronomy was wrong for this day of September 26, 2023, then the meaning of this feast day is still intact.

The following four paragraphs are taken from Wikipedia: h*ttp:// en.wikipedia.org/wiki/Yom_Kippur*

"Yom Kippur (Hebrew: פּוּרִיּוֹם כ , IPA: ['jom ki'pur]), also known as the Day of Atonement, is the holiest day of the year for religious Jews. Its central themes are atonement and repentance. Jews traditionally observe this holy day with a 25-hour period of fasting and intensive prayer, often spending most of the day in synagogue services. Yom Kippur completes the annual period known in Judaism as the High Holy Days.

Yom Kippur is the tenth day of the month of Tishrei. According to Jewish tradition, God inscribes each person's fate for the coming year into a "book" on Rosh Hashanah, and waits until Yom Kippur to "seal" the verdict. During the Days of Awe, a Jew tries to amend his or her behavior and seek forgiveness for wrongs done against God (bein adam leMakom) and against other human beings (bein adam lechavero). The evening and day of Yom Kippur are set aside for public and private petitions and confessions of guilt (Vidui). At the end of Yom Kippur, one considers one's self absolved by God.

Yom Kippur is considered one of the holiest of Jewish holidays and it is observed by many secular Jews who may not observe other holidays. Many secular Jews fast and attend synagogue on Yom Kippur, where the number of worshippers attending is often double or triple [citation needed] the normal attendance.

In a nutshell, the name "Yom Kippur" means "Day of Atonement," and that pretty much explains what the holiday is. It is a day set aside to "afflict the soul," to atone for the sins of the past year. In Days of Awe, it is believed that God opens His "books" in which God inscribes all of our names. On Yom Kippur, the judgment entered in these books is sealed. This day is, essentially, your last appeal, your last chance to change the judgment, to demonstrate your repentance and make amends."

At this time it must be understood that all of Israel will be saved at the Second Coming of the Messiah (Rom. 11:25-32; Isa. 66:7-8; Zech. 12:10 – Zech. 13:1). "All Israel shall be saved" ...This refers to the whole nation that will be alive in Palestine when Christ comes (Zech. 12:10 – Zech. 13:1; 14:1-15; Mt. 24:39; Isa. 66:7-8).

It is at that time that all the rest of Israel will be gathered (Isa. 11:1-12; 66:19-21; Mt. 24:31).

We aren't trying to use human reasoning for any of this. We only use Scripture studies, but what better day could there possibly be for the day when all of Israel will repent. The Day of Atonement is the perfect day to fulfill this High Holy Day. All the Yom Kippur's prior to this one have only been dress rehearsals. Let me re-insert a fact that all students of eschatology can agree upon based upon the above Scripture references. At the Second Coming of Christ, on that exact day, all of Israel will see the Lord coming in the sky. They will believe, and they will repent!!! Again, what better day of the year for the Second Coming than on Yom Kippur (The Day of Atonement)? It just so happens this is the day that coincides with all the math, eschatology, and astronomy to fit September 26, 2019.

Neilah is the closing or final service of Yom Kippur. It is the Jewish belief that the gates of heaven are open during the days of repentance to receive our prayers for forgiveness and that they close after the neilah service. (Specifically, they are open on Rosh HaShanah to let the righteous into Heaven and remain open until the neilah service of Yom Kippur.) When the final blast of the shofar (the Shofar HaGadol, the Great Trumpet) is heard at the end of the neilah service, those who have observed the day with sincerity should feel that they have been inscribed and sealed in the Book of Life.

The Day of Atonement was the most solemn of all the feast days. It was the day of cleansing for the nation and for the sanctuary. On this day alone, once a year, the high priest entered into the holiest of all, the Holy of Holies in the temple, within the veil of the temple, with the blood of the Lord's goat, the sin offering. Here he sprinkled the blood on the mercy seat. The blood of the sin offering on the great Day of Atonement brought about the cleansing of all sin for the priesthood, the sanctuary, and Israel as a nation (Lev. 16:29-34). Israel was restored on the 40th and last day of Teshuvah, and the

10th and last day of the Days of Awe (from Rosh Hashanah – Yom Kippur)

Teshuvah is the Hebrew word assigned to the 40 days preceding Yom Kippur, the Day of the Covering, or Atonement. Originally, it only comprised the 10 days between Rosh Hashanah and Yom Kippur (Days of Awe). But Jewish tradition extended this time of repentance that all might come to the place of salvation. Look at the Hebrew: Teshuvah - The root word is the Hebrew "shoov," which means to return. It combines both aspects of forgiveness: turning from evil and turning toward good. The Jews make restitution during this period with those they have offended. Ridding oneself of guilt is a goal of Teshuvah.

Not only have the fall feasts not been fulfilled by their prophetic future, but even the days leading up to them are shining in the sun to be noticed, and screaming to be heard. Only the willfully ignorant will look at them and quickly dismiss the knowledge they hold concerning the prophetic future of the end times.

There are a lot of studies out there about the 40 Days of Teshuvah. I've given enough information to prove the evidence, but if you want more, I will suggest a book I read in 2007 called, 40 Days of Teshuvah, by Perry Stone and Bill Cloud. Here is a quick excerpt: "Most Christians are not familiar with the Hebraic concepts of the Bible, especially the seven appointed feasts and the yearly cycles ordained by God. Few Christians have heard about the new moon cycles and how Israel's calendar and prophetic future were hidden in the lunar cycles. Understanding the new moon unlocks deeper revelation of the seven main feasts. Three of these, the fall feasts, are introduced during the season of Teshuvah. This time is called the Days of Awe and Seasons of Joy."

Feasts Of The Lord / Appointed Times

MILLENNIAL REIGN BEGINS ON THE FEAST OF TABERNACLES

This is not proof of a 2016 Rapture, or a 2023 Second Coming, but it will be helpful to those who don't know why The Feast Of Tabernacles is thought to be the fulfillment of the first day Jesus begins the Millennial Reign of 1,000 years of peace on earth. Note: Sukkot is Hebrew for The Feast Of Tabernacles. If Sukkot is fulfilled in 2023 by the start of the Millennial Reign, then it will be on the October 1 and will continue for seven days.

This will begin five days after the Second Coming (Zech. 14:1-5) and every year after that from everlasting to everlasting … "And it shall come to pass, that every one that is left of all the nations which came against Jerusalem shall even go up from year to year to worship the King, the LORD of hosts, and to keep the feast of tabernacles" (Zech. 14:16).

The day the saints came back to earth was Zechariah 14:1-5, on the Day of Atonement, hopefully September 26, 2023. The day of atonement is also called 'Yom Kippur,' which is five days before the feast of tabernacles, also called 'Sukkot.' It appears that there is an immediate gathering for the Lord that takes five days to gather for after Christ first sets His feet back on earth (Zech. 14:1-5).

The seventh and final feast of the Lord is the feast of tabernacles. It occurs five days after the Day of Atonement on the fifteenth of Tishri (October). This feast is also called the Feast of In gathering (Ex. 23:16; 34:22), the Feast to the Lord (Lev. 23:39; Judges 21:9), the Feast of Booths, or simply "the feast" (Lev. 23:36; Dt. 16:13; 1 Kings 8:2; 2 Chr. 5:3, 7:8; Neh. 8:14; Isa. 30:29; Ezek. 45:23, 25) because it was so well known. After the return from Exile, Ezra read the law and led the Israelites in acts of penitence during the Feast of Tabernacles (Neh. 8:13-18). The dedication of Solomon's' Temple also took place (I Kings 8:2) during this feast. Later, Josephus referred to the Feast of Tabernacles as the holiest and greatest of the Hebrew feasts.

On the first day of the feast, each participant had to collect twigs of myrtle, willow, and palm in the area of Jerusalem for construction of their booth (Neh. 8:13-18). These "huts" or "booths" were constructed from bulrushes as joyful reminders of the temporary housing erected by their forefathers during the Exodus wanderings (Lev. 23:40-41; Dt. 16:14). The "booth" in Scripture is a symbol of protection, preservation, and shelter from heat and storm (Ps. 27:5; 31:20; Isa. 4:6). The rejoicing community included family, servants, orphans, widows, Levites, and sojourners (Dt. 16:13-15). Besides the construction of the booths, other festivities included the in gathering of the labor of the field (Ex. 23:16), the in gathering of the threshing floor and wine press (Dt. 16:13), and the in gathering of the fruit of the earth (Lev. 23:39). Samples of the fall crop were hung in each family's booth to acknowledge God's faithfulness in providing for His people.

On the eighth and final day of the feast, the high priest of Israel, in a great processional made up of priests and tens of thousands of worshipers, descended from the Temple Mount to pause briefly at the Pool of Siloam. A pitcher was filled with water, and the procession continued via a different route back to the Temple Mount. Here, in the midst of great ceremony, the high priest poured the water out of the pitcher onto the altar. Since in Israel the rains normally stop in March, there is no rain for almost seven months! If God does not provide the "early" rains in October and November, there will be no spring crop, and famine is at the doorstep. Therefore, this ceremony was intended to invoke God's blessing on the nation by providing life-giving water.

It is in connection with the Feast of Tabernacles and this eighth day that the gospel of John records a fascinating event. John wrote: "In the last day (eighth day), that great day of the feast, Jesus stood and cried out, saying, If any man thirst, let him come unto me, and drink. He that believeth on me, as the scripture hath said, out of his heart shall flow rivers of living water" (Jn. 7:37-38). The Son of God was saying in the clearest possible way that He alone was the source of life and blessing; that He could meet every need of the human heart.

Another ritual included the lighting of huge Menorahs at the Court of the Women. This is the probable background for Jesus' statement: "I am the light of the world" (Jn. 8:12). The water and the "pillar of light" provided during the wilderness wandering (when people dwelt in tabernacles) was temporary and in contrast to the continuing water and light claimed by Jesus during this feast which commemorated that wandering period.

The eschatological visions which speak of the coming of all nations to worship at Jerusalem refer to the feast of tabernacles on the occasion of their pilgrimage (Zech. 14:16-21). This feast speaks eloquently of Christ's millennial Kingdom - of a new beginning without the ravages of the curse of sin. In that day, the earth will give her full bounty, all animals will be docile (Isa. 65:25), armies will no longer march, every man will sit under his own fig tree (Micah 4:4), and righteousness will become a reality in the earth.

> And it shall come to pass, that every one that is left of all the nations which came against Jerusalem shall even go up from year to year to worship the King, the LORD of hosts, and to keep the feast of tabernacles" (Zech. 14:16).

In the last verses (Zech. 14:16-19) we have the explanation of what will happen to those who are left of all the nations who will fight against Jerusalem under the Antichrist. If they have not taken the mark of the beast (Rev. 14:9-11), and if they have not persecuted Christ's brethren, the Jews (Mt. 25:31-46), and if they are otherwise worthy of entrance into the kingdom, they will be left here to live as natural men on earth, to multiply and replenish the earth, as God originally commanded (Gen. 1:26-31).

They will be permitted to establish themselves in the earth and live through the entire 1,000 years, if they remain obedient, not committing any sin worthy of death (Isa. 65:20-25). They will be required to go up (at least representatives) to Jerusalem to worship the King, the Lord of hosts, and to keep the feast of tabernacles yearly (Zech. 14:16). If they do not go up as required, there will be no rain upon their land (Zech. 14:17-19). If any rebel with Satan at the end of the 1,000 years, then fire will come down from God out of heaven and devour them (Rev. 20:7-10).

> In that day shall there be upon the bells of the horses, HOLINESS UNTO THE LORD; and the pots in the LORD'S house shall be like the bowls before the altar (Zech. 14:20).

"The last two verses in Zechariah (Zech. 14:20-21), simply explain the absolute holiness of the kingdom. The word holiness itself will be on the bells of the horses and on every pot in Jerusalem. Sacrifices will be continued as a memorial to the work of Christ on the cross, as explained in Ezekiel 40 – Ezekiel 46. There will never be a Canaanite in the eternal temple, the Lord's eternal capital (Ezek. 43:7).

The theory that saints will spend eternity in heaven, and that all things in the future will be spiritual only, is contradicted throughout Scripture. It is clear that God made all material creations and the living creatures in them to continue forever, as they were created. Here we have many natural and earthly things mentioned as continuing -- bells, horses, men, bowls, houses, pots, animal sacrifices, and other things which must be understood literally in connection with the Millennium and the New Earth period, as we understand them now.

God made a contract with Noah stating that all animals and men would continue forever, as well as all seasons on the earth (Gen. 8:22; 9:1-16). Hundreds of plain, simple statements in Scripture confirm the fact that God's plan for natural man is eternal. Had there been no fall, as by Adam and Eve, there would have been no sin, or death for sin, and therefore no resurrection for people who had died before all things became restored. Furthermore, there would be no resurrected saints reigning over eternal coming generations. As it is now, the plan will be carried out with resurrected saints ruling as kings and priests under God and Christ; from the planet earth they will help the Godhead to administer the affairs of all creations in space" (Dake Annotated Reference Bible).

CHAPTER 4

UNDERSTANDING THE RAPTURE / TRIBULATION GAP

Believing the rapture begins the 70th Week is commonly believed by the church. However, there is more evidence supporting a gap between the catching away of the righteous and the start of Daniel's 70th Week. It only stands to reason that the rapture will not be on day one of the Daniel's 70th Week.

What does begin the Seven Year Tribulation, or Daniel's 70th Week? It is the signing of the seven year peace treaty made for Israel's and signed by the Antichrist (Dan. 9:24-27). The rapture happens first, and then the man of sin is revealed (2 Thess. 2:7-8). It just doesn't make sense to have a world-wide event where millions vanished across the world, and then on the same day, a leader establishes a seven year peace treaty with Israel. The Antichrist will not be revealed until the ten kingdoms are formed from the old Roman Empire. Could it be that the events are seconds, or minutes apart, and that's why it could happen on the same day? I'm going to say no, and here is why.

Before the Antichrist is known, there must be a re-bordering of the Old Roman Empire. You may need to google "Old Roman Empire borders." As you can see, the Old Roman Empire includes parts of three continents: Europe, Asia, and Africa. We can get further into this in the pages ahead, but all that has to be understood now is that the Antichrist will be in charge of one of the ten kingdoms in order to make the covenant with Israel. This will be the old Syrian territory. If the church ever sees these ten territories of the revised Roman Empire, then we know the rapture is at the door. As it stands, I believe a dramatic change of power and borders will result from an unprecedented world-wide event, like millions vanishing without a trace.

Biblically, the unknown time between the rapture and the start of the Tribulation could be as long as 30, 100, or even 1,000 years. Scripture gives no absolutes about this. However, it is my belief the two events will happen in the fall of the same year. We do know the rapture will take place before the Tribulation, before the reign of Antichrist, before the fulfillment of Matthew 24 - Matthew 25; Revelation 4:2 - Revelation 22:5, and before the fulfillment of many other prophecies. The rapture is next on the prophetic time-line.

There are a number of scriptures in the Bible making it crystal clear the rapture will take place before the tribulation. Here are a few examples from Christ and the New Testament writers. We have shown this to be sound doctrine from books 1-2 of the Millions Vanished series. Noah was sealed in the arc seven days before the judgment of the world-wide flood came upon the earth. It didn't start raining as soon as the righteous were safe (Gen. 7:1-10). Lot is a different story. He and his family were safe enough away from the cities for God to send His wrath against Sodom and Gomorrah. This judgment was immediate. So, there is precedence for such a delay of the beginning of the 70th Week.

There is a great reason for an unknown period of time between the rapture of the church and the beginning of Daniel's 70th week / the Seven Year Tribulation. Why might there be time in between the Rapture and the beginning of the Tribulation? The key event that starts off this tribulation period is the signing of the 7 year treaty with Israel by Antichrist (Dan. 9:27). Also, the Rapture in Revelation has to be placed directly after the church is finally spoken of, which is Revelation 4:1, when the things that will take place after the church age are revealed. The Seven Year Tribulation begins and ends from Revelation 6:1 – Revelation 20:6. The time from Revelation 4:1 – Revelation 6:1 can be seen as a time of delay in between. This is literally when the Judgment Seat of Christ will take place as seen by the crowned saints. Presently, crowns have not been given to saints in heaven.

I've even heard such speculation from a couple of sources. One of the sources is *Prophecy in the News*. They also believe there is a gap of time in between the rapture and the beginning of the Tribulation. For example: In the scenario that the rapture is on feast of trumpets in 2016, then the few days from October 4 – October 26, 2016 would allow time for the 144,000 (Rev. 7:1-8) to get saved, allow time for the Antichrist to explain and solve things, come to power by the demonic help of the Beast that comes out of the Abyss (Rev. 9:11; 11:7; 17:8), leading to the signing of a seven year peace treaty and time for the great deception (2 Thess. 2:7-12), which is a visible fleet of UFO's around the world that pose as beings from another galaxy, but are really demonic and merely from another dimension (Eph. 6:12; Col. 1:16-18) (Book 4 teaches this).

The feast of trumpets is on October 3-4 in 2016, which is based upon the sighting of the new moon, so the day may fall on October 5. 2016 is just an example for teaching purposes. I hope it did happen in 2016, but if not, then so be it. Passover in 3 ½ years falls on April 8, 2020, so we just need to subtract 1,260 days to find out when the Antichrist signs a treaty with Israel, beginning the 70th Week. This will be October 26, 2016. The gap of time will then be about 3 weeks. Keep reading throughout this book and all this will come together.

There is also a gap in between the end of the Tribulation and the Second Coming. Like the rapture, the common belief is that the Second Coming ends the 70th Week. This is not a big deal for doctrine, but it is a big deal for figuring out a correct time-line for those daring enough to do so. I salute you! Counting 1,260 days into the future from Passover, 2020 will land you on September 20, 2023. This is when the two witnesses, Enoch and Elijah, will end their ministry and be killed (Rev. 11:1-13).

The Second Coming will land on September 26, 2023, because this is the day of atonement. The two witnesses rise from death and rise to the sky in front of their enemies 3 ½ days later on September 24, 2023. They attend the marriage supper of the Lamb with all resurrected saints and come back to fight against Antichrist two days later. In this scenario, the gap of time in between the end of Daniel's 70th Week and the Second Coming will be six days long. You've just gotten a small taste in making a biblical timeline, but the full course is still yet to come.

The beginning of the Millennial Reign has also been mistakenly thought of as starting at the Seconding Coming, but there is a gap of time even between the Second Coming and the official start of the Millennial Reign. Five days is set between the feast of atonement and the feast of tabernacles. We covered this in chapter 3, but this makes another great case for the understanding of gaps of days between the major events surrounding the Second Coming.

In conclusion, the rapture does not begin the 70th Week. The 70th Week does not end at the Second Coming. The Second Coming does not begin the Millennial Reign. The gap between the rapture and the beginning of the Tribulation can be known by subtracting 1,260 days from Passover, and then counting the days between that date and the feast of trumpets (feast 5 / appointed time 5 from Leviticus 23). The gap between the end of the 70th Week and the Second Coming is known by adding 1,260 days to Passover, and then counting the days between that date and the feast of atonement (feast 6 / appointed time 6 from Leviticus 23). The beginning of the Millennial Reign is always going to be 5 days after the Second Coming on the feast of tabernacles (feast 7 / appointed time 7 from Leviticus 23).

Chapter 5

BOOK 2'S COVER UNVEILED

I'm biased about this cover. I designed it and **Quest Publications** made it a reality. I think it's the most eye-catching book cover I've ever laid my eyes on. It was a gamble to create a cover like this, in that I already knew its meaning would go mostly unknown. To the watcher, I believed it would compel them, as most are familiar with the new moon and it's meaning for the timing of the rapture with pre-tribbers.

The rest of the moons are still a mystery to those who are familiar with the new moon rapture. No matter what your understanding currently is when using the moon as a prophetic time marker, you have chosen the right book. I write simple for all levels. Those who understand all the Bible scholar's lingo can understand me, and so can the most common man, which I include myself with.

I recently heard a wise man say, "There is always an easier word you can use in place of a big one. If a six year old doesn't understand what you're talking about, then simplify it." The whole point of writing about the Bible is to help everyone have a clear understanding, not to give an author an image of superiority. Everyone has their gifts and calling to advance the kingdom of God.

I saved this teaching for this chapter in this book because we had to learn the feast days of the Lord first. You'll never look at book 2's cover the same after this. It's like a treasure map hidden in plain sight.

Book 2's Cover Unveiled

This information will be revolutionary if you are prone to searching for the book-ends of the Seven Year Tribulation. We're going to build upon this teaching in the chapter entitled, Putting the Biblical Time-Line Together. Refer back to the book 2 cover for the visual needed.

A partial lunar eclipse was chosen for preterism. This won't help us discover the future timing of the rapture, mid-point of the Tribulation, or any other future event, but it is relevant. The moon is a time marker for some important prophetic events coming up. Remember, two of the seven reasons the moon was created is for signs and to inform us when the appointed times are coming (Gen. 1:14-16; Col. 2:16-17).

The destruction of Jerusalem by the Romans occurred in 70 AD. The Jewish historian Josephus reported a partial lunar eclipse on Passover of that year. Passover is the first feast mentioned in the list of seven in Leviticus 23. Passover is also the first feast, or appointed time, that was fulfilled by Jesus with His death on the cross. There is another important Passover date coming up in this chapter. Many preterists believe the rapture happened in 70 AD, along with most prophecy, if not all. Wrong as that is, Jesus' predicted the destruction of Jerusalem, which did take place in 70 AD, and the partial blood red moon on Passover was no coincidence.

Waning crescent was chosen for the partial rapture theory. This theory was shown incorrect in book 2, so there is no significance of the waning crescent moon. It just looks like a partial moon to me, so it was chosen for the rapture view's name "partial rapture." They hold to multiple raptures of the church throughout the Seven Year Tribulation.

A total solar eclipse was chosen for the pan-tribulation rapture. As with the partial rapture theory, there is not a significant moon given, but the next four are highly momentous and crucial for the watcher. This view has no definite timeline, so naturally there can be no moon rightfully assigned. A pan-tribulation view says the rapture will happen when it happens. They avoid any and all dispute by pleading impartiality. This eclipse was chosen because it is of the moon hiding the light of the sun so that darkness blankets the earth. This is appropriate for those who shun the light of Scripture that reveals the timing of the rapture. They have chosen darkness to blind their eyes from this truth.

The feast of trumpets is when the rapture will occur in a soon coming year, maybe this year. This feast happens immediately after a new moon. A new moon is when the moon is directly in between the sun and the earth. The moon gives off no natural light, so we cannot see any of the light of the sun reflecting off the moon. The feast of trumpets officially begins with the sighting of the first sliver of light from the new moon. This has to be seen by two witnesses in Israel.

The mid-point of the Seven Year Tribulation will fall on a full moon. How do I know this? Because the revelation of knowing the rapture will happen in the fall, with the revelation that the Second Coming will fulfill the 6th feast, the day of atonement, also in the fall, puts the mid-point in the spring. What better day in the spring than on Passover? The day Jesus gained ultimate victory over the devil is also the greatest day of sacrifice for the Jews, who will have re-instituted the sacrifices by then in their temple (Dan. 9:24-27; Mat. 24:15; Rev. 11:1-3).

Passover is when the Antichrist will enter the temple, stop daily sacrifices, ending the Israeli covenant he signed with them, and declares himself to be God. The mid-point of the Tribulation will be on Passover, which is always on a full moon. The Jewish calendar is lunar, meaning it is solely based on the moon cycle. Passover will never be on the same day on our calendar in back to back years. Passover is always on the full moon, when the earth is in between the sun and the moon. With the moon being directly on the furthest side of the earth from the sun in a straight line, we can see all the sunlight reflecting off the moon.

Book 2's Cover Unveiled

By understanding when the mid-point of the Tribulation is, we can now assign accurate days to the beginning and end of the Tribulation. This is where many miss it who seek to date find, even when they understand the fulfillment of the fall feast days. They may begin with the feast of trumpets and add 2,520 days (1,260 + 1,260), or they may begin at the Second Coming on the feast of the great day of atonement and subtract 2,520 day. The variations differ depending on the number of days used: 1,260 (Dan. 7:25; 12:7; Rev. 11:2-3; 12:6, 14; 13:5), 1,290 (Dan. 12:11), 1,335 (Dan. 12:12), or 2,300 (Dan. 8:14). This will always create a gap of days in between the rapture and the beginning of the Tribulation, as well as a gap of days in between the end of the Tribulation and the Second Coming.

A total lunar eclipse is what is known as a blood moon. This is when the pre-wrath rapture view happens (Rev. 6:12). They believe this happens just before the end of the Tribulation, so I place it in that order on the book cover. This moon will happen, but it will be toward the beginning of the Tribulation. Also, there will not be a rapture during this blood moon, sun darkening, firestorm falling, earth shattering event (Rev. 6:12-17).

Revelation 6 is actually toward the beginning of the Tribulation. We'll dive deeper into the chronological sequential order of the Book of Revelation in the chapter 10, section 5, and in chapter 11, entitled, *How to Put a Biblical Time-Line Together*. An innumerable amount of incorrect doctrines and time-lines have come from not understanding how Revelation was given.

The post-tribulation view received a new moon for visual effect. In truth, this was symbolic of the darkness of the moon immediately after the Tribulation.

> Immediately after the tribulation of those days shall the sun be darkened, and the moon shall not give her light, and the stars shall fall from heaven, and the powers of the heavens shall be shaken (Mat. 24:29).

The moon will not be in a normal eclipse as I'll show you. The moon will also not be a new moon. She will simply not give her light, nor will the sun. The feast of trumpets is always after the sighting of the first sliver of the new moon. The day of atonement is always ten days later. The last feast day to be fulfilled is the feast of tabernacles, which occurs five days after the day of atonement. To put it another way, the feast of trumpets is day 1. The feast of atonement is day 10. The feast of tabernacles is day 15.

The moon cycle is about 29.5 days long, so 15 days after the new moon of the feast of trumpets is the feast of tabernacles, which always lands on a full moon. Day 1 is a new moon. Day 15 is a full moon. Day 10 is a moon that is 2/3 full, or 1/3 empty if you're negative (just kidding). The point is that the Second Coming is going to fulfill the feast of atonement, which is on day 10. The sun and moon can only be darkened to not give light on earth by an eclipse. A full solar eclipse, or a full lunar eclipse can only happen on day 1 or day 15. This is when the sun, earth, and moon are in conjunction with each other.

There can never be a total eclipse on the day of atonement, which is when the Second Coming takes place. So what is it that blocks the light of the sun and the moon at the same time in concordance with being pelted with many asteroids (Mat. 24:29)? Is it possible the sun with literally stop shining? This cannot be, for God created a solar covenant with man (Gen. 1:14-18; 8:22; Ps. 89:34-37; Jere. 31:35-37; 33:19-26). In addition to eternal seasons of fruitfulness, it promised that man would continue forever, as long as the solar system endures. These promises were made to Noah, David, and Jeremiah as seen in Scripture references above.

Some believe there will be no need for the sun one day because God will be the light we will use when He brings the New Jerusalem to earth after the Millennial Reign (Rev. 21:1-7, 9-10; Rev. 22:1-5). However, the sun and the moon will shine forever. Not only will they continue to give and reflect light, but that light will be seven times brighter than it is now (Isa. 30:26).

There is no clear explanation in Scripture to what causes the darkness of both the sun and the moon. If it were just those two events then the theory of nuclear war may work. The idea is that the smoke from the war of Armageddon will darken the sky. However, the stars will also be falling. This can be nothing else than meteors. Literal language is being used, so Jesus is not using symbolic language for angels falling or for missiles.

Two times are the stars spoken of as falling to the earth while the sun is darkened. The first time is at the beginning of the Tribulation during the 6th seal (Rev. 6:13). The second time is at the coming of Christ soon after the Tribulation (Mt. 24:29-31). There will be several years between the two events. Naturally, references to stars falling to earth do not refer to real stars, all of which are much bigger than our own planet. These are meteors, asteroids, or shooting stars.

I believe the likely cause of both events involving darkness of the sun, meteors pelting the earth as the earth and even the heavens shake, will come about from a heavenly body. This heavenly body could be a planet, a dwarf star, or a giant meteor. We know this is not far-fetched, as there are two meteors thrown to the earth during the trumpet judgments (Rev. 8:8, 10). There is a belief accepted by many, yet ridiculed by more, that we have a binary star in our solar system. This means we have two stars, which is the norm for many solar systems.

Planet X is the name. Nibiru is also a common term for the rogue planet that could be a dwarf star. I won't give a detailed study of it here, but at the risk of being discredited by many, I truthfully see more evidence for it than against it. It makes its way around the sun every few hundred or few thousand years in a long elliptical orbit that takes it very far outside the orbit of Pluto. If this is true, then it will explain the many astronomical events during the Tribulation.

It is theorized to come in close to the sun as it passes the earth. Then, taking around seven years to make its pass around the sun before it passes by the earth once more as it heads back out of our commonly known solar system. This can explain the meteors pelting the earth at the beginning of the Tribulation when the sun is darkened (Rev. 6:12-17). Maybe the rogue heavenly body shoots between the sun and the earth to block the sun and eclipse the moon in order to cause a blood moon effect.

If the body is very large, the gravitational pull of a Planet X would drag space debris with it, which would account for the shooting stars hitting the earth. If the heavenly body passes through the asteroid belt, then the result would be cataclysmic for the earth as it flies by us. The gravitational pull would also account for the earthquakes that also accompany the darkening of the sun and shooting stars about seven years apart (Rev. 6:12; Mat. 24:29-31).

There is much more information on this topic from a Christian and biblical viewpoint, but this will suffice for our subject. Keeping your hand on the pulse of stories like this is a great way to watch.

CHAPTER 6

THE DOCTRINE OF IMMINENCY

There has been a time in my life when I examined everything the church has taught me. I did this out of duty, not unbelief. I wanted to be able to back up my beliefs with Scripture. There has never been a day in my life when I have ever doubted the authoritative, infallibility, and Holy Spirit inspired book we call, The Bible. Even in this, I have examined the critics and defenders of the authenticity of the Bible. We must! How can we know we have not been deceived if we never search the things out that we have been taught (Acts 17:11)?

The Doctrine of Imminency is no exception. I have studied the origins of this widely accepted belief, as well as searching it out in the Scriptures. My searching has conclusively found it to be false. I'll tell you where this doctrine came from and why it is untrue. I'd like to first point out that this doctrine is not dangerous, which is highly unusual for a false doctrine. The good from it is that it is a motivation for constant holiness in view of the belief that Christ could come back on any old day to rapture the church; though, this motivation is quickly outweighed by those who believe they can actually be caught in sin and still be raptured. The bad from this doctrine is that it keeps God's people blinded to the prophetic times.

Why would you accept a belief that the rapture will be the fulfillment of the feast of trumpets if you believe the rapture is not an appointed time of God? Believing the Doctrine of Imminency makes you reject such truths, because those who hold it's teachings believe the rapture is not on a definite time-table. Rather than accepting the knowledge of the fulfillment of the feast days, they believe the rapture is going to come about based upon things happening on this planet. God will then say it is time after one of the many things triggering the rapture occur. Some ideas say the rapture won't happen until the Day of the Saints, Sudden Destruction, Great Revival, A United Church, The Wealth of the Wicked (being given to the righteous), or the Fullness of the Gentiles. And if one believes the rapture is middle or post tribulation, then that is even more willful blindness upon those who believe the Doctrine of Imminency, because the events that take place in the Tribulation will be known by those who know Scripture.

I won't go into great detail with this, but I will give some points and leave it with you, the reader. The only thing we have left to look for prophetically is the rapture. There are no other prophecies that need fulfilling for this event. This has always been the case, even when Israel was not a reborn nation yet. The rapture happens at least 7 years before the Second Coming, but this does not mean exactly 7 years before. Nowhere in the Bible does it say how long before the 70th Week of Daniel that the rapture will happen, only that it will happen before the last seven year period. So, it is in this sense that the rapture could be considered imminent.

If you do believe as I do, that the rapture is an appointed time of God and it will be fulfilled by the feast of trumpets, then you will understand why it would be impossible to believe the event could happen on any old day. If you understand times, ages, and dispensations, then you would also not choose any old year. In the simplest explanation, this is why the Doctrine of Imminency is false. Understanding the appointed times, or feast days, is foundational end time knowledge and a must have key in order to unlock many end-time mysteries.

The Doctrine Of Imminency

The rapture will occur at sunset on the feast of trumpets as its fulfillment. Sunset in Israel is when the last trumpet is blown. This feast is next in line as given in Leviticus 23. If you know God and study His Word, then you know His ways. They are orderly, not random. The feast of trumpets is also the only appointed time that uses a specific trumpet, called the last trump.

I write all of this in retrospect of studying these things out. To be fair and unbiased, I will show you my findings when searching for the scriptures people use to support this belief. The following verses are used to prove the Doctrine of Imminency. Read them well and we'll examine their truths after each text proof for the Doctrine of Imminency.

> Behold, I shew you a mystery; We shall not all sleep, but we shall all be changed, In a moment, in the twinkling of an eye, at the last trump: for the trumpet shall sound, and the dead shall be raised incorruptible, and we shall be changed. For this corruptible must put on incorruption, and this mortal must put on immortality. So when this corruptible shall have put on incorruption, and this mortal shall have put on immortality, then shall be brought to pass the saying that is written, Death is swallowed up in victory (1 Cor. 15:51-54).

This is one of the top two most recognized rapture passages that reflects nothing for an imminent rapture. This is mistakenly used as proof of an imminent rapture because it's giving us the knowledge that this event will happen in a split second, or the twinkling of an eye. True as this fact is, it in no way indicates an absolute that the rapture can happen on any day at any time. On the contrary, this passage gives us the biggest key to understanding the timing of the rapture to be at a specif time of an unknown year.

That time is at the last trump, which again is the time of the feast of trumpets. Specifically, the last trump is blown at sunset to end the feast, so the timing given is down to the minute. Since 2008,

I have always looked up when the sun will set in Israel on the day in September or October that ends this feast day.

> For our conversation is in heaven; from whence also we look for the Saviour, the Lord Jesus Christ: Who shall change our vile body, that it may be fashioned like unto his glorious body, according to the working whereby he is able even to subdue all things unto himself (Phil. 3:20-21).

> Looking for that blessed hope, and the glorious appearing of the great God and our Saviour Jesus Christ (Tit. 2:13).

Both of these references speak of the same thing, which is that it's scriptural to look for the rapture, or coming of the Lord in the air for the saints (Php. 3:20; Tit. 2:13). Both references express the action of looking for the rapture, but neither say the event could happen at any time. To play the devil's advocate, they also do not say the rapture will happen on the feast of trumpets, but Paul is the author of all 5 of these text proofs of an imminent rapture.

Imminent means that something could happen very soon, or without delay. The Doctrine of Imminence according to that standard is true, but the modern understanding that it could happen on any day is false. Any year? As far as I know, this is true. The only absolute truth revealed to us in these times is that the rapture cannot happen on any day, for it is an appointed time to be fulfilled on the feast of trumpets, during sunset, at the last trump, in a specifically appointed year not known to us yet.

> So that ye come behind in no gift; waiting for the coming of our Lord Jesus Christ (1 Cor. 1:7).

> And to wait for his Son from heaven, whom he raised from the dead, even Jesus, which delivered us from the wrath to come (1 Thess. 1:10).

The Doctrine Of Imminency

I'll take these two proofs used for an imminent rapture together, as they say the same thing. We are to be waiting for the coming of our Lord Jesus Christ. This is quite contrary to ignoring the subject because you hope to see your kids have kids. The great blessed hope comes before the hope of living out your life here on earth with no change in the Church Age. The Greek word for "waiting" is apekdechomai (GSN-<G553>), which means to be eagerly expecting. It is used in nearly every instance of looking for the coming of the Lord, or the future hope of salvation (Rom. 8:19). Many watchers eagerly wait for the rapture, while only expecting it on the feast of trumpets.

These five verses are all I've found to uphold the Doctrine of Imminence, though they lack any proof to say this event will occur on any old day. We are to wait for His coming while looking and watching. This event will happen in an atom of time when it happens, but no Scripture teaches that this event will happen on any given day. Had I not received the revelation of the feast days and the literal last trump blown on the feast of trumpets, then I admittedly would believe the doctrine to be true. It is doubtful that I would have even thought of examining this doctrine since it's been told to me as an absolute truth since I was a child. We must be careful and examine everything (2 Tim. 2:15).

We may say, and it would be entirely scriptural, that there are no signs of the rapture, but there are many events preceding the Second Coming that will be known as they are being fulfilled. There never was a sign or a prophecy stated that had to come to pass, or be fulfilled before the rapture. The rapture could have taken place on any year in the past, or in the future, without a sign or prophecy having to be fulfilled. If there are certain prophecies to be fulfilled before the rapture, then we must look for those events to be fulfilled first, instead of looking for the rapture.

We do know by certain indications that many of the prophecies for the Second Coming to shortly come to pass are now beginning to be fulfilled, thus showing us that we are very near. If the Second Coming is near, the rapture is even closer, for the rapture will take place at least seven years before then. As you can see, the thought is very true that there is no prophecy that has to be fulfilled before the rapture, but this still does not validate the belief that it can happen, or will happen on any given day.

As a watcher who believes the rapture can only happen on a single moment of time once in any given year, unknown to me, I still look and watch for this day. It is still a motivation to constantly and consistently live out my faith in perfect obedience to the New Covenant made by the blood of Jesus. Tomorrow is not promised to any of us. We live as if the rapture could happen at any moment. This is a great mixture of the love and fear shown toward the Almighty God.

Chapter 7

AM I DATE-SETTING?

Remember how some Pharisees tried to trip Jesus up (Mk. 12:13; Mat. 19:3; 22:23-46)? He was wise and understood their motivation, giving Him trick questions... Condemned if you do, and condemned if you don't questions. Jesus was sincere, fearless, and brave in teaching the whole truth of God (Mk. 12:13-14). This is how I pattern my life. So to answer the death blow of being associated with date-setters, I remember how Jesus handled Himself and pray for that wisdom.

Just like all these topics, there are many layers to this question. It is extremely taboo to be a date-setter. While I'm not giving a point on the calendar for the definite rapture, I am saying it can only happen at one specific time of the year. To many, this puts me in a dangerous class.

I know many prominent teachers who believe the rapture will happen on a feast day, but come short of saying it is an absolute. They do this to keep followers and avoid being put in a taboo class of date-setters. On one hand, this is wise, while on the other hand, it is showing fear. Again, I pray I have a good balance with a subject so many are ignorant about due to a lifetime of being taught no one knows the day or hour, so why speculate? Biblically, that reference is always referring to the Second Coming.

The bottom line is no, I am not date-setting. It is true that many have said that this date or that date will bring the rapture. They spoke as a watcher, but were also unwise by speaking with an absolute. I think most watchers now days have seen such evidence for the rapture that all have fallen in that trap at one point or another. Some have said that they aren't date-setting, they are date finding. I agree with this line of thinking. It is my belief that all of the great days of the Lord, from the events of the First Coming to the events of the Second Coming, are all appointed times (Gen. 1:14; Mat. 8:29; Acts 17:26) that have their foreshadowing found in the seven feasts of the Lord (Lev. 23). The first four feasts had their fulfillment's during the time period of the First Coming. The last three will be fulfilled by the events surrounding the Second Coming.

In Colossians 2:16-17 we are reminded that the feasts and Sabbaths are a shadow of things to come. In Matthew 16:3, Jesus rebukes the Pharisees as hypocrites for not discerning "signs of the times," as prophesied in Scripture regarding His Coming. Were these "Feasts of the Lord" only meant to be sacrificial offerings of bulls & goats, or were they a foreshadow / typology of God's redemptive plan? Feasts… aka Solemn Appointed Times with the Lord (Leviticus 23:1-4). The Hebrew word translated "Feasts" means Appointed Times. According to Deuteronomy 16:16, God commands us to keep His Feasts and appear before the Lord with thanksgiving "forever" (Ex. 12:14). We can see the Second Coming in Zechariah 14:1-5 (Feast of Atonement). Shortly following in Zechariah 14:16 we see the Feast of Tabernacles 5 days later that will occur yearly throughout the Millennial Reign. This one in Zechariah 14 will be the beginning of the Millennial Reign. After the rapture, the Second Coming will be easily known to the day by those who gain understanding. This is why Satan prompts the Antichrist to change the times as seen in the Book of Daniel (Dan. 7:25).

There are 3 times more prophecies about the Second Coming than that of the First Coming, yet the magi ("3" wise men) read the signs. If one has a good understanding of the feast days, then one would automatically conclude the day of the rapture and the Second

Am I Date-setting?

Coming, unless they want to watch with a blindfold on. This is not to say we can know the year with any amount of certainty.

We know the generation is now. There are hundreds of signs that God forewarned us about. The greatest clue is that of the rebirth of national Israel in 1948. All we are looking for is the year. It is perfectly good to give watch dates. To give any one day as an absolute is completely foolish. Nevertheless, watchers will always receive rebukes from those who believe any date given is forbidden, yet this is not what we were told.

Jesus was not rebuking people for watching and piecing the puzzle together when He said no one knows the day or hour, or He would have rebuked his disciples for asking about the sign of His Coming and the end of the age (Mat. 24:1-3). Instead of a rebuke, we have the most part of Matthew 24-25; Mark 13; and Luke 21 giving many clues to the events of His Coming. Don't stop there. These signs are spread across the pages of time and Scripture.

For instance, an unknown heavenly body caused darkness for three hours at the exact time Jesus was hanging on the cross. This was on Passover, when the moon is full. A full moon is when the earth is in the middle of the sun and the moon. The moon did not block the sun. There was a lunar eclipse in 70 AD on Passover, the year the second temple was destroyed. There were two blood red total lunar eclipses in 32 AD. One on Passover, and one on Tabernacles. Two partial lunar eclipses were in the following year of 33 AD. Not a coincidence, the partial eclipses also happened on Passover and Tabernacles, the first and seventh feasts of the Lord (Lev. 23).

I am not date-setting, I am awake, sober, and watching as I see the end of this age coming closer. With that said, I have been a date finder, not a date-setter. There have been years that stuck out like a sore thumb, so naturally I have proclaimed the feast of trumpets in those respective years could be the rapture.

It sure looked that way in 2008 when there were three years in a row of total solar eclipses in 2008 – 2010 on Av 1. This is the day on the Jewish calendar that Nebuchadnezzar destroyed the Temple. 600 years later, Rome destroyed the temple on the 9th of Av. All the Jews were kicked out of England in 1290 on the 9th of Av, as well as Spain in 1492. World War I started on the 9th of Av. Hitler's proclamation to kill the Jews came on the 9th of Av. This is the same day Israel rejected the land 3,500 years ago.

Av 1 sits in the middle of Tammuz 17 to Av 9. Tammuz and Av are names of months on the Jewish calendar. The rabbis like to call these three weeks "The dark time," or "Between the straits." Moses had found the people worshiping the golden calf on Jewish calendar day of the 17th of Tammuz. Also from Av 1st – Av 9th there are to be no comforts to be enjoyed. No bathing, no clean clothes, no shoes, and they must read from the Book of Lamentations during those days.

Major events occurring in the "dark days" between Tammuz 17 to Av 9 is vast, and beyond coincidence. There are days and times being signaled to us if we are awake and watching. Seven years later was the 2014 – 2015 total lunar eclipses all landing on Passover and the feast of tabernacles. This gained the new terminology of being called a prophetic tetrad, or a biblical tetrad.

The beginning of the three years in a row of a total solar eclipse landing on the same day on the Jewish calendar in 2008, then ending a rare strand of total lunar eclipses in 2015 points to a 7 year period. 2008 and 2015 were both high watch years for the rapture on the feast of trumpets. Should we dance around the term "date-setter" when all these facts are known? We know the season if we are not in darkness (1 Thess. 5:1-5). We know the day of the rapture, Second Coming, and the first day of the Millennial Reign (Gen. 1:14; Lev. 23; Col. 2:16-17; 1 Thess. 4:16-17; 1 Cor. 15:52), so looking for the year based on signs and clues from the Bible is only a natural progression of watching for His Coming (Mk. 13:34-37).

Am I Date-setting?

If a year sticks out based on a seven year cycle of stock market or bond crashes, then I'm looking at that next 7th year. If that year falls at the same time as the end of a rare tetrad of four blood moons, then I'm sounding the alarm. I believe being called a date-setter for this view is like being called a bigot for not embracing lesbianism, gays, bisexuality, and transgenders. It is a way of silencing what is not wanted. I believe an appointed time is just that, a time appointed and known before hand. Jesus may not have known those years on earth, but He sure does now. I am not a date-setter. I am seeking to find that day. The date has already been set by God in the plan of dispensations for man during the divine counsel of the Trinity before the foundations of the world (Eph. 1:4-5; 1 Pt. 1:20).

CHAPTER 8

THAT DAY AND HOUR KNOWETH NO MAN

Here is the most common belief about looking for the rapture: "We know the times and seasons of it, but not the day or the hour. Men will not know the exact day or the hour of His coming. This will always be the case, as predicted by Jesus in Matthew 24:36, 39, 42-51; 25:13. Jesus Christ and the angels do not know the day or hour of the rapture (Mk. 13:32). It is, therefore, folly for any man to make predictions and set dates for the return of Jesus Christ for the saints or for the end of the times of the Gentiles."

> But of that day and hour knoweth no man, no, not the angels of heaven, but my Father only (Mat. 24:36).

> Watch therefore: for ye know not what hour your Lord doth come (Mat. 24:42).

> Watch therefore, for ye know neither the day nor the hour wherein the Son of man cometh (Mat. 25:13).

> But of that day and that hour knoweth no man, no, not the angels which are in heaven, neither the Son, but the Father (Mk. 13:32).

The truth is that the church is supposed to be reading the signs of the time (Lk. 12:56; 1 Thess. 5:1-5). We are not supposed to be dead (Rev. 3:1-6). We are not supposed to be lukewarm (Rev. 3:15-16). We are not supposed to be asleep (Mk. 13:36; 1 Cor. 15:33-34; 1 Thess. 5:6-8). We are supposed to be watching (Mk. 13:34-37; Lk. 21:34-36; 1 Thess. 5:6; Tit. 2:11-13; Rev. 3:2). Jesus is not supposed to come to Christians as a thief in the night (1 Thess. 5:2-4; Rev. 3:3; 16:15).

Let's thoroughly address the most common "rapture quote" known to man. It is, "No one knows the day or the hour." However, this phrase does not mean that we are supposed to be end-time ignorant. First thing to acknowledge is that Jesus was always referring to the Second Coming, never once referring to the rapture. Jesus only referred to the rapture two times (Jn. 14:1-3; Lk. 21:36), but never revealed this mystery in His day. He left that for Paul to reveal (1 Cor. 15:51-54).

First, let's look at Matthew 24 to prove the fact that these references are always speaking of the Second Coming, not the rapture seven years prior. The dialogue of this chapter begins with three questions brought to Jesus by His disciple. These are the three questions asked: When will Jerusalem be destroyed? This question is not answered by Matthew. It is answered in Luke 21:12-24. What will be the sign of Your coming? Answered in Matthew 24:4-26, 37-39. What will happen when You come? Answered in Matthew 24:27-31, 40-51; 25:1-46.

"What shall be the sign of thy coming?" Parousia (GSN-<G3952>) is Greek for "coming," meaning personal visible presence or reappearing. There will be two appearances Christians refer to. The first will be the rapture, which is a personal coming in the air (not to the earth) for the saints (1 Thess. 2:19; 3:13; 4:13-17; 5:23; 1 Cor. 15:23, 51-58; 2 Thess. 2:1,7-8; Jas. 5:7-8; 1 Jn. 2:28; Jn. 14:1-3). The second will be the Second Coming to earth with His saints to reign (Mt. 24:3, 27-51; 25:31-46; Jude 1:14; Rev. 19:11-21; Zech. 14:1-5).

There are twenty-four signs of the Second Coming foretold from Jesus' answer in Matthew 24. Let me point out the obvious for the analytical thinkers. Jesus did not rebuke them for asking. Why would He, since He is the One Who also commanded them to watch for His Coming (Mk. 13:34-37)? By watching for the signs of the Second Coming, we can better know when to expect the rapture, or the next "parousia" coming. These signs will be fulfilled in Daniel's 70th Week, but their increase in this century alone points to the nearness of their fulfillment's.

These are the twenty-four signs of the Second Coming, not the rapture: deceptions (Mt. 24:4-5, 11, 24); false Christs (Mt. 24:5, 23-26); wars and rumors of wars (Mt. 24:6-7); famines (Mt. 24:7; Rev. 6:5-6); pestilences (Mt. 24:7; Rev. 6:8); earthquakes (Mt. 24:7; Rev. 6:12-17); anti-semitism (Mt. 24:9; Mk. 13:9, 13); offenses (Mt. 24:10; cp. Mt. 18:1-10); betrayals (Mt. 24:9; Mk. 13:12); hatred (Mt. 24:10; 2 Tim. 3:1-9); false prophets (Mt. 24:11, 24; Rev. 13); lawlessness abounding (Mt. 24:12); love decreasing (Mt. 24:12-13; 2 Tim. 3); increased missionary work (Mt. 24:14); abomination of desolation (Mt. 24:15; Dan. 9:27; 2 Thess. 2:4; Rev. 13); new Jewish nation in Judea (Mt. 24:9, 15-26; Ezek. 37; Dan. 9:27); new Jewish temple (Mt. 24:15, 26; Rev. 11:1-2; Dan. 8:9-13; 9:27; 11:45; 2 Thess. 2:4); Great Tribulation of 3 1/2 years (Mt. 24:21; Dan. 12:1; Rev. 12:1 - Rev. 19:21); martyrdoms (Mt. 24:9, 22; Dan. 8:24; Rev. 7:9-17; 11:7; 15:2-4; 20:4-6); flight of Jews from Judea (Mt. 24:16-21; Rev. 12:6, 14; Isa. 16:1-5; Ps. 60:4-8; Dan. 11:40-45; Ezek. 20:33-38; Hos. 2:14-16); increased satanic powers (Mt. 24:24; 2 Thess. 2:8-12; Rev. 13; 16:14; 19:20); surfeiting (Mt. 24:38; Lk. 17:28; 21:34); sex crimes (Mt. 24:38; Lk. 17:27); and procrastination and lethargy (Mt. 24:39).

All these 24 signs are given as clues, not as rebukes for seeking to know when Jesus is coming back. Matthew 24:36, being one of the more commonly used references to no one knowing the day or the hour is after the definite timing is given. "For as the lightning cometh out of the east, and shineth even unto the west; so shall also the coming of the Son of man be. For wheresoever the carcase is, there will the eagles be gathered together. Immediately after the tribulation of those days..." (Mat. 24:27-29). Where the dead bodies are slain at Armageddon the birds will be gathered together to eat them (Job 39:30; Ezek. 39:17-22; Lk. 17:34-37; Rev. 19:17-21). The rapture will have taken place seven years before this.

The rational question one should ask next is, "Then the Second Coming cannot be known but you say it will be on the day of atonement?" All will be shortly addressed, then quickly made known.

Five verses later, in Matthew 24:41, we see that a group of people were taken like the flood, which "took them all away." Even though we see that this is immediately after the Tribulation (Mat. 24:29-31), pre-tribbers still use this as a rapture reference. The flood destroyed many (Mat. 24:39; Lk. 17:27). We know the flood destroyed the people it took away. So the Second Coming will not rapture, but destroy many at the battle of Armageddon to make the carcasses that will be eaten by the fowls of Matthew 24:28 (Lk. 17:34-37; Ezek. 39:17-22; Mat. 24:28; Rev. 19:17-21). At Armageddon, many will be left to continue living on earth when Christ reigns (Zech. 14:16-21; Mat. 25:34,46; Isa. 2:2-4; 66:19-21; Rev. 20:4-10), not destroyed, like Noah and his family were left and not destroyed.

Matthew 24:40-42 are some of the most misunderstood verses in Scripture. This is because people interpret them in connection with the rapture instead of the Second Coming. None of the context in all of Matthew 24 – Matthew 25, or Mark 13 is related to the rapture. Yet, the "no one knowing the day or the hour" references are always spoken of in the 20th and 21st century as being related to the rapture (24:36, 39, 42-51; 25:13; Mk. 13:32).

Therefore, regardless of how much these verses sound like the rapture of the church, they could not refer to that event. These verses are very Jewish in nature. They refer to the literal Coming of Christ to destroy the ungodly, Just like the flood did in the days of Noah. "Then" (at the Coming of Jesus with the saints and the holy angels to put an end to wickedness as did the flood) shall two be in the field when the one shall be taken and the other left. "Watch therefore," for ye know not what hour your Lord doth come. Don't be like the evil servant who thought the delay of his master had been delayed, for he compromised his righteousness to worry about sinful feelings and fulfilled sinful desires. For that servant, weeping and gnashing of teeth (Mat. 24:42-51).

> And take heed to yourselves, lest at any time your hearts be overcharged with surfeiting, and drunkenness, and cares of this life, and *so* that day come upon you unawares. For as a snare shall it come on all them that dwell on the face of the whole earth (Lk. 21:34-35).

Why should we take these verses out of their proper setting, which is at the Second Coming of Christ with the saints, and make them refer to the Coming of Christ for the saints? Why do we have to use such passage to prove that there will be a rapture? There are plenty of authentic rapture references. We don't need to claim these Second Coming references are rapture references for any reason. Therefore, why should we base a doctrine upon a passage that does not concern the subject of the rapture?

We may say, and be entirely scriptural, that there are no signs of the rapture as there are of the Second Coming. None of the signs and prophecies stated in Scripture and listed in Matthew 24 happen before the rapture, for they refer to the events happening on earth during the 70th Week of Daniel (Rev. 1:1; 6:1 – 22:6; Lk. 21:36). There never was a sign stated that had to come to pass, nor a prophecy to be fulfilled before the rapture. The rapture could have taken place in the past, at any time since and it can take place at any time now, or in the future, without a sign or prophecy having to be fulfilled. If there are certain prophecies to be fulfilled before the rapture, then we must look for those events to be fulfilled first instead of looking for the rapture.

As we know from prophecy, Israel will be gathered in their own land and have control over Jerusalem (Dan. 8:13-14; 9:27; 11:45; 12:11; Mat. 24:15; 2Th. 2:4; Rev. 11-12; 13:11-18). Since these events have occurred many decades ago, there is nothing to watch for except the events surrounding the 70th Week of Daniel (Dan. 9:24-27). It is possible that some of the above signs and prophecies may come to pass before the rapture, but that remains to be seen. We do know by certain indications, that some of the prophecies are now beginning to be fulfilled, or increasing rapidly, thus showing us that the Second Coming is very near. And if the Second Coming is near, the rapture is nearer, for the rapture will take place at least seven years before the revelation.

The rapture can take place any time, as proved by the fact that the early Christians were looking for the rapture in their day (Phil. 3:20-21; Tit. 2:13). They did not make one statement that certain events must take place before the rapture, so all the modern theories are wrong that teach that certain signs must come to pass, that certain prophecies must be fulfilled, that the Antichrist must first come, that the Tribulation must come first and be completed, and that a revival must first come to get the church ready for the rapture. This is altogether out of order with the doctrine of the rapture.

The following is a quick excerpt from *http://kingdomengineers. com/2011/08/matthew-24/* and entitled, *Matthew 24 - The Irony Of Quoting, "No Man Knows The Day Or Hour."*

"Be ye therefore ready also: for the Son of man cometh at an hour when ye think not (Luke 12:40)." This post is about understanding the return of Jesus Christ. It is ironic that the above quote from Scripture

is almost universally used by many Christians as a reason to stop any conversation about the end-times. They don't want to hear about it. They don't want to think about it. So, they use this quote as an excuse not to watch for the Return of Jesus Christ.

It is ironic because this quote is from those same sections of Scripture where Jesus Christ Himself exhorts us to watch for His return! It is ironic because this quote, in context, was used by Jesus as a reason to watch for His return. But don't take my word for it, take it to God's Word and see the truth for yourself: So likewise ye, when ye shall see all these things, know that it is near, even at the doors (Mat.24:33). But of that day and hour knoweth no man, no, not the angels of heaven, but my Father only (Mat.24:36).

Watch therefore: for ye know not what hour your Lord doth come (Mat.24:42). *Therefore be ye also ready: for in such an hour as ye think not the Son of man cometh* (Mat.24:44). *Watch therefore, for ye know neither the day nor the hour wherein the Son of man cometh* (Mat.25:13). *So ye in like manner, when ye shall see these things come to pass, know that it is nigh, even at the doors* (Mark 13:29). *But of that day and that hour knoweth no man, no, not the angels which are in heaven, neither the Son, but the Father* (Mark 13:32).

Take ye heed, watch and pray: for ye know not when the time is. Watch ye therefore: for ye know not when the master of the house cometh, at even, or at midnight, or at the cockcrowing, or in the morning. Lest coming suddenly he find you sleeping. And what I say unto you I say unto all, Watch (Mark 13:32-37). Blessed are those servants, whom the lord when he cometh shall find watching: verily I say unto you, that he shall gird himself, and make them to sit down to meat, and will come forth and serve them (Lk. 12:37). Be ye therefore ready also: for the Son of man cometh at an hour when ye think not (Luke 12:40). The lord of that servant will come in a day when he looketh not for him, and at an hour when he is not aware, and will cut him in sunder, and will appoint him his portion with the unbelievers (Luke 12:46).

The primary focus on each of these chapters is the exhortation to watch. It is indeed ironic that people use the quoted verse as a reason not to watch. Now that you know the truth (that Jesus exhorts us all to watch), and you are without excuse, know this, we are in the end-times and His return is near, even at the door. Read the rest of those chapters and look at the world events around you. Israel is God's time clock and it started ticking when Israel became a nation again in 1948. But don't expect to be informed about this in the lame-stream media. Turn off your televisions and search the internet for conservative and Christian news websites.

This is the end of article from *http://kingdomengineers.com/2011/08/matthew-24/* I just wanted to show another source from someone pointing out this simple truth.

DOES JESUS NOT KNOW THE RAPTURE DAY

He is omniscient, meaning all knowing. Many people will still say Jesus said He didn't know and even the angels don't know the day or the hour. The common belief is He is at the right hand of God the Father and is waiting on the command to get His bride. The truth is that Jesus is not in heaven with this knowledge being withheld from Him. The truth is, Jesus will come back for His spotless church (Eph. 5:27), not His spotless bride (no reference found).

Christian men and women alike fantasize about being the bride of Christ. The truth should be loved over a fantasy. There should be nothing disappointing about the bride being the Holy City, the New Jerusalem. The church will be a part of the bride for eternity. Not the church alone, but all redeemed men and women will be a part of the bride from Abel until the last one saved at the end of the future Tribulation. Old Testament saints were also promised the New Jerusalem (Heb. 11:10-16).

And there came unto me one of the seven angels which had the seven vials full of the seven last plagues, and talked with me, saying, Come hither, <u>I will shew thee the bride, the Lamb's wife</u>. And he carried me away in the spirit to a great and high mountain, <u>and shewed me that great city, the holy Jerusalem, descending out of heaven from God</u>, Having the glory of God: and <u>her</u> light *was* like unto a stone most precious, even like a jasper stone, clear as crystal (Rev. 21:9-11).

Let us be glad and rejoice, and give honour to him: for the marriage of the Lamb is come, and his wife hath made herself ready. And to her was granted that she should be arrayed in fine linen, clean and white: for the fine linen is the righteousness of saints (Rev. 19:7-8).

This explains that His wife is made up of the saints of all ages from Abel to the last one in the first resurrection; those who will go to live in the New Jerusalem (Heb. 11:10-16; 12:22-23; 13:14; Rev. 21:2,9-10). Revelation 22:17 tells us the Holy Spirit and the bride (the Holy City), say "Come!" The New Jerusalem, the Lamb's wife (Rev. 21:2, 9-10), is ready and prepared for the redeemed of all ages to have their part in her. Jesus is not unaware of when His Father will send Him. Jesus was fully aware of the appointed times on earth pertaining His earthly ministry. He no doubt knows when He will fulfill the fall feasts of the Lord as He is now omniscient again. I will explain what I mean by "again."

Dr. David Jeremiah, who should need no introduction, believes Jesus does know the appointed times and merely didn't know at that time because He had emptied Himself out from being omniscient when He left heaven to take on flesh. This statement couldn't be any more true when examining it to Scripture.

Philippians 2:7 says Jesus made himself of no reputation. This is often referred to in theological circles as the kenosis of Christ. Greek: kenoo (GSN-<G2758>), to empty out, drain. It is translated "make void" (Rom. 4:14; 1 Cor. 9:15); "make of none effect" (1 Cor. 1:17); "be in vain" (2 Cor. 9:3); and "make of no reputation," meaning, He emptied Himself (Phil. 2:7). What was Christ emptied from?

Jesus was the Word in the dateless past, and has never emptied Himself from His divine nature, for He was God not only from all eternity (Mic. 5:1-2; Jn. 1:1-2; Heb. 1:8; Rev. 1:8-11), but God manifest in flesh during His life on earth (Isa. 7:14; 9:6-7; Mt. 1:18-25; Jn. 1:1-2, 14; 1 Tim. 3:16).

In the next five Scripture filled paragraphs, Finis Jennings Dake shows that "Christ emptied Himself of: equality with God (Php. 2:6-7; Jn. 14:28; 1 Cor. 11:3); God-form or God-body, the spirit body that He lived in from eternity, to take human-form (Php. 2:6-8; 3:21; Mt. 1:18-25; Lk. 1:35; Jn. 1:14; Lk. 24:37-40; Zech. 13:6; Gal. 4:4; Rom. 8:3); immortality of body (1 Cor. 15:3; Ps. 16:10; 1 Pet. 2:24; 3:18); the glory that He had with the Father before the world was (Jn. 12:23; 17:5; Mt. 16:27; Php. 2:5-11); His authority in heaven and in earth, which was given back to Him after the resurrection (Mt. 28:18; Php. 2:9-11; Eph. 1:20-23; 1 Pet. 3:22); and His divine attributes and outward powers that He had with the Father from eternity. He had no power to do miracles until He received the Holy Spirit in all fullness (Jn. 2:11; 3:34; Isa. 11:1-2; 42:1-7; 61:1-2; Lk. 3:21-22; 4:16-21; Mt. 12:28; Acts 10:38). He could do nothing of Himself in all His earthly life.

He attributed all His works, doctrines, powers, etc. to the Father through the anointing of the Holy Spirit (Jn. 8:28). This is all proved by the following facts in Scripture. He was limited to the status of a man (Php. 2:6-8; Heb. 2:14-18; 5:8-9). He was God's agent using God's power of attorney (Jn. 8:28; Acts 10:38). He was our example that we should walk in His steps (1 Pet. 2:21) The temptations prove that He was limited as a man so that He could overcome as a man and not as God (Heb. 4:14-16; 5:7-9). Isaiah (Isa. 7:14-16) speaks of the Messiah being born without knowledge enough to know to refuse the evil and choose the good. Isaiah (Isa. 11:2; 53:1-12) speaks of the Messiah being limited as an ordinary baby, showing that God would give Him the spirit of wisdom, understanding, counsel, might, knowledge, and fear of the Lord. If He had these attributes as God from all eternity and did not lay them aside in becoming man when was this ever true of Him?

Isaiah (Isa. 50:4-11) also predicted that the Messiah would be born without the tongue of the learned, without knowing how to speak a word in season to help any soul, and that He would be wakened day by day to increase in knowledge and wisdom. Isaiah (Isa. 42:1-7; 61:12-2) speaks of Messiah receiving His power to manifest divine acts by the anointing of the Holy Spirit and not by retaining His own former natural attributes and powers. Is it necessary for God to be anointed with the Holy Spirit to do what He is naturally capable of doing? If it became necessary to anoint Jesus during His earthly life, then it proves He did not retain His former glory and attributes which He had from all eternity when He emptied Himself to become like men in all things (Php. 2:6-8; Heb. 2:14-18; 5:8-9).

History records that Christ was limited as a baby and grew in body, soul, and spirit (mind, 1 Cor. 2:11), grace, wisdom, stature, and favor with God and man (Lk. 2:40,52). Even after His manhood, His full anointing and gifts of the Spirit, He was still limited in knowledge (Mk. 13:32). He even learned obedience by the things He suffered (Heb. 4:14-16; 5:7-9). He did not claim the attributes of God, but only the anointing of the Spirit to do His works (Jn. 8:28; Mt. 12:28; Lk. 4:16-21). Others stated this was the source of His power (Jn. 3:34; Acts 10:38). Most scriptures used in theological texts proving that Christ had divine attributes on earth are statements true of Him since His glory has been restored and do not prove anything during His life on earth.

All scriptures related to His earthly life can be explained as referring to the exercise of the gifts of the Spirit and not natural attributes. The fact that Christ promised all believers power to do the works He did proves that it was through the anointing of the Spirit, not by His deity and natural attributes, that He did His works (Mt. 10:1-20; 16:18; 18:18; Lk. 10; 24:49; Mk. 16:15-20; Jn. 14:12-15; Acts 1:4-8). His exaltation to original glory and the highest place under God the Father is proof of His lowest humiliation and earthly limitation short of being God by nature (Php. 2:9-11; Eph. 1:20-23; Col. 1:15- 23; Col. 1:15-23; 1 Pet. 3:22)."

Surely, Jesus does know the exact day and hour now of the future appointed times of the end-times, just as surely as He knew the appointed times of the First Coming were to be fulfilled in the spring of His 33rd year (as Jesus foretold of His death in Matthew 26:2 says, "Ye know that after two days is the feast of the Passover, and the Son of man is betrayed to be crucified"). Jesus said in Revelation that He will come back soon. If He did not know when, then it may be 10,000 years away and He would not have been able to say soon, not even by His standards. He was limited by His state of humanity on earth, but surely He was not as limited after He was glorified and sitting at the right hand of God the Father. Jesus did get the revelation from the Father to give to John more than 60 years after He had been living back in heaven.

As far as the angels not knowing, I agree. When Jesus spoke these words, the rapture was still a mystery to human and angelic beings, but not to Christ (Lk. 21:34-36; Jn. 14:1-3). The revelation was later given to Paul, which he revealed in many places. Paul taught the disciples as reflected by James, Peter, and John referencing the rapture. Taught by Paul (1 Cor. 15:23, 51-54; 2 Cor. 5:1-8; Eph. 5:27; Phil. 3:11, 20-21; 1 Thess. 2:19; 3:13; 4:13-17; 5:9, 23; 2 Thess. 2:1, 7; Col. 3:4). Taught by James, Peter, and John (Jas. 5:7-8; 1 Jn. 2:28; 3:2; 1 Pt. 5:4; Rev. 4:1).

The angels who were rebellious taught of the end of the age to ancient civilizations as a means of deceiving mankind. Of course the end of the age knowledge is true, but the origin and ending of it all is a lie from their mouths. They certainly didn't know the day or the hour, but they clearly understood dispensations, since they have been around for a long and unknown period of time. They were on the planet heaven when god created the earth (Gen. 1:1; Job 38:4-7). They understand doctrines, dispensations, advanced technology as proven by their spacecraft (UFO's), and the ways of an orderly God who hung every star in its place for a specific purpose (Gen. 1:14; Isa. 40:26). The stars and all the heavenly bodies were created to be governed by us, and will be in the eternal future (Ps. 8). The appointed times set in Leviticus 23 were also unknown to them in my opinion. I'm sure they caught on after the First Coming events.

They know the dispensation ends around 2012, but didn't know about the rapture or the appointed times. It is also clear that the fallen beings (fallen angels and demons) knew when the appointed time was not by their own confession to Jesus that it was not the appointed time for their destruction found in Matthew.

> And, behold, they cried out, saying, What have we to do with thee, Jesus, thou Son of God? art thou come hither to torment us before the time (Mat. 8:29)?

Now, if they knew it was not the time, it stands to reason that they would know the time. It is my conclusion that this can only be known by dispensation markers drawn out to all in the heavens. The Galactic Alignment is happening from 1980 – 2016, though Dec. 21, 2012 receives the credit for this 36 year long event that takes place once every 25,920 years. This began the astronomical new age and is an indicator that the Church Age is almost over. We will fully study this out in book 4, *Signs of His Coming*.

Another thing is that maybe Jesus did know the rapture would be on the feast of trumpets, He clearly understood the fulfillment's of the feasts of the Lord (Gen. 1:14; Lev. 23; Mat. 26:2; Col. 2:16-17), but was limited in the knowledge of the years in which the age of the church ends. Knowing the rapture (or the Second Coming, which is what He was really referring to) is on the feast of trumpets, or the day of atonement still means you don't know the day or the hour if you don't know the year. Example: if you know the Second Coming is on a Tuesday at sunset, do you know the actual day or the hour? No, you don't, but you know it will be fulfilled on a Tuesday at sunset. There are many Tuesdays and many future hours that fall on a sunset.

As we all know, you can't make a doctrine from one verse, so let's examine the command to watch. As a student of the Word, it has never made sense to me that God has given so many clues to His coming (both 1st and 2nd), yet the church seems proud that they are in darkness regarding when the Rapture and/or Second Coming will be. If the church is supposed to be ignorant of such things, then it seems like Jesus would have rebuked His disciples for asking Him what the sign of His coming and the end of the world would be (Mat. 24:3).

He gave 24 signs of His Second Coming from Matthew 24:4-26, 37-39. At that time, He also explained, what would happen when He comes back at the end of the [world] Greek: aion, age, a period of time long or short. It refers to the end of this age, as do all the other places where "the end of the world" is used (Mt. 12:32; 13:39-40, 49; 24:3; 28:20). This age will end at the Second Coming (Mt. 24:29-31; 25:31-46; Rev. 19:11-21; Zech. 14:1-5), but the earth and man will continue forever (Gen. 8:22; 9:12; Eccl. 1:4; Ps. 104:5; Isa. 9:6-7; Dan. 7:13-14; Rev. 11:15; 21:3 - Rev. 22:5). Jesus explained a lot in reference to His Second Coming. There are no rebukes.

Why would he give us this forewarning that "there shall be signs in the sun, and in the moon, and in the stars" if we are not supposed to study it and know? If we don't know the biblical calendar, then we will remain clueless as to what God is doing, which has never been His intent (Amos 3:7). If man was to remain ignorant, then prophecy would be an unknown concept. The rest of this chapter will transform your mind by the Word of God if you are still in doubt. At least, that is my prayer as I reiterate some crucial statements.

The church is supposed to be reading the signs of the time. We are not supposed to be dead, we are not supposed to be lukewarm, and we are not supposed to be asleep. We are supposed to be watching. Jesus is not supposed to come to Christians as a thief in the night. "But of that day and hour knoweth no man, no, not the angels of heaven, but my Father only" (Mat. 24:36). I will say this again about this widely known and poorly used verse… Jesus is STILL talking about His Second Advent, as in reference to the question from His disciples… "And as he sat upon the mount of Olives, the disciples came unto him privately, saying, Tell us, when shall these things be? and what shall be the sign of thy coming, and of the end of the world?"

At this point, the disciples had no idea about the rapture and were not asking about something completely unknown to them. But this still leaves us with, "Then the Second Coming will never be known to us in regards to the day or the hour. I can say with 100% boldness that those who have decided to follow Christ, after the rapture, will no doubt have a very good idea about the time frame of the Second Coming. Would the naysayers still tell them not to try and figure it out. What if they just counted seven years to have a clue? Let's carry on.

"Watch therefore, for ye know neither the day nor the hour wherein the Son of man cometh" (Mat. 25:13). This is a command to watch in view of the Second Coming. Matthew 25:13 is in view of what was spoken from Matthew 25:1-12, and is called the parable of the ten virgins. The ones not watching and ready were the five foolish virgins. In contrast, the five wise virgins entered into the kingdom because of their readiness and watchfulness. That's the only point of the parable. Remain watchful. Stay holy, pure, and faithful as a virgin waiting for her bridegroom.

> But of that day and that hour knoweth no man, no, not the angels which are in heaven, neither the Son, but the Father. Take ye heed, watch and pray: for ye know not when the time

is. For the Son of man is as a man taking a far journey, who left his house, and gave authority to his servants, and to every man his work, and commanded the porter to watch. Watch ye therefore: for ye know not when the master of the house cometh, at even, or at midnight, or at the cockcrowing, or in the morning: Lest coming suddenly he find you sleeping. And what I say unto you I say unto all, Watch (Mk. 13:32-37).

Again, many commands to stay awake and watch… hardly the ignorant and blind Christian mindset that has impaired full Christian growth and maturity. The pulpits are mostly silenced on Sunday morning because humbleness by ignorance on end-times has overcome the multitudes. We are to stay awake, alert, vigilant, and sober. The goodman of the house will be awake and watching for the literal visible coming to the earth with the raptured saints. A thief will not catch him unaware (Mat. 24:42-44).

Watch therefore: for ye know not what hour your Lord doth come. But know this, that if the goodman of the house had known in what watch the thief would come, he would have watched, and would not have suffered his house to be broken up. Therefore be ye also ready: for in such an hour as ye think not the Son of man cometh. Who then is a faithful and wise servant, whom his lord hath made ruler over his household, to give them meat in due season? Blessed is that servant, whom his lord when he cometh shall find so doing. Verily I say unto you, That he shall make him ruler over all his goods. But and if that evil servant shall say in his heart, My lord delayeth his coming; And shall begin to smite his fellowservants, and to eat and drink with the drunken; The lord of that servant shall come in a day when he looketh not for him, and in an hour that he is not aware of, And shall cut him asunder, and appoint him his portion with the hypocrites: there shall be weeping and gnashing of teeth (Mt. 24:42-51).

But of the times and the seasons, brethren, ye have no need that I write unto you. For yourselves know perfectly that the day of the Lord so cometh as a thief in the night. For when they shall say,

Peace and safety; then sudden destruction cometh upon them, as travail upon a woman with child; and they shall not escape. But ye, brethren, are not in darkness, that that day should overtake you as a thief. Ye are all the children of light, and the children of the day: we are not of the night, nor of darkness (1 Thess. 5:1-5).

The faithful who are walking in righteousness and looking for the return of our Lord will not be blind concerning the times or seasons. Jesus will not come as a thief in the night to the watchful. The ones who are the goodmen of the house, the wise virgins, the watchful, will escape the wrath to come (1 Thess. 4:16-17; 5:9 - surrounding verses).

And unto the angel of the church in Sardis write; These things saith he that hath the seven Spirits of God, and the seven stars; I know thy works, that thou hast a name that thou livest, and art dead. Be watchful, and strengthen the things which remain, that are ready to die: for I have not found thy works perfect before God. Remember therefore how thou hast received and heard, and hold fast, and repent. If therefore thou shalt not watch, I will come on thee as a thief, and thou shalt not know what hour I will come upon thee (Rev.3:1-3).

THE DEAD CHURCH IS NOT WATCHFUL.

Because thou sayest, I am rich, and increased with goods, and have need of nothing; and knowest not that thou art wretched, and miserable, and poor, and blind, and naked: I counsel thee to buy of me gold tried in the fire, that thou mayest be rich; and white raiment, that thou mayest be clothed, and that the shame of thy nakedness do not appear; and anoint thine eyes with eyesalve, that thou mayest see (Rev. 3:17-18).

THE LUKEWARM CHURCH IS NOT WATCHING.

Behold, I come as a thief. Blessed is he that watcheth, and keepeth his garments, lest he walk naked, and they see his shame (Rev. 16:15).

CHAPTER 9

EVENTS PEOPLE ARE WAITING ON BEFORE THE RAPTURE

Many Christians are still waiting for a few things to happen before the rapture, yet many of these same people would also align their theology with the Doctrine of Imminence, that the rapture could happen any day now. Let's read Scripture and start getting our beliefs in order. A sign-less event needs no known event to precede it. However, we will see if there is any validity in the events many believe must come to pass before the blessed day when Jesus comes back to get His spotless church.

Exposing false doctrines is important in the end-times, especially in this day when we are told to be on high alert (Mat. 24:24; 2 Cor. 11:3-4, 12-15; Gal. 1:6-7; Col. 2:6-8; 1 Tim. 4:1; 2 Tim. 3:1-5, 12-14; 4:1-5). I'm not trying to write a book based on that, just like the Bible is not purposed for solely shining light on deceived people who are deceiving others. However, when the subjects come up, we must address them to clean up the theology in many minds, hoping to divert some. These events are: The Day of the Saints; Sudden Destruction; A Great Revival; A United Church; The Wealth of the Wicked; and The Fullness of the Gentiles.

1. THE DAY OF THE SAINTS

There is a book about this lesser known doctrine by Dr. Bill Hamon. I can't find where or when this doctrine came from, but it is essentially the belief that the saints will walk in complete victory here on earth before the rapture happens. Bill Hamon says, "Many Christians are looking for 'the Day of the Lord' but before that day comes the Lord is preparing His Bride for His Divine purposes in the earth. All creation longs for that day—The Day of the Saints. This day is on God's prophetic timetable and is the day when the Saints will fulfill all the Scriptures regarding Christ's glorious church."

There are a few things wrong with his statement. First, I'll go on record and say that anyone following this man should cease and desist immediately. His doctrines are not aligned with Scripture, but are accepted because he also teaches that modern "apostles" and "prophets" give the church new doctrines that supplement those given by the original apostles and prophets. In *Apostles, Prophets and the Coming Moves of God*, Hamon says:

> "He [Paul] also reveals that this anointing for divine revelation was not just given to the prophets of old but has now been equally given to Christ's Holy Apostles and Prophets in His Church" (page 140).

This teaching, that new doctrines are needed to supplement Scripture, is a mark of the cults of Christianity, like Mormonism. In contrast, Protestants believe that Christians get their teachings from the Bible alone, which God revealed through the original prophets and apostles (2 Pt. 1:19-21; 2 Tim. 3:15-17).

As for the rapture view he holds, which is important to understand if you are one to believe the "Day of the Saints" will happen before the rapture, Harmon says, "Rapture teaching is one of the most faith deadening teachings ever preached. It has the most neutralizing affect on a Christian's aggressive growth process. We have a lot to do in this Earth and there is going to be a lot of stuff that we need to do in eternity. If you don't have a big comprehensive vision, both restorationally and eternally, then what motivation is there to do much except try to win a few souls to get a big reward in heaven?"

His rapture views are not stated as far as I have found. He has gone on record and told of four rapture views, of which he says the pre-tribulation rapture is the one he would choose if it were up to him. From all I've read and from what he teaches, I'd say the day of the saints doctrine parallels the teaching that hails the church as the ones who will bring in the kingdom of God. He seems to believe the church will be changed and put on immortality after they have conquered the world with their dominionism and power.

Dominion Theology, also called "Kingdom Now Theology," is a false teaching stating that man is commissioned to bring the entire world under the dominion of Christianity, by force if necessary, and then, hand over the Christianized world to Jesus when He comes. He believes the power of the saints at their climax, right before they are changed to immortality, will match that of the prophets in the Old Testament. Based on all implications from his teachings, I won't give much time on here, his rapture view indicates that he believes the saints will be changed, but not go to heaven at all, for the saints brought the kingdom of heaven to earth.

Hamon teaches that Christ can't return to earth until Christians form a "militant" army, under the leadership of modern apostles and prophets, that will physically subdue the earth and start to establish God's kingdom in the earth's governments. Hamon compares this army to the Crusaders, who he describes as the church's only bright lights during the Dark Ages.

God's end-times army will achieve victory, in part, by striking God's enemies with blindness and calling down natural disasters on them — causing entire nations to convert to Christ, according to Hamon. The apostles and prophets will be so powerful that Christians who come into their presence with sin in their lives will be struck dead. All members of the army will become sinless and extremely powerful, as they become more and more enlightened through new doctrines given by the apostles and prophets, finally attaining their own immortality (this is Hamon's unorthodox take on the rapture). See these teachings in Hamon's book *Apostles, Prophets and the Coming Moves of God*.

Hamon promotes one of the more distorted doctrines, the manifested sons of God doctrine. Their interpretation of this verse is unique in church history. There is no rapture, but people will be changed into eternal beings right here on earth to do miraculous works like Jesus to overcome the devil and the world system before, and in order to make ready the Lord's physical return to earth and the Millennial Reign of Christ and His saints. Not unlike Hymenaeus, Alexander and Philetus (1 Tim. 1:19-20; 2 Tim. 2:17-19), Hamon, Wagner, and the other leaders of the Apostles and Prophets Movement, believe in a totally different view of the end of this age, with no rapture, no Great Tribulation, and no Antichrist (as you will read – they will defeat him for Jesus, sparing the earth of his horrendous reign and mark, 666).

The Day of the Saints is contrary to the clear description of the wrath of God that is happening during the last seven years of the Dispensation of Grace (Rev. 6 – Rev. 19). The saints who are saints at the sounding of the trumpet of God are not subjected to go through His wrath (Lk. 21:34-36; 1 Thess. 4:13 – 5:11; 2 Thess. 2:1-8; Rev. 4:1). The one's who repent of sinful living and actually follow Jesus during the Tribulation will be subjected to much persecution. A great multitude will be killed (Rev. 6:8-11; 7:9-17; 13:7, 15-18; 15:2-4; 17:6; 20:4; Mat. 24:9-13, 22; Dan. 7:21-27; 8:24; 9:27; 12:7). This is hardly even vaguely close to what Hamon is teaching. The only thing close to being comparable is the Two Witnesses, who are themselves killed before they are changed to immortality (Rev. 11:7-12).

To be truthful, it was as recent as February 2015 when I first heard of the Day of the Saints. A very strong Christian woman I know told me she now believed this was true, so she was not thinking the rapture could happen yet, even though she had been hopeful of a feast of trumpets rapture in 2015 due to the Shemitah and 2014 – 2015 blood red moons on feast days. Ironically, she is a pre-tribulationalist, yet Hamon is far from it. I asked her where in Scripture does it hint of this mighty end-time move of saints being endowed with great power, while revival is dominant through the lands. She surprised me with her answer. She pointed to Acts 2.

I'll explain very simply why Acts 2:16-21 is not pointed to a great move of the saints before the rapture, but why Hamon could use this passage as a proof of a great move of the saints before the rapture. Here is more of my conversation with this friend of mine after I encouraged her to remain strong in Christ, because 2015's feast of trumpets looked perfect for the rapture of the church. She replied, "I hope and pray the rapture is this year. I think there will be an outpouring first. If the outpouring has started by Pentecost, I think we can be sure the rapture is this year."

I replied, "A revival would be great before the rapture, but one thing for sure is that there will be a great revival / awakening due to the rapture when most who are believers are left behind because they are not followers. From my experience, the non believers far out number the believers, and the believers far out number the followers. It's a belief I wish I was wrong about. Tribulation revival (Rev. 6:8-11; 7:9-17; 13:7, 15-18; 15:2-4; 17:6; 20:4; Mat. 24:9-13, 22; Dan. 7:21-27; 8:24; 9:27; 12:7), side by side w the apostasy (2 Thess. 2:1-3, 8-12; Rev. 6:12-17; 9:20-21; 16:8-11)."

She replied, "In the last few months, I have had the glory / power of the Lord fill my hands (seemed like fire shooting out of my palms) outside church and I have laid hands on people about five separate times and they were healed instantly. I think it is the beginnings of the outpouring. Chuck Pierce came up to me yesterday at church in Cleveland and told me that when he saw me, he saw my family and family line and that he saw me doing works that would astound me. Last week, one night I had three repeat dream / visions where I saw on a white piece of paper, or booklet with all caps, big bold letters of 'FLOOD.' I think it means the Holy Spirit is about to flood soon. Also, I was feeling in the past month like there is adjustments going on in the palms of my hands. I have asked around and heard from two people they used to hear the 'old folks' talk about that. Anyway, I am super excited and feel that the most exciting time of my life is about to happen!"

As far as I'm teaching here, let me say that healing is absolutely part of the gospel program (Isa. 53; Mat. 8:17; 1 Pet. 2:24). Currently, it's been 1 ½ years since these messages were exchanged with her and I have heard nothing else from her about this. She is a good woman and I hope she is on track doctrinally. The problem is that Hamon is not a pre-tribber, and neither is Chuck Pierce, who prophesied over her in Cleveland. I'm not one to hold to prophecies from people who contradict Scripture, not just with the rapture, but in many areas if you want to research them out on your own.

I just can't understand a pre-tribber changing any rapture timing views based on the teachings of people who don't believe in a pre-tribulation rapture. Actually, Hamon doesn't seem to even believe in a rapture, just a change in body from mortality to immortality. As you learned in book 1, a rapture is a transporting from one place to another. Chuck Pierce seems to believe in one of the raptures we spoke of in book 1, which is the transporting of your spirit from earth to heaven. This is not a rapture in the first resurrection. The next paragraph is a short statement of Pierce's rapture beliefs. He had been talking about preterism, a rapture timing belief we learned about in book 2. He then switches to hyper-preterism.

"Hyper-Preterist teaching usually begins when individuals in the Body begin to find error in teaching related to what we in the Western world call "The Rapture." This is not so much a reaction to the historic teaching on the rapture, but to the sometimes unbalanced popularization of the rapture resulting from such books as the "Left Behind" series. I believe what is really being rejected by Preterists is the idea of escapism. I have always rejected this as well, but I do know that there is Biblical revelation alluding to a "rapturous spirit." I believe the church will look like Stephen in the Book of Acts. We will be moving forward to transform and influence society and government and become more and more persecuted. Governments will clash. Therefore, as Stephen wore the "GLORY of GOD" as he ascended, so will we."

With all I've read, he seems to hold to a similar view of preterism, though he is not into replacement theology. He is a domionist who believes the saints must rise to political and spiritual dominance before Jesus physically will rule on earth. He claims we are living in the Book of Revelation, though this doesn't mean he believes we are in the last seven years of the Church Age. I believe he doesn't believe in a literal seven years. It is my opinion that he is also not speaking of living in Revelation 2-3 only, as is representing the Church Age, but rather is including with that the chapters after that as well. Many believe the whole of Revelation is happening over an extended period of time, much greater in length than 7 years.

The following is from h*tp://dominion-theology.blogspot.com/* ... "Dominionists are being urged to take a full part in all areas of the world system in order to change it from within. This can't be done without the obedience of all its followers, so a system of leadership [discipleship] must be introduced to ensure every Christian is under authority and unable to err from the teaching. This leadership model is the New Apostolic Reformation headed by the International Coalition of Apostles under head "apostle" C. Peter Wagner.

It excludes from the 'one world kingdom' all those who disagree with Dominionism teaching. In effect, it disinherits all other Christians from the Body of Christ. Some Dominionist fellowships teach that their Church is the only valid one, that the door to salvation is through the Church, (not Jesus Christ the Savior!) and that everyone outside of the system is outside of the Kingdom of God. In addition to being clearly unscriptural, it leads to human arrogance and rivalry, and replaces obedience to God with submission to men.

An empire-building, self-seeking arrogance pervades much of the Dominionism leadership, and they have proven themselves closed to correction. Greed, corruption, immorality and spiritual abuses have thrived in this climate - and the teaching which focuses so much on the earth as our inheritance has led many to become so in love with this present world as to adopt most all its values.

The doctrines of the New Apostolic Reformation have been promulgated by C. Peter Wagner, Cindy Jacobs, Chuck Pierce, Bill Hamon, a group known as the "Kansas City Prophets," the Vineyard Fellowship, and many others. At the highest echelons these organizations all have interlocking boards of directors. Two noteworthy internal venues for disseminating false prophecies and new doctrines include The Elijah List and Joel News. False prophets regularly pump out new "prophecies" and "decrees" to shore up the kingdom mandate. These "prophecies" are a major avenue for communicating "God's plan" for the next step in kingdom-building. False apostles have been anointed, appointed as leaders of regions around the globe, and charged with wielding the King's authority." (end quote)

Dominionism is highly part of The New Apostolic Reformation (NAR), which has inherited and accelerated two transformative currents within conservative Christianity over the past several decades. One is a revised theology of the End Times. The other is the energized, empowered, and highly politicized variety of evangelicalism that has emerged from this theology.

"DeMar promotes the idea that Christians are to take over the world, whether or not Jesus said that "My kingdom is not of this world." DeMar says, "If modern day Bible prophecy 'experts' are correct that we are living in the 'Last Days,' then why bother trying to fix a broken world that is about to be thrown on the ash heap of history? Why concern ourselves with education, healthcare, the economy, or peace in the Mideast? Why polish brass on a sinking ship?...American Vision believes that 'Last Days Madness' has caused Christians to retreat from the public sphere and has temporarily hindered the Church from making a real impact in America and around the world." However, he doesn't say this in the promotional material that goes out deceptively causing people to think they're attending a Bible prophecy conference when they're paying for an anti-Bible-Prophecy conference.

This conference is one of many put together by American Vision, the organization of Gary DeMar, known for his anti-rapture, anti-pre-millinnial stands on Bible Prophecy. American Vision hosts a number of faith-busting events during the year, including a Hawaiian cruise where your expectancy of the Lord's return can be decimated by the likes of other Re-constructionists like Gary North and D. James Kennedy.

And DeMar will make his products available to those who attend and bring their credit cards with them. His resource table will include such classics as his books, *End Times Fiction* and *The Left Behind Hoax*. Then, you could also purchase Hanegraaff's Preterist fiction, *The Last Disciple*, that boasts of single handedly reclaiming Bible Prophecy for the view that there is no Bible prophecy left to be fulfilled."

See more at: *http://www.apostasyalert.org/REFLECTIONS/conferences.htm*

These men are all affiliated in the same movement, as well as many of the same organizations and conferences. I've spent much more time on this than I wanted to, but this must be known to keep other Christians with sound doctrine on the right course. This friend of mine that now believes in the Day of the Saints before the rapture has been persuaded by men who don't even hold her view of the rapture They straight up mock the rapture all together. They are mocking God (2 Pt. 3). As far as Acts 2:16-20 is concerned to prove a great move of the saints before the rapture, let's look it over a bit and determine what is being foretold.

> 16 But this is that which was spoken by the prophet Joel; 17 And it shall come to pass in the last days, saith God, I will pour out of my Spirit upon all flesh: and your sons and your daughters shall prophesy, and your young men shall see visions, and your old men shall dream dreams: 18 And on my servants and on my handmaidens I will pour out in those days of my Spirit; and they shall prophesy: 19 And I will shew wonders in heaven above, and signs in the earth beneath; blood, and fire, and vapour of smoke: 20 The sun shall be turned into darkness, and the moon into blood, before that great and notable day of the Lord come (Acts 2:16-20).

The timing of these great events is before the Day of the Lord. No one would argue this, so I guess the great indifference of when these events will occur is in the definition of the Day of the Lord. These kind of misunderstandings are why many false teachings are born, birthing even more false doctrines. This is why I spent many pages in this book for watchers in explaining what many end-time terminologies are and when they will take place. I show the many different references of the Day of the Lord in chapter 10. For now, know that the Day of the Lord finds it's timing to begin at the Second Coming, lasting until the end of the Millennial Reign.

Because of this fact, we know the reference to the last days (vs. 17) is speaking of the Seven Year Tribulation. What was spoken to the prophet Joel that will happen in the last days (vs. 16-17)? It is three great outpourings of the Holy Spirit: on the day of Pentecost and many years following this day (Acts 2:1 - Acts 28:31); during the future tribulation (Joel 2:28-32; Acts 2:16-21); and during the Millennium (Isa. 32:15; 44:3; Ezek. 36:26-27; 39:29; Zech. 12:10).

This was partially fulfilled in the 1st century, but will be completely fulfilled in the Tribulation when God will be fulfilling also Acts 2:19-21; Rev. 6:9-11; 7:1-17; 15:2-4).

There are fourteen end-time expressions through Scripture, and it is up to context and harmonizing all references on a subject to determine the exact timing referenced. As noted in the Dake Annotated Reference Bible, they are: latter times - last years ending this age before the Millennium (1 Tim. 4:1), latter years - Armageddon and the end of this age (Ezek. 38:8, 16), latter days - the future tribulation (Num. 24:14; Dt. 4:30; 31:29; Jer. 23:20; 30:24; 48:47; 49:39; Dan. 2:28; 10:14), latter day - Millennium (Job 19:25), latter days - Millennium (Hos. 3:5), last days - end of this age preceding the Millennium (Dan. 8:19; 2 Tim. 3:1; Jas. 5:3; 2 Pet. 3:3; Jude 1:18), last day - the rapture, at least seven years before the Millennium and Second Coming (Jn. 6:39-40, 44, 54; 11:24), last days - the Tribulation period or last seven years of this age (Acts 2:16-21), last days - First Coming (Heb. 1:1-2), last times - first coming (1 Pet. 1:20), last time - apostolic times and the whole church age (1 Jn. 2:18, last time - second coming (1 Pet. 1:5), last days - Millennium (Gen. 49:1; Isa. 2:1; Mic. 4:1), and last day - end of the Millennium (Jn. 12:48; cp. with Rev. 20:7-15).

More proof of the timing of Acts 2:16-21 being in the Seven Year Tribulation can be seen from verses 19-20. As we learned from book 2, the rapture is definitely before the revealing of the Antichrist, who is revealed by the signing of the seven year covenant with Israel (Dan. 9:27; 2 Thess. 2:1-8; Rev. 4:1; 6:2). Acts 2:19 says, "And I will shew wonders in heaven above, and signs in the earth beneath; blood, and fire, and vapour of smoke." The rapture is in Revelation 4:1. Here are references in Acts as compared with the Book of Revelation and Ezekiel: blood (Rev. 8:7-8; 11:6; 16:3-6; Ezek. 38:22); fire (Rev. 8:5-8; 9:17-18; 11:5; 16:8; 18:8); and vapour of smoke (Rev. 9:2-3, 17-18; 18:9, 18; 19:3).

Events People Are Waiting On Before The Rapture

Acts 2:20 says, "The sun shall be turned into darkness, and the moon into blood, before that great and notable day of the Lord come." Here are the references as compared to what's happening in the Book of Revelation and Matthew: sun shall be turned into darkness (Rev. 6:12; 8:12; 9:2; 16:10; Mat. 24:29); moon into blood (Rev. 6:12; 8:12; 16:10; Mat. 24:29); and the Second Coming, or great and notable Day of the Lord (Mat. 24:29-31; 25:31-46; Rev. 19:11).

I'd like to conclude with one more significant proof from the prophet Joel. In Joel 2:1-11, we have a supernatural army that will ride across the earth on the Day of the Lord (Joel 2:1-11). Many theories have spread their wings and flown people away from sound doctrine. These people are the saints of God coming with Him to do battle with rebels of the earth and take it back completely at the Second Coming (Rev. 19:11-21). Many have concluded this "Joel's Army" to be saints proclaiming their dominion over the earth during the time of the Tribulation. The fact is that saints will not be ruling dominant during the Tribulation.

Many will die a martyrs death, not in battle when the sword will not wound them (Joel 2:8). Did you know that Joel 2:8 really does say the blade will not hurt them? This is because this army has gained immortality of the body in the first resurrection, which ends before the Day of the Lord. The blade will cut many heads off of saints in the days before the Second Coming (Rev. 6:8-11; 7:9-17; 13:7, 15-18; 15:2-4; 17:6; 20:4; Mat. 24:9-13, 22; Dan. 7:21-27; 8:24; 9:27; 12:7), so context of the subject, as well as having the correct time-line Scripture is referring to is that important.

2. Sudden Destruction

For yourselves know perfectly that the day of the Lord so cometh as a thief in the night. For when they shall say, Peace and safety; then sudden destruction cometh upon them, as travail upon a woman with child; and they shall not escape (1 Thess. 5:2-3).

When Antichrist shall have conquered the 10 kingdoms inside the Roman Empire in the first 3 ½ years of Daniel's 70th Week (Dan. 7:23-24; Rev. 13 and Rev. 17), and by these kingdoms shall have conquered Russia and the other nations north and east of the Roman empire in the last 3 ½ years of Daniel's 70th Week (Dan. 11:40-45), it will be time for the world to be saying "Peace and safety." They will think that getting rid of Israel (Zech. 14) will mean no further wars. They will then look forward to a period of peace and prosperity, but the Lord will come suddenly when Jerusalem is half taken and sudden destruction will be upon all the nations at Armageddon (Zech. 14; Joel 3; Rev. 19:11-21).

The references of "peace and safety," and "sudden destruction" are often used with watchers of the rapture. They believe the "peace and safety" reference is speaking of the seven year peace covenant made with Israel and signed by the Antichrist (Dan. 9:27). Therefore, whenever a politician or the United Nations mentions peace and safety, many watchers get anxiously excited. Most pre-tribbers naturally believe the rapture will happen before that covenant is made. They are correct.

2 Thessalonians 5:3 ends with, "they shall not escape." The destruction will be spread across the nations. The cities of the nations will fall by a great earthquake. Hail will fall weighing over 100 lbs., and 5 out of 6 people in the armies of the nations at Armageddon will be obliterated (Ezek. 39:2; Zech. 14:1-5, 16-21; Rev. 19:11-21).

Not all will be killed, for many will be left alive to come into the Millennium (Zech. 14:16-21; Isa. 2:1-4; Mt. 25:31-46).

There is a dominant theme of the rapture found from 1 Thessalonians 4:13 – 5:11, so it makes sense that sudden destruction is mistakenly associated with the rapture. Let us also note that this day of sudden destruction shall not overtake a follower of Jesus living by the Spirit, not the flesh.

> But ye, brethren, are not in darkness, that that day should overtake you as a thief. Ye are all the children of light, and the children of the day: we are not of the night, nor of darkness (1 Thess. 5:4-5).

Verse 2 tells us the Day of the Lord will come as a thief in the night. Again, this is referring to the Second Coming, which begins the Day of the Lord. God has not appointed Christians to go through the Tribulation wrath, the Sudden Destruction of 1 Thessalonians 5:2-3; Revelation 6:1 – Revelation 19:21; Matthew 24:15-21, or the wrath of eternal hell, but to be delivered by rapture so that whether we live or die we should live together with Him forever (1 Thess. 5:9-10; 4:13-18; 2 Thess. 2:7-8; Rev. 4:1).

Referring to Jesus' Second Coming as a thief in the night is an expression used in 1 Thessalonians 5:2-4; 2 Peter 3:10; Revelation 3:3; 16:15. Each time it refers to the Day of the Lord coming as a thief, except Revelation 3:3, where it refers to judgment on the church of Sardis. Jesus also referred to His Coming as a thief in Matthew 24:43. It is only a reference used to describe those who are not watching, not sober, not awake, and not fighting the fight of faith and laying hold of eternal life by continuing in Christ and enduring until the end (1 Thess. 5:6-11; Mat. 10:22; Jn. 15:1-6; 1 Tim. 6:12; 1 Cor. 9:24-27).

Christians are not in ignorance and darkness about the day of the Lord (1 Thess. 5:1-2, 4-5, 9). The rapture takes place at least seven years before the Second Coming, which begins the Day of the

Lord (2 Thess. 2:7, Rev. 4:1). Therefore, they will not be here for that day to overtake them as a thief like it will the ungodly (1 Thess. 5:2-5).

In conclusion, sudden destruction is the wrong event to be looking for when watching for the rapture. It will be of no value to the watcher.

3. A Great Revival

Even more still have it in their minds that the rapture won't be happening until a great outpouring of the Holy Spirit that brings a great revival. This is much like the Day of the Saints and uses the same scriptural text, so we won't spend much more time setting this doctrine straight. Nowhere in Scripture does it speak of a great revival before the rapture. They get this doctrine from Acts 2:16-21, which is happening during the Seven Year Tribulation. Again, the day of the rapture has been fixed and appointed when the Trinity set in order the plan of salvation and dispensations before the foundations of the world were laid (Eph. 1:4-5; 1 Pt. 1:20). It had to be, for They hung the sun and the moon and set their timing in motion, which foretells the signs and the appointed times (Gen. 1:14).

If there were a great revival before the rapture, then Acts 2:16-21 would be a prophesy that must be fulfilled before the rapture, pointing to the closeness of the rapture itself to a world who mostly believes in the Doctrine of Imminency. Confusing isn't it? If you go below the surface of many people's beliefs, then the implications often contradict each other. It will only be the rapture that will cause people to wake up to the reality of what has hit them. God makes it clear this revival won't happen before the rapture.

The great revival is the great multitude of saints that come out of the Tribulation period. They are mostly martyrs (Rev. 6:9-11; 7:9-

17; 15:2-4; 20:4-6), though many people will enter the Millennial Reign (Zech. 14:16-21; Isa. 2:1-4; Mt. 25:31-46). Many still will apostatize from the faith (2 Thess. 2:1-3, 8-12; Rev. 6:12-17; 9:20-21; 16:8-11). If a revival occurs before the rapture, then that would be fantastic. However, there is no prophecy in all of Scripture that points to this, only a wrong understanding of when the Day of the Lord will actually happen. For those who believe the Day of the Lord is the Tribulation, then it makes sense for them that the great outpouring of the Holy Spirit happens before the Day of the Lord, or Seven Year Tribulation, because that would happen before the rapture whether you were pre-trib, partial view, mid-trib, pre-wrath, post-trib, or pan-trib.

4. A United Church

Many still are waiting for the church to merge into global unity. This is a doctrine created from Ephesians 5:27, which says Jesus will present a glorious church to Himself, not having spot, or wrinkle, or any such thing; but that it should be holy and without blemish. "Glorious Church" comes from the Greek: endoxos (GSN-<G1741>). Here; Lk. 7:25; 13:17; 1 Cor. 4:10. The Dake Annotated Reference Bible says the church is now glorious because of the glorious gospel (1 Cor. 4:4; 1Tim. 1:11), the glorious power of God working in it (Col. 1:11) to make it pure, holy, spotless, and without blemish. It will be presented to Christ a glorious church because of the glorious liberty of all children of God (Rom. 8:21), and the glorious bodies that saints will receive (Phil. 3:21).

The church these people have in mind isn't going to merge from the literal tens of thousands of Christian denominations into one church with one mind like the early church (Acts 1-4). The perfect church, or glorious church are all the different individuals around the earth, through the generations, that follow Christ in righteousness… follow, not just believe. There's a difference. People make up His church, not denominations. These people are already united into the body of Christ. Many people who are Methodists, Baptists, Presbyterians, Church of God, Assembly of God, and many more denominations make up the glorious church already. Many from the same denominations are not part of the glorious church because they do not follow the New Covenant and Jesus' commands (Jn. 8:31-34; 15:14; Eph. 5:27; 1 Jn. 2:3-6; 3:5-10).

Some denominations are straight up heretical and some are cults. What won't be happening is unity in all of professing Christendom. This is a move that the pope has sought out for in the past few years. The problem is in the compromises Christians would be making for unity. This unity for man will bring division from God. Jesus said He came to bring division, not peace (Lk. 12:51). The gospel's message will never bring about unity in the world. How much division is there among same denominations when it comes to doctrines? This is quickly found out for those who dare to speak doctrine with believers.

This is the Age of Profession, when the tares will grow among the wheat (Mat. 13:24-30). The only way for unity is to avoid teaching or speaking sound doctrine to grow the body of Christ. The only way for unity in this age is to stop caring about the Word of God being taught and to just love people who are on their way to hell. But of course, this is not love for them or for God (Jn. 8:31; 14:23-24; 1 Jn. 2:3-6; Mat. 28:18-20). As said before, but worthy of repeating, the glorious church is already unified (Eph. 5:27; Jn. 17; 1 Thess. 5:23). Many will be added to the glorious church up until the day of the rapture. Many will even fall away (1 Pt. 4:17-19).

Jesus prayed for His followers to be one with Him and God the Father, just as Jesus and the Father are one. What "one" means here is "unity." Many believe unifying all denominations who profess Christ will be an answer to His prayer, but it is actually already being answered throughout the centuries. His followers are the ones who went beyond believing, and began following in righteous living (Eph. 5:27; Tit. 2:11-12; 1 Jn. 2:3-6; 3:1-10).

> 11 And now I am no more in the world, but these are in the world, and I come to thee. Holy Father, keep through thine own name those whom thou hast given me, that they may be one, as we are. 12 While I was with them in the world, I kept them in thy name: those that thou gavest me I have kept, and none of them is lost, but the son of perdition; that the scripture might be fulfilled. 13 And now come I to thee; and these things I speak in the world, that they might have my joy fulfilled in themselves. 14 I have given them thy word; and the world hath hated them, because they are not of the world, even as I am not of the world. 15 I pray not that thou shouldest take them out of the world, but that thou shouldest keep them from the evil. 16 They are not of the world, even as I am not of the world. 17 Sanctify them through thy truth: thy word is truth. 18 As thou hast sent me into the world, even so have I also sent them into the world. 19 And for their sakes I sanctify myself, that they also might be sanctified through the truth (Jn. 17:11-19).

5. THE WEALTH OF THE WICKED

Others are waiting on the wealth of the wicked to be transferred to the righteous before the end of the Church Age. C. Peter Wagner is one of the key proponents of the view that the transfer of the "wealth of the wicked" is a pre-millennial event and is specifically meant for the church. Many others through the years have heard this taught and seem to have been instantly enticed by the lure of God giving them unprecedented wealth. The dominant verse used is located in Proverbs.

A good man leaveth an inheritance to his children's children: and the wealth of the sinner is laid up for the just (Proverbs 13:22).

Peter Wagner's association of churches is under his senior apostolic authority. Dr. Wagner, who was also a major thrust behind the "Church Growth Movement," (NAR) "New Apostolic Reformation" and the "Third Wave," has found an astonishing amount of influence. Supposedly, this wealth transfer is a glorious development of the last days that enervates and honors the church.

This is all too familiar terminology after reading about the "Day of the Saints." Peter is a leader in the false teaching of dominionism. He is affiliated with Chuck Pierce, the man spoken of from my friend who now believes in the Day of the Saints, which she unknowingly is unaware of the roots that doctrine stems from. You don't have to be a part of one of the many deceiving end-time movements to inherit their folly. These doctrines have crept into the churches, as have many others that have become mainstream, like "Once Saved, Always Saved" (Gen. 3:4; 1 Cor. 9:24 – 10:11).

Peter Wagner has said, "[…] the body of Christ needs to come into alignment with God's declared purpose to release unprecedented amounts of wealth for the extension of His kingdom on earth." C. Peter Wagner, Personal invitation to this author to participate in an ad hoc "invitation-only" Apostolic Round-table on Kingdom Wealth, in Colorado, October 2004. On file with The Mulberry Ministry.

So, why do people use this as an event that has to happen before the rapture? Simple, it is taught as an event that will happen before Jesus will come back. By conclusion, and without analyzing, examining, or looking at implications or exhausted teachings from the senders of such messages, people conclude that it will happen before the rapture because the rapture will happen before Jesus will come to earth, and the Tribulation won't be good for the saints. If these same people would research the end-time views of the "prophets" of such doctrine, they would see that these men's beliefs are far away from their own.

Proverbs 13:22 merely says that a good man leaves an inheritance through the following generations, which includes the heritage of a godly life-style and a good name. Not all the righteous have material wealth, so it could not be speaking of this alone. Because of the inheritance of the entire earth that the righteous will receive, all of what the sinners and the wicked now have will be ours one day, but not prior to the rapture or the Second Coming. The saints will reign on earth with Christ (Dan. 7:13-14, 18, 27), and at that time and straight into the eternal future, the wealth of the earth will not belong to the wicked (Rev. 21:8).

If you're reading this book, then you are probably not new to the Christian faith. I'm sure you've heard that you can't build a doctrine from one verse. This is exactly what has been done here. What has happened here is typical with teachers who have an agenda, or a preconceived notion. They begin with their doctrine of choice and find verses to support it.

The famous end-time chapters from the gospels never once speak of the church becoming rich from receiving the wealth of the wicked. Revelation never once hints to this either. On the contrary, we know the times will be extremely difficult. There is only one time we see a wealthy group of people or a city in the detailed chronological Book of Revelation, and this is literal Babylon (Rev. 18). There is more written on mystery Babylon (Rev. 17) and literal Babylon (Rev. 18) in chapter 10. Literal Babylon is not a city full of saints. Any saints living in this city are told to get out before it is destroyed at the end of the Tribulation (18:4). She has shed the blood of the saints (18:24), so the saints will not be rich, or ruling the land.

The dominionism movement believes they are to operate before the Second Coming like Moses, Elijah, and Elisha. They believe the earth will be overcome with the saints in authority, government, and wealth. They believe this will happen before Jesus comes back. Revelation shows the commerce city of the earth being ran by the wicked up until the very end of the Tribulation. This city is not taken by the saints for her wealth. No, it is destroyed by an earthquake (Rev. 16:17-21), by supernatural destruction (Rev. 16:17-21; 18:8, 10, 17, 19, 21; Isa. 13:6-13; Jer. 50:20, 40; 51:8), suddenly in one hour (Rev. 18:8-19; Isa. 13:19; Jer. 50:40; 51:8), by fire from heaven (Rev. 18:8-18; Isa. 13:19; Jer. 50:40), with violence (Rev. 18:21), by the earth swallowing her (Rev. 18:21; Jer. 51:62-64), and by God (Rev. 18:8,20), as He destroyed Sodom (Isa. 13:19; Jer. 50:40). She will never be inhabited again (Isa. 13:20; Jer. 50:39-40; 51:29,37,43).

The reason many of these false teachers believe Revelation doesn't stand in the way of their view is because they believe they have new revelation, or they happen to believe much of Revelation has either been fulfilled, or it is just too spiritual to be interpreted literally. If you can't build a doctrine from a single verse, then let's look at other verses that speak of wealth being given to the righteous.

> Then you will look and be radiant, your heart will throb and swell with joy; the wealth on the seas will be brought to you, to you the riches of the nations will come (Isaiah 60:5).

> Your gates will always stand open, they will never be shut, day or night, so that men may bring you the wealth of the nations—their kings led in triumphal procession (Isaiah 60:11).

> Thou shalt also suck the milk of the Gentiles, and shalt suck the breast of kings: and thou shalt know that I the LORD am thy Saviour and thy Redeemer, the mighty One of Jacob (Isa. 60:16).

This simply means that Israel will receive the riches of the Gentiles to help in the restoration of Jerusalem and all of Palestine, and to carry on the universal missionary program of the Millennium (Isa. 60:5-7, 16; 2:2-4; 52:7; Zech. 8:12).

> You will feed on the wealth of nations, and in their riches you will boast (Isa. 61:6).

> I will extend peace to her like a river, and the wealth of nations like a flooding stream (Isa. 66:12).

> Rise and thresh, O Daughter of Zion, for I will give you horns of iron; I will give you hoofs of bronze and you will break to pieces many nations. You will devote their ill-gotten gains to the LORD, their wealth to the Lord of all the earth (Micah 4.13).

> The wealth of all the surrounding nations will be collected—great quantities of gold and silver and clothing (Zech. 14:14).

> The abundance of the riches of Jerusalem under the Messiah, when all nations will shower gifts upon Israel to honor Him in His building up of the nations, in fulfillment of prophecy. Peace will flow like a river and the glory of the Gentiles like a flowing stream (Isa. 66:12).

> Jerusalem will be comforted as by a mother comforting a needy child (Isa. 66:12-14).

All these scriptures are speaking of the same thing. Israel is the focus here, not the church. This transfer is happening after the Second Coming and at the beginning of the Millennial Reign. The glorious (authentic) church as a whole will continue to be persecuted until they are taken at the rapture (Rev. 4:1), and then many saints who were not saints at the rapture will be heavily persecuted until the Second Coming (Dan. 7:25; Rev. 6:9-11; 7:9-17). Then, the saints of all ages will rule and reign as kings and priests with all the wealth of the world (Dan. 7:13-14; Rom. 8:14).

6. The Fullness Of The Gentiles

The Times of the Gentiles will end (Dan. 9:27; 12:1-7; Mt. 24:31; Lk. 21:24; Rev. 11:1-2). All agree to this. I guess the area of disagreement would be the understanding of when the Time of the Gentiles ends. If all understood this simple fact, then the Time of the Gentiles would have no traction in determining when the rapture will be.

To understand the answer further, we must have the understanding of when the Time of the Gentiles actually began. Some are waiting for the fullness of the Gentiles to come in based on one or two verses. Others believe the Time of the Gentile will last 2,520 years, so they want to know the year it began. We will give simple conclusions to these questions. This is one of the two more famous verses from Paul.

> For I would not, brethren, that ye should be ignorant of this mystery, lest ye should be wise in your own conceits; <u>that blindness in part is happened to Israel</u>, until <u>the fullness of the Gentiles be come in</u> (Rom. 11:25).

If all understood when the blindness of Israel goes away, then this wouldn't be a question. They were blind to who Jesus was, and they will be until the Second Coming. This is actually a very well known and accepted fact. They will all believe at His Coming when they shall see Him coming in the clouds. They will fulfill Psalms 118 that was partially fulfilled at Jesus' First Coming. The revealed secret here is of the blindness of Israel until Christ comes, when she will be restored (Rom. 11:25-29; Isa. 66:7-8; Zech. 12:10 - Zech. 13:1; 14:1-21). But how do we know? Just read the rest of the verse.

Events People Are Waiting On Before The Rapture

And so <u>all Israel shall be saved</u>: as it is written, <u>There shall come out of Sion the Deliverer, and shall turn away ungodliness from Jacob</u> (Rom. 11:26).

This is a plain reference to the Second Coming, when the Deliverer shall deliver Israel from the ungodly armies of Antichrist that march to annihilate her. This is when Israel shall see Jesus, His armies of saints and faithful angels, and will all be saved by their believe and crying out for Him to save them.. The Time of the Gentiles will finally be over.

<u>Save now, I beseech thee, O LORD: O LORD, I beseech thee</u>, send now prosperity. <u>Blessed *be* he that cometh in the name of the LORD</u>: we have blessed you out of the house of the LORD (Ps. 118:25-26).

These words were sung by the Jews at the feast of tabernacles, when carrying green branches in their hands (Ps. 118:25-26). This was partially fulfilled by Jesus' First Coming when the people thought Jesus would save them from Roman rule. Verse 26 was sung when Christ made His entrance into Jerusalem (Mt. 21:9). (Ps. 118:26, fulfilled, and quoted in Mt. 21:9; 23:39; Mk. 11:9; Lk. 13:35; 19:38; Jn. 12:13). If the Time of the Gentiles ends at the Second Coming, then God is not waiting for a certain number of Gentiles to be saved before the rapture. It couldn't be any more simple.

The Times of the Gentiles is the administration of the Gentiles, as the rod of chastening upon Israel, to further God's purpose concerning them. When did this begin? It began with Israel's first oppression by the Gentiles in Egypt, and will continue with the history of Israel through this Dispensation of Grace. It will end at the return of the Messiah in glory when he will deliver Israel from the Gentiles and exalt them as the head of all nations in the Millennium and forever (Lk. 21:24; Rom. 11:25; Rev. 19:11 – Rev. 20:10).

The dispensation of the Gentiles is mentioned only in Luke 21:24, which has the same meaning as the fullness of the Gentiles in Romans 11:25. The term in Romans is also taken to mean that a time will come when God will no longer save Gentiles, only Jews. There are no such doctrine in all of Scripture. People have always had grace to be redeemed while air is still filling their mortal lungs and their heart still pumps blood. During the future tribulation both Jews and Gentiles can and will be saved (Acts 2:16-21; Rom. 1:16; 10:11-13; Rev. 7:9-17).

The term "the fullness of the Gentiles" could not mean that God will some day cut off Gentiles from salvation and become a vicious tyrant, damning the souls of men in eternity regardless of what those men may desire to do about their own destiny. This term always refers to political domination over the Jews by the Gentiles, off and on, from the Egyptian bondage to the Second Coming. The whole length of "the times of the Gentiles" will be more than 3,800 years and has run through the Egyptian, Assyrian, Babylonian, Medo-Persian, Grecian, and Roman empires and will continue through the two empires that are yet future-the Revised Roman and the Revived Grecian.

It is broadly taught that the times of the Gentiles are 2,520 years, based upon a theory about the seven times of Leviticus 26, where God predicted that when Israel sinned He would punish them seven times for their sins. It is believed that a prophetic year is 360 days long and that these days can double as years for a hidden time-frame for deciphering the time left in the Church Age. Therefore, a year of 360 days is made a period of 360 years.

Seven periods of 360 years makes 2,520 years. Many have taught that these 2,520 years began with the fall of Jerusalem under Nebuchadnezzar about 606 B.C. since Daniel is the one first writing about all this. Daniel wrote of the oppression from his day on, but this is not stating that the oppression began in Daniel's day. Many starting years have been taught, therefore many endings for the times of the Gentiles have been proclaimed. The following are some of the dates given in modern books of prophetic students for the ending of the times of the Gentiles: 1914, 1917, 1918, 1925, 1927, 1932, 1935, 1937, 1938, 1942, 1945, 1948, 1954, 1958, etc.

To reiterate, some persists in the misunderstanding of this doctrine by the belief the fullness of the Gentiles refers to the number of people who become believers during the Church Age. When this number is reached, the rapture will take place. There is no doctrine found in the Bible that is formed by only one verse and the day of the rapture, Second Coming, and the beginning of the Millennial Reign have been predetermined since the beginning of time (1 Pt. 1:20). These three events will be fulfilled by the last three feasts of the Lord in the order in which they were written in Leviticus 23.

In Revelation 13:1-18; 17:8-13, John illustrates the whole length of the times of the Gentiles with the dragon and the beast that had seven heads and ten horns. The seven heads and the beast itself are explained to be eight world kingdoms to oppress Israel from the Egyptian bondage to the Second Coming. The times of the Gentiles began with the oppression of Israel in Egypt and will continue through the kingdom of Antichrist and end at the Second Coming.

The whole length of the times of the Gentiles will be more than 3,800 years and has run through the Egyptian, Assyrian, Babylonian, Medo-Persian, Grecian, and Roman empires and will continue through the two empires that are still in the future. They are the Revised Roman Empire and the Revived Grecian Empire. This proves the 2,520 year period of the Time of the Gentiles is not grounded in good understanding. We cannot find the day of the rapture by determining the beginning of the Jewish oppression.

Chapter 10

FOUNDATIONS FOR BUILDING A BIBLICAL TIME-LINE

How do you put together a biblical time-line? Simply answered, you put together all the pieces of the puzzle God so generously gave us in His Word. Prophecy is as uncomplicated as history. If you can understand simple history, then you can understand prophecy. History is the study of past events, particularly in human affairs. Prophecy is simply history told before it happens.

We will be learning how to put together a biblical time-line in the next chapter. Before this happens, the foundation must be sure. Doctrine must be known and understood (2 Tim. 2:15; Rev. 22:18-19). There are countless time-lines, but one faulty belief will totally throw it off it's path. I've seen great ideas on the course of a sure path sway from the straight path over something as simple as thinking a verse is speaking of the Tribulation when it was in fact speaking of the Millennial Reign. The ignorance came from not realizing the boundaries of the time frame given for the Day of the Lord.

There are only a few subjects we'll get control of before moving forward. Books can be written on for all these subjects and many more subjects could have been included. It is my hope that these chosen few will build you up in biblical strength of understanding. The pertinent information selected has to do with your watcher training in building a sound biblical time-line. I hope these condensed studies will encourage you to study beyond the writings of these pages.

1. Names and Time Frames for the 7 Year Tribulation

This needs to be basic information for anyone who's been attending any church for at least one year. Sadly, foundational knowledge is ignored completely across the board. This goes double if not triple for any and all end-time knowledge for understanding. I've talked to Christians who have been churched for sixty years, yet have no concept of what Daniel's 70th Week is, nor can they even recall hearing the term. I am astonished!

There are other terms used for half of the Tribulation that are often confused for the whole of the Tribulation. Common and easy misunderstandings, or a total lack of ever hearing some terms like these can greatly throw off time frames and events.

Daniel's 70th Week

There are so many things to teach concerning the whole of Daniel's 70th Week, but I'm committed to keeping my eyes on the target. However, often I give added value when I go off course slightly. I suppose you'll be okay if you learn more than you have to. This is how a fuller comprehension of the Bible happens. Some of my best ideas have come when I was going on rabbit trails. You can start on the subject of sanctification and end up learning what happened to the souls of giants after they died. This is a good thing! This is how to learn the fun way, adventure style.

Daniel's 70th Week is used synonymous with the Seven Year Tribulation, however their days are not identical. The Seven Year Tribulation of the last seven years of the Dispensation of Grace will last a few more days than Daniel's 70th Week. I often use these two terms interchangeably. For all practical, everyday prophecy teachings, this is alright. However, when looking to make a precise time-line, we'll need to identify the exact specifications for each term. This is eschatology expert series. If you can comprehend the next few paragraphs, you'll be far more advanced than every leading prophecy expert out there as identified by the mainstream church.

We get the doctrinal term "Daniel's 70th Week" from Daniel 9:24-27. This was a direct prophecy of events given from the mouth of Gabriel, a chief angel who was sent from God. The prophecy concerns Israel and Jerusalem from Daniel's time until the end of all the persecution of Daniel's people, the Jews (Dan. 9:22-23). The point of the vision was to give wisdom and understanding concerning the future of Israel and last day events. This is still the case, for the last week, or seven years has not yet happened. Daniel was commanded to understand the vision and believe it, so we are to do the same.

If you don't have a clear understanding of this one chapter, then many other prophecies cannot be fully understood. Daniel's whole book is well beyond what is needed to authenticate the whole Bible as inspired, and God as true. Daniel 9:24 gives us the the time frame of Seventy Weeks. The phrase "seventy weeks" literally means "seventy sevens" (Hebrew: for "week" is shabuwa` (HSN-<H7620>), seven). "Seventy weeks are determined upon thy people and upon thy holy city..." (Dan. 9:24). What has to be determined is the amount of time one "seven" amounts to. Is it a week of seven days, or a "week" of seven years? It is seventy sections of seven years because Daniel's prayer concerned years, not days (Dan. 9:2).

The seventy periods of seven years add up to 490 years and are divided into three sections. The first division is a period of seven sevens. This equates to 49 years and has been determined for the rebuilding of Jerusalem (Dan. 9:25). The second division is a period of sixty-two sevens, which equates to 434 years from the completion of the city at the end of the 49 years to the time the Messiah is cut off or crucified for men (Dan. 9:25-26). If you look at simple history, you can see that the decree to rebuild Jerusalem, which is when the 70 Weeks began, lets you know the Messiah will be killed exactly 483 years later. This is how the "three wise men" knew the Messiah should be born soon.

The last period of seven years is the 70th period of seventy sevens. This last seven years is Daniel's 70th Week, or the Seven Year Tribulation. Daniel 9 is how we understand the tribulation of God's wrath will last seven years. Many are more familiar with the doctrinal term of "7 Year Tribulation," but few can accurately explain where we get this term from, as it doesn't appear in the Bible in those words.

The gap of time in between the 69th Week of Daniel and the 70th Week of Daniel is the Church Age. Romans 11:17-24 confirms for us that Israel was cut off when they rejected their Messiah. God will fully direct His attention back on Israel during the last seven years of this dispensation in order to bring them to repentance and fulfill the six things of Daniel 9:24. The church will be raptured many days before the 70th Week begins, but the tribulation will begin immediately. This is the gap in between the rapture and the beginning of Daniel's 70th Week, which will begin when the Antichrist signs the seven year covenant with Israel to protect them from the revised Roman Empire that will have formed before the 70th Week begins.

The last period of seven is divided into two parts, the first half and the last half, which is clearly explained to be 3 ½ years (Dan. 7:25; 12:7; Rev. 11:1-3; 12:6, 14; 13:5). The references foretelling of 3 ½ years always speaks of the last half of Daniel's 70th Week. The language used to describe the last 3 ½ years is as follows: "a time and times and the dividing of time" (Dan. 7:25); "a time, times, and an half" (Dan. 12:7); "forty and two months" (Rev. 11:2; 13:5); "a thousand two hundred and threescore days" (Rev. 11:3; 12:6); and "a time, and times, and half a time" (Rev. 12:14).

During this time the vision will be completed and the end of the age will come. The "time, times, and an half," or the 3 ½ years (Dan. 12:7), are the 42 months of Antichrist's war on Israel till God purges every enemy from Israel making the Jewish people willing to do God's will (Ezek. 20:33-38; Zech. 13:9; Mal. 3:3). If the last half of the 70th week is 3 ½ years, then the first half is also 3 ½ years, making the one seven period from Daniel 9:27 to be 7 years. If the last period of seventy sevens is 7 years, then all sevens are referring to years, making Daniel's 70 weeks a period of 490 years long.

Daniel's 70th Week can be rightfully equated with the Seven Year Tribulation, but the 70th Week will be a precise length of time consisting of 2,520 days: 1,260 x's 2 = 2,520 (Rev. 11:3; 12:6). There is a gap of time between the rapture of the church and the 70th Week of Daniel, as read in a previous chapter. The church is the hinderer of lawlessness and will be the ones withholding the wrath of God (1 Thess. 5:9; 2 Thess. 2:7-8). The Tribulation will begin directly after the rapture, and the world powers will see their opportunity to create order out of chaos. The New World Order will make their move, redefining borders of the Old Roman Empire, persecuting Israel, which is why the Antichrist makes a covenant with her. He secretly wants to overthrow the other kings and will use Israel to defeat them.

This will begin to come alive in the next chapter when we apply this knowledge to show you how it harmonizes. Seven years is determined for both the Seven Year Tribulation and the 70th Week of Daniel. The 70th Week consists of 7 years of 360 days, while the Tribulation is closer to 7 years of 365 days. The rapture will be on the feast of trumpets, while the Second Coming will be on the feast of atonement. The Day of Atonement is 10 days after the feast of trumpets. So, the time between the rapture and the Second Coming would appear to be seven years and ten days apart.

However, God's calendar is based on the moon, meaning it is a lunar calendar. The feasts are determined by the moon, so the feast of trumpets is never on the same day on our Gregorian calendar in back to back years. Likewise, neither are the other feasts. The amount of days in between the rapture and the Second Coming will vary by a few days with every set of seven year periods. This will make complete sense by following the educational time-line in the next chapter. For example, if the rapture happens on the feast of trumpets in 2016 (Sept. 3-4 or Oct. 3-4), then there are either 22 or 52 days of tribulation before the Antichrist signs the 7 year covenant with Israel, beginning Daniel's 70th Week.

The 2,520 days of the 70th Week are finished on September 20, 2023, but the Second Coming on the day of atonement is on September 26, 2023. This allows a 6 day gap between the end of the 70th Week and the end of God's wrath and tribulation on the earth. The 22 or 52 days, plus the 6 days at the end mean the Seven Year Tribulation lasts for 2,548 days, or 2,578 days. This would average a year being either 364 days long, or 368.3 days long. Either way, the Tribulation is still 7 years in duration.

The reason for the two possible dates for the rapture on the feast of trumpets is because their calendar is lunar and the months don't allow for more than 30 days since a moon cycle is roughly 29 ½ days in duration. 2016 is akin to our leap year. Some of their years add a 13th month to balance their calendar.

To recap, the Tribulation will start to impact Israel ahead of Daniel's 70th Week. How long before is determined by simply finding your seven year period from fall to fall, then finding the date of Passover in the spring, halfway in between your seven year time-frame. Subtract 1,260 days from Passover and that is the day Antichrist signs the seven year treaty, beginning the 70th Week of Daniel. Find the days in between that day and the feast of trumpets, which is when the rapture happens, and you'll know when tribulation begins.

This is when I theorize the New World Order making it's move to change the borders in three continents of North Africa, West

Asia, and Europe to form the Revised Roman Empire. Order out of Chaos. There is no greater chaos from now to then that could cause an acceptance of this plan. Millions vanishing will cause the next great revival (Acts 2:16-21; Rev. 6:9-11; 7:9-17), the next great apostasy (2 Thess. 2:10-12; Rev. 6:2-11; 9:20-21; 17:1-18; 18:1-24), and the next great economic crash that could cause the world powers to come together in that area of the globe.

When Antichrist rises at the beginning of the Week, Israel will be undergoing persecution from the ten kings of Revised Rome controlled by Mystery Babylon. When Antichrist comes he will make a 7-year covenant with Israel assuring them of protection in their continued establishment as a nation (Daniel 9:27). Because the Jews will not submit to Mystery Babylon, there will be a widespread persecution and they shall be "hated of all nations" during the time of the beginning of sorrows when Antichrist will be endeavoring to conquer all these nations (Mat. 24:4-12). Antichrist will need Jewish moral and financial support in his rise over these nations of ten kings, so he will make an confederation with them for seven years.

The 1,260 days of the last half of the 70th Week will end when the two witnesses are killed, but the Second Coming will not be on that day, for their dead bodies are laid in the streets for 3 ½ days until they are resurrected and rise to heaven (Rev. 11:7-12). The Antichrist has waged war with Israel and assembles all his defeated and conquered armies to march against her. The 3 ½ days after the death of the two witnesses further proves a gap of time in between the end of the 70th Week and the Second Coming. This tells us the Tribulation continues a few days beyond the 70th Week. Therefore, the time of the Tribulation will be during the whole of Daniel's 70th Week (Dan. 9:27), yet the tribulation will end at the Second Coming (Mat. 24:29-31; Rev. 19:11-21), while the 70th Week ends a little before this.

The Great Tribulation

The Great Tribulation is the last half of the Seven Year Tribulation. It is called great because it is a time of greater persecution for Israel. The Great Tribulation is synonymous with Jacob's Trouble. You may have heard of these terms, or it may be new to you. We are going to look at the Scriptures used to validate these terms. Unlike the doctrinal terms of "Seven Year Tribulation" and "Daniel's 70th Week," the doctrinal terms of "Great Tribulation" and "Jacob's Trouble" are found word for word in scriptural text. The Great Tribulation is where we get the term used more than them all, the Seven Year Tribulation. The Great Tribulation clearly being 3 ½ years in duration, the natural execution of language was to call Daniel's 70th Week, "The Seven Year Tribulation."

> And I said unto him, Sir, thou knowest. And he said to me, These are they which came out of <u>great tribulation</u>, and have washed their robes, and made them white in the blood of the Lamb (Rev. 7:14).

Revelation 7 is a parenthetical passage introducing the 144,000 and the martyred tribulation saints who come out of the the Great Tribulation, referring to the last 3 1/2 years of Daniel's 70th Week (Mt. 24:15-22; Dan. 12:1; Jer. 30:6-9). All the events of Revelation 11:15 - Revelation 19:21 take place during this time.

> And at that time shall Michael stand up, the great prince which standeth for the children of thy people: and there shall be <u>a time of trouble, such as never was since there was a nation even to that same time</u>: and at that time thy people shall be delivered, every one that shall be found written in the book (Dan. 12:1).

This is another reference to the Great Tribulation and the 144,000, just like in Revelation 7. The 144,000 are the only Jews who are redeemed right before the mid-point of Daniel's 70th Week.

They will be caught up to heaven to be delivered from this time of great tribulation (Rev. 12:5). They are the man-child of Revelation 12, as we have learned in book 1 of this series.

Michael, the chief prince of the atmosphere over Israel (Dan. 12:1; 10:21; Rev. 12:7-12) stands up for Israel at this moment, because this is when Antichrist steps into the Jewish temple, stopping sacrifices, declaring himself to be God, and breaks covenant with Israel to destroy her. This occurs right after he defeats the other three kings from the Old Grecian Empire and the other six kings give him their authority to avoid war. The man of sin will not need Israel after that and this is why he breaks covenant and reveals his true intentions (Dan. 8:13-14; 9:24-27; 11:45; 12:1-2; Mat. 24:15; 2 Thess. 2:4; Rev. 13; 17).

> 15 When ye therefore shall see <u>the abomination of desolation, spoken of by Daniel the prophet, stand in the holy place</u>, (whoso readeth, let him understand:) 16 Then let them which be in Judaea flee into the mountains: 17 Let him which is on the housetop not come down to take any thing out of his house: 18 Neither let him which is in the field return back to take his clothes. 19 And woe unto them that are with child, and to them that give suck in those days! 20 But pray ye that your flight be not in the winter, neither on the sabbath day: 21 For then shall be <u>great tribulation, such as was not since the beginning of the world to this time, no, nor ever shall be</u>. 22 And except those days should be shortened, there should no flesh be saved: but for the elect's sake those days shall be shortened (Mat. 24:15-22).

For then, the great tribulation of the last 3 ½ years of this age will begin (Dan. 9:27; 11:40-45; 12:1, 7, 11; Jer. 30:4-7; Rev. 7:14; 11:1 - Rev. 19:21).

Jacob's Trouble

Ask ye now, and see whether a man doth travail with child? wherefore do I see every man with his hands on his loins, as a woman in travail, and all faces are turned into paleness? 7Alas! for <u>that day is great</u>, so that <u>none is like it</u>: it is even <u>the time of Jacob's trouble</u>; but he shall be saved out of it. 8 For it shall come to pass in that day, saith the LORD of hosts, that I will break his yoke from off thy neck, and will burst thy bonds, and strangers shall no more serve themselves of him: 9 But they shall serve the LORD their God, and David their king, whom I will raise up unto them (Jer. 30:6-9).

A man travailing with child always pictures the most horrible tribulation upon a nation (Jer. 30:6-7; 4:31; 6:24; 13:21; 22:23; 49:24; 50:43; Mic. 4:9-10; 5:3; Ps. 48:6; Isa. 13:8; 21:3; 42:14; 66:7-8; Rev. 12:2). Jacob is the name of Abraham's grandson. Isaac is his father. Jacob's name was changed to Israel and his sons became the forefathers of the tribes of Israel. It is called Jacob's Trouble in verse 7, but it literally means Israel's Trouble. The time of Jacob's trouble, like the time of great tribulation, will be the last three and a half years of this age, the last half of Daniel's 70th week, and the time when Antichrist will enter Israel and take over the temple as his capital building, to be worshiped there as God (Dan. 7:27; 11:40-45; 12:1-7; Mt. 24:15-31; 2 Thess. 2:1-12; Rev. 12:1 - Rev. 20:6).

"In that day," from verse 8, refers to the Second Coming of Jesus, when God will break the yoke of Antichrist off the neck of Israel and he will come to an end. This will be on the last day of that great tribulation against Israel. If Jesus did not come back at the time He does, then no flesh of Israel would be saved, but for the elect's sake (context here is Israel), the persecution in those days shall be stopped short of total annihilation for Israel (Mat. 24:22).

An accurate vocabulary of biblical terminology can be known through a little study. This will avoid great confusion while watching.

To recap, the last seven years of this age begin when the Church Age ends. The Dispensation of Grace continues on for another seven years until the Dispensation of Divine Government begins at the Second Coming. The Dispensation of Divine Government is synonymous with the Millennial Reign of Christ. The last seven years is Daniel's 70th Week, or the Seven Year Tribulation. The last 3 ½ years of the Dispensation of Grace and the 70th Week of Daniel is called Jacob's Trouble, which is synonymous with the Great Tribulation. The Day of the Lord has no part of Daniel's 70th Week, the Seven Year Tribulation, Jacob's Trouble, or the Great Tribulation. The Day of the Lord overlaps the Millennial Reign, or Dispensation of Divine Government.

2. 1,260; 1,290; 1,335 Days of Daniel 12

There are three time periods of days given in Daniel 12. If the purpose and timing of these days remains a guess for watchers, then time-lines will continue to suffer. More important than that, we will remain blind and ignorant to God's truths. Some people are even putting the Second Coming on the 1,290th day. The simplicity of the days makes it confusing for people. We naturally think everything from the Book of Daniel and Revelation has to be a riddle. Anything straight forward must not mean what it says, so we make things more complicated than God intended. Years become days, and days become years.

The "time, times, and an half," or the 3 ½ years of Daniel 12:7 are the 42 months of Antichrist's war on Israel during the Great Tribulation. The next period is an increase of 30 days to be added to the 1,260 days (Dan. 12:11). Nothing specific is told to be happening during this month of space beyond Daniel's 70th Week, though we can know many things the saints will be doing from other passages throughout the Bible. The last period from Daniel 12:7-

13 is 1,335 days, an increase of 45 days to the second period. The addition of 75 days to the 1,260 days will complete the 1,335 days that occur in Daniel 12. The 1,335th day will be the actual day of the announcement and declaration of the kingdom, when those who have lived through the Tribulation will be blessed. This is when Jesus will say to the sheep nations:

> Come, ye blessed of My Father, inherit the kingdom prepared for you from the foundation of the world (Matthew 25:34).

For educational purposes, if the 70th Week is from 2016 – 2023, then this day will fall on December 4, 2023, and be just in time for Hanukkah. The construction of the Millennial temple is one of the many things that will be taking place in the extra 75 days after the 1,260 days (Ezekiel 40-46; Zech. 6:12-13). Blessed is the man that waits and lives up to the end of the 1,335 days (Daniel 12:12), for he will have a part in the events of the days after the 1,335th day (Daniel 12:13). As seen, one half of the Tribulation will not be 1,260 days, while the other half is 1,290 days long. I've seen this many times through my years, but the authority from Scripture denies this.

3. 2,300 Days of Daniel 8:14

And he said unto me, Unto two thousand and three hundred days; then shall the sanctuary be cleansed (Dan. 8:14).

I've seen many weird theories with the time-frame of the 2,300 days. I don't speak to insult, I understand what confusion feels like when reading Daniel and Revelation. The 2,300 seems to be 2,300 days by this verse alone, but the Book of Daniel always interprets itself. The days are literally half this number at 1,150 days. This is 110 days shy of the conclusion of the 1,260 days. All time periods given of days always refer to the Great Tribulation, or the last half of the 70th Week. At the end of the 2,300 evenings and mornings (3 years, 2 months, and 10 days; Dan. 8:11-13, 26) the sanctuary shall be cleansed of the abomination of desolation (Dan. 8:13-14; 9:27; 11:45; 12:11; Mt. 24:15; 2 Thess. 2:4; Rev. 13:11-18).

We have to understand what causes the temple to be defiled in the first place. It is when the abomination of desolation walks in and declares himself God. When does this happen? This happens on day 1 of the 1,260 days, which will be on a soon coming Passover. Daniel 8:26 explains the vision to referring to evenings and mornings. There will be 1,150 evenings and 1,150 mornings, which together equate to the 2,300 days until the sanctuary is cleansed again.

This must be the case since it is clear the beginning of the 2,300 days is in the middle of the Tribulation and the math would put the cleansing of the sanctuary to be about 3 years after the Second Coming if it were 2,300 full days. It must be accepted that the sanctuary will have been cleansed long before that day. After all, the temple of the Tribulation time will have been destroyed by earthquakes at the end of the Tribulation, and then the Millennial temple will be quickly constructed (Zech. 6:12-13; 14:1-5; Ezek. 40 – Ezek. 48).

It appears as though the remnant who remained in Israel and did not flee when the Antichrist broke his covenant with them are the ones who take the temple back. This will most likely be due to him being busied with fighting the armies of the north for the most part of the Great Tribulation. They are keeping him busy during this time and are the one's God used to distract Antichrist from destroying Israel when he sought to destroy her after he broke covenant with them (Rev. 12 – Rev. 13).

It is clear that Judah will have an army fighting at Jerusalem when Antichrist comes down from the north (Ezek. 38 – Ezek. 39) to retake Jerusalem (Zech. 14:14), so the taking back of the temple is very plausible. No scripture says that the abomination of desolation will actually be in the temple 1,260 days. So, if Daniel 8:14, 26 says the daily sacrifices will be taken away after 2,300 evenings and mornings, then this is the simple and only answer to be found. Not one of these days secretly means years, so we won't even go there.

4. Will The Days Be Shortened?

> And <u>except those days should be shortened</u>, there should no flesh be saved: but for the elect's sake those days shall be shortened (Matthew 24:22).

> And <u>except that the Lord had shortened those days</u>, no flesh should be saved: but for the elect's sake, whom He hath chosen, <u>He hath shortened the days</u> (Mark 13:20).

Understanding of the "shortened days" is crucial when taking the step forward to explore a biblical timeline for the Seven Tear Tribulation. It only takes one wrong move to completely destroy accuracy of a timeline. I've seen many that exchange literal, plain facts for human reasoning. You have to stick with the pieces of the puzzle in the box to make the outcome of the puzzle match the picture on the box.

There are those who believe the number of days during the Tribulation will fall short of the 2,520 days that are in the seven year period of Daniel's 70th Week. The day count comes from Daniel in his book and from John in the Book of Revelation. There are 1,260 days in half of that period, so naturally, there will be double that, or 2,520 days in Daniel's 70th Week, or the Seven Year Tribulation.

Others have interpreted the days themselves being shortened, in that the hours in each day will be fewer. I'll use 16 hours as an example since this is what I've seen many times. Some use Revelation

8:12 as the foundation for their theory that the days will be shortened by one-third. There is no authority for this theory from that verse or any other. But some believe the earth will spin faster because of the hit of the asteroid, or perhaps due to the magnetic pull from a binary red dwarf star passing by our planet, called Planet X. Though this Planet X, often called Nibiru, may be true, it will not shorten the hours of our day by speeding up the rotation.

The precision of the earth's rotation of earth was set by God to maintain life. If the earth speeds up by 50 %, then we would have a day lasting 16 hours. Many changes would occur. Seasons: Along with the rotation of earth its atmosphere also rotates. This causes the flow of atmospheric winds across the globe. With rotation speeding up, there will be a devastating change in seasons, causing typhoons, heavy rainfall, and many other devastating changes. Ocean level: Due to earth's rotation, ocean level is maintained on central (non-polar) regions of earth. Increasing rotation means more water will start flowing from the polar regions into the non-polar regions, causing a number of countries to be submerged in oceans.

Temperature: With increase in rotation days and nights will become shorter. Temperature will be on extremes. Either very hot or cold. Human body: Our body is synced with the speed of earth. Increasing the rotation speed will cause us to not be able to adapt to the new momentum and we will perish. Satellites will be out of alignment, such as our most important satellite, the moon. This will add to the chaotic tides and ocean levels. The earth's electromagnetism will change to all of mankind's demise and many other unpredictable changes.

The days will not be shortened by number of hours in a day by the acceleration of the earth's rotation, nor will the literal 24 hour, 2,520 days be one day less than 2,520 days. This is very easy to prove and verify. These days are 1,150 (Dan. 8:13-14), 1260 days (Dan. 12:7), 1290 days (Dan. 12:11), & 1335 days (Dan. 12:12). All day counts are always speaking of the last three and a half years beginning at the middle of Daniel's 70th Week. This is when the Antichrist breaks his covenant with Israel. This is when the Two Witnesses stand against this man of sin to protect Israel (Rev. 11:1-3). The "time, times, and an half, " or the 3 ½ years (Dan. 12:7), are the 42 months of Antichrist's war on Israel till God purges every rebel from the nation making her willing to do His will (Ezek. 20:33-38; Zech. 13:9; Mal. 3:3).

There's always a lot of hypothesis concerning Jesus's words from Mark 13:20 and Matthew 24:22. Because of these speculations, prophecy watchers' studies and watch dates are compromised. The persecution itself will be cut short, not the 1,260 days themselves. If it were the days themselves, then why was Daniel told 1,260 days? Did God change His foreknowledge or His mind many hundreds of years later when Jesus spoke these words (Mat. 24:22; Mk. 13:20)?

The Book of Daniel was written from Babylon and Shushan about 616 B.C. to 536 B.C. by Daniel, a captive prince from Judah (Dan. 1:3-6). Daniel was also an interpreter of dreams and visions (Dan. 1:17; 2:12-49; 4:8-27; 5:10-31), prime minister under several kings (Dan. 2:46-49; 5:29; 6:1-3), and a prophet of God (Dan. 7:28; 8:1; 9:21-23; 10:1-12; 12:4-13). He prophesied of the Gentile world kingdoms from his day to the Millennium and eternal kingdom of God on earth (Dan. 2:38-45; 7:17-27; 8:20-25; 9:24-27; Dan. 11:40 – Dan. 12:13). He accurately wrote down what he was told concerning the day periods from the middle of the Tribulation forward.

So, did Jesus contradict Scripture with what was told to Daniel? This seems to be the thought by watchers who insist the days are what will be shortened, or the hours of the days will be shortened. Can we examine the validity of this? Oh yeas we can! The revelation of the number of days that will be in the Tribulation are not only recorded in Daniel, but also in the Book of Revelation.

Revelation was written on Patmos island, about 95 - 96 A.D. (Rev. 1:9) by the apostle John (Rev. 1:1). The purpose was to give an unveiling from Jesus Christ, which God gave to Him to show unto His servants things (events) which must shortly come to pass (Rev. 1:1). What I am presenting is that Jesus confirmed the number of days that were told to Daniel some 600 to 700 years earlier (Rev. 11:1-3; 12:6, 14; 13:5; Dan. 7:25; 12:7). If this is the case, then when Jesus spoke to John some six decades after He taught Mark 13:20 & Matthew 24:22, it must be clear that the persecution will be cut short, not the 1260 days themselves (Rev. 11:1-3; 12:6, 14; 13:5; Dan. 7:25; 12:7).

Antichrist could easily destroy Israel in a short time after he breaks his covenant with them, if God were not to interfere by opening up the earth to swallow forces of the Antichrist who are trailing Israel to annihilate her (Rev. 12). It is God Who will supernaturally cause the ground to open up and swallow the armies of the dragon and Antichrist as they flee after Israel when she goes into the wilderness of Moab and Edom to escape (Dan. 11:41; Isa. 16:1-5; Mat. 24:16; Rev. 12:14-17). The Antichrist will be enraged by this and focus his rage on those in Israel who did not flee.

God will assist the remnant of the woman which does not take flight into the wilderness. God then stirs up the countries of the north and east against the Antichrist. He will then leave the remnant during the last 3 ½ years, going forth to conquer these nations. They will keep him engaged during this time, taking the Antichrist's focus off of Israel. The wars against the north countries in the north and east is how the remnant in Israel retake much of Jerusalem to cleanse the temple after 2,300 evenings and mornings (1,150 days, or 3 years, 2 months, and 10 days; Dan. 8:11-13, 26).

Then, after conquering these countries at the last part of the seven years, he will lead all his conquered foes and many other nations against Jerusalem to destroy it, but God will come and put an end to the Gentile dominion and deliver Israel (Zech. 14; Rev. 19). This war between Antichrist and countries of the north and east will cause the persecution of Israel to be shortened as in Matthew 24:22.

The days are precisely given and ordained. The next period is an addition of 30 days to the 1,260 days of the above mentioned period (Dan. 12:11). The last period is 1,335 days, an addition of 45 days to the second period. The extra 75 days (the 30 days and 45 days) added to the 1,260 days will complete the 1,335 days of Daniel 12:7-13, the last day of which will be the actual day of the proclamation of the kingdom, when men who have lived through the Tribulation will be blessed. It is the actual time when Christ will say to the sheep nations: "Come, ye blessed of My Father, inherit the kingdom prepared for you from the foundation of the world" (Mat. 25:34). Again, these extra 75 days will be taken up by certain events necessary to the actual proclamation of the kingdom. Oh, glorious day!

From the time the daily sacrifice will be taken away (Dan. 12:11; 8:9-14; 9:27), and from the setting up of the abomination of desolation there will be three periods: 1,260 days (Daniel 12:7); 1,290 days (Daniel 12:11); 1,335 days (Daniel 12:12). Blessed is the man that waits and lives up to the end of the 1,335 days (Dan. 12:12). You'll have part in many amazing events following the 1,260 days, and being accepted into the kingdom of heaven for eternity after the 1,335 days (Dan. 12:13). This is of course conditional upon natural man's willingness to accept the conditions of fully submitting to God and His ways (Isa. 65:20). The biblical events of the 75 extra days are listed at the end of the next chapter (ch. 11).

5. Understanding the Order of the Book of Revelation

It is more important now than ever before to have a good understanding of when the events in the Book of Revelation take place. As I write this, the church is at the very end of Revelation 3 in a symbolic way. Literally, the Church Age is almost over and will come to an abrupt end as millions vanish and billions are left behind.

This section's function serves at least three main purposes. First, so the reader of this during this age will be helped to not be caught off guard. Second, many end-time time-lines are messy. Knowing the sequence of events as they are placed in Revelation will help you examine your latest insight and see if it is in harmony with Scripture. For example, I once theorized that all eyes would see Jesus at His Coming because all the saints and angels would be traveling with Him in space, which may take more than 24 hours to ride from heaven to earth.

The light this would bring would look like a star getting closer and closer. I later read that His Coming would be as fast as lightning (Mat. 24:27), and we would all be riding through a portal from heaven to earth (Rev. 19:11). This portal is how the raptured saints get to heaven (Rev. 4:1). Little details like that make or break our creative ideas. We have to stick with Scripture. It's more impressive than anything we can conjure up, but we have to read it and know how to study it in the manner God intends. Read carefully to understand the sequence of events that will soon unfold.

Revelation was written by the apostle John (Rev. 1:1) on Patmos island (Rev. 1:9), about 95 - 96 A.D. This is the unveiling of information from Jesus Christ, which God gave to Him to show unto His servants, events that must shortly come to pass (Rev. 1:1). These "things," or events, are taking place from John's time and will continue to transpire through to the eternal events of the new heaven and new earth (2 Pt. 3:1-13; Rev. 20 – Rev. 22). The events are in sequential order with parenthetical passages inserted between the main events.

A parenthetical passage explains certain things with better detail, and explains when they are going to happen along with the main events, but are not the same as these main events. Often, the consecutive order of events and continuity of the focus subject can be better comprehended if the student temporarily ignores the parenthetical passages. However, since the parenthetical events do take place somewhere within the sequential order of the main events, they cannot be dropped out indefinitely. It must be understood that such passages are very important, since they are given from God the Father, to Jesus the Son, for people like us to have a good understanding about the events soon to come that will end this dispensation.

The best example I can give is that of the book itself. The Bible didn't have to have Revelation added to it. After all, we have end-time prophecies throughout the Word, even the Book of Daniel is extremely detailed if you let it interpret itself, for the answers to what the symbolism means are always interpreted within the book itself. However, the Book of Revelation adds even more detail to the prophecies we already had.

This is what parenthetical passages do for us. They give greater insight to the truths we already have. Parenthetical passages in the Book of Revelation should not be dissected from within the time frame of the events in which they are given. For example, the woman and man-child in Revelation 12 must be happening in the middle of the Tribulation, not two thousand years ago when Jesus was born. Another example is the 200 million "man" army of Revelation 9. It cannot be the same as the armies from the east in the Battle of Armageddon, for chapter 9 is happening in the first half of the Tribulation, while chapter 16's battle is happening at the end of the Tribulation.

Parenthetical passages may not take place at the exact time they are recorded. They do take place sometime within those events in which they are listed with. The chronological order of the Book of Revelation should not be disturbed by moving events from one place in the book to another. For instance, the entire story of the two witnesses as far as Revelation is concerned has been told in chapter

11. God saw fit for their entire story to be told in a nutshell at the beginning of the Great Tribulation, which is in the middle of the Seven Year Tribulation.

Had I written the last half of the story of Daniel's 70th Week, I would have kept placing their story throughout the last 3 ½ years as their story unfolds. However, this is not how God saw fit to give us the information we need, and His ways are far greater than mine (Job 38 – Job 42; Prov. 3:5-6). The two witnesses are a great illustration for understanding what a parenthetical passage is, regardless of your belief as to when their ministry will be (first half, or last half). It is quiet clear that 3 ½ years is not all in Revelation 11 alone. The events are continuous from Revelation 10 – Revelation 19.

Revelation has been divided into three clearly-defined sections (Rev. 1:19). First, "The things which thou hast seen," which is the vision of Christ in the midst of the candlesticks (Rev. 1:12-20). Second, "The things which are," which is referring to the church, for John's time of receiving the vision and revelation was during the Church Age, which has not yet ended. The seven letters to the seven churches in Asia Minor, or present Turkey, is to whom the whole book is addressed (Rev. 2:1- Rev. 3:22). These messages to the churches apply to the whole church age and until the rapture of the church just before the future Tribulation and coming of the Antichrist, who will be here for the last seven years of this age (Dan. 9:27; 2 Thess. 2:7-12; Rev. 6:1 – Rev. 19:21).

Third, "The things which shall be hereafter," which are the events after the rapture of the church (Rev. 4:1 - Rev. 22:5). These include the scenes in heaven (Rev. 4 - Rev. 5), the seven seals and their parenthetical statements (Rev. 4:1 - Rev. 19:21), the Millennium (Rev. 20), and the new heaven and new earth (Rev. 21:1 - Rev. 22:5), and events of the conclusion (Rev. 22:6-21). Revelation 4:1 begins after the church is spoken of for the last time in Revelation 1 – Revelation 3. Greek: meta (NT:3326) tauta (NT:5023), after these things. This Greek phrase is used at the beginning and at the end of Revelation 4:1, thus: "After these things (after writing the things concerning the churches of Revelation 2 & 3), I looked ... a door was opened in heaven: and the first voice ... said, Come up hither, and I will show thee things which must be after these things,: that is, after the churches (Rev. 4:1).

This confirms and settles the question as to the time of the fulfillment of all the events of Revelation 4 – Revelation 22. They must be after these things, that is all things concerning the churches, or after the rapture of the church. The church is no longer on earth when the events of Revelation 4 – Revelation 22 take place. The Church Age is represented by the prophetic application (Rev. 1:3) of the seven churches (Rev. 2 – Rev. 3). Revelation 4:1 is when the rapture takes place in Revelation and is the place that ends the Church Age.

Christ said the things of Revelation 4 – Revelation 22 "must be hereafter," that is, after the churches, as proved above and also by Revelation 1:19, which is the key to understanding the three main divisions of Revelation. If this is true, then the church is raptured before these things of Revelation 4 – Revelation 22, and after the things of the churches of Revelation 2 – Revelation 3. If "the things which are," from Revelation 1:19, concern the church (Rev. 2 – Rev. 3), then the "things which must be after" "the things which are" must concern events after the churches. The church must be here during the time of the fulfillment of the things concerning the churches, and it must not be here during the fulfillment of the things after the churches. Then the church is raptured in Revelation 4:1 between "the things which are" (Rev. 2 – Rev. 3) and "the things which must be hereafter," that is, after the churches (Rev. 4 – Rev. 22).

If the events past Revelation 4:1 must be after the things of the churches, then the events will not be fulfilled along with the things of the churches. This means that every event of Revelation 4 - Revelation 22 must be fulfilled after the rapture of the church.

It also means that no historical or present event could possibly be a fulfillment of any event of Revelation 4 - Revelation 22.

Some hold to a view called, "The Hermeneutical Spiral." Prominent teacher, David Platt, teaches this. Wiki defines it like this: "The hermeneutic circle (German: hermeneutischer Zirkel) describes the process of understanding a text hermeneutically. It refers to the idea that one's understanding of the text as a whole is established by reference to the individual parts and one's understanding of each individual part by reference to the whole. Neither the whole text nor any individual part can be understood without reference to one another, and hence, it is a circle. However, this circular character of interpretation does not make it impossible to interpret a text; rather, it stresses that the meaning of a text must be found within its cultural, historical, and literary context."

For our understanding, hermeneutics is simply how you interpret the Bible. For us, we let Revelation 1:19 be the key to this interpretation that it's clearly meant to be. We interpret the Bible literally when at all possible. If language is clearly symbolic, metaphoric, or figurative, then we seek to find the literal truth God is giving from the symbolism, etc. The Bible often interprets itself in those instances. Therefore, Revelation 12 is not referring to Mary giving birth to Jesus who was then raptured. The point of that is out of harmony with the key to Revelation (Rev. 1:19). It would also make no sense for that little bit of history to be thrown in there.

I heard David Platt on Thy Word radio broadcasting teach on Revelation by way of his spiral interpretation. The judgments are not only future events to him, for they have been happening through time from beginning to the end and all around through time like a spiral. The plaques of Exodus are like the plaques of Revelation, so in what time have they happened and are being referred too? He says God gives Revelation to his people as a stunning picture of the glory of Christ and of God's sovereign rule over history.

Foundations For Building A Biblical Time-line

God clearly communicated that He is giving us a revealing of future events that will happen after the church has been raptured (Rev. 1:1, 19; 4:1). The spiral interpretation leads to all meaning systems being open-ended systems of signs referring to signs referring to signs. No concept can therefore have an ultimate, unequivocal meaning. There would be no parenthetical passages in Revelation with an open-ended system like that.

Take note of the parenthetical passages inserted between the main events, which explain certain things that are to happen along with the main events, but are not the same as these events. Here is a list for a clear understanding that will help you be the watcher Jesus commanded and called you to be (Lk. 21:36; Mk. 13:34-37).

Parenthetical passage 1 - (Revelation 7:1-17)

Parenthetical passage 2 - (Revelation 8:2-6)

Parenthetical passage 3 - (Revelation 8:13)

Parenthetical passage 4 - (Revelation 10:1 - 11:14)

Parenthetical passage 5 - (Revelation 14:1-20)

Parenthetical passage 6 - (Revelation 15:2-4)

Parenthetical passage 7 - (Revelation 16:13-16)

Parenthetical passage 8 - (Revelation 17:1 - 18:24)

Parenthetical passage 9 - (Revelation 19:1-10)

To recap, as well as continue on with sectioning off Revelation's sequential order, "The things which thou hast seen" are referring to Revelation 1. "The things which are" are referring to the literal churches in Asia Minor at the end of the 1st century, as well as instructions for the church during the entire Church Age (Rev. 2 – Rev. 3). "The things which shall be hereafter" is referring to the things after the churches, or after the rapture (Rev. 4:1).

Revelation 4 – Revelation 5 begin the Tribulation, but are the scenes in heaven. The first 3 ½ years of the Seven Year Tribulation take place in order from Revelation 6:1 – Revelation 9:21. This is the lesser tribulation time because Israel is protected during this time. Revelation 10:1 – Revelation 11:14 is the 4th parenthetical passage in the book and takes place in the middle of the Tribulation. It explains certain events which are not the contents of the judgments of the seals, trumpets, or vials, but happen along with the main events of this period. It breaks the main vision of the trumpets and is inserted between the 6th and 7th trumpets, as the 1st parenthetical passage is inserted between the 6th and 7th seals (Rev. 7:1-17).

Revelation 11:15 – Revelation 19:21 takes place during the last 3 ½ years of the Seven Year Tribulation. This is Jacob's Trouble, or the Great Tribulation, because the tribulation on Israel is so great during this time. So, Revelation 10 – Revelation 19 is the entirety of the last 3 ½ years of the Dispensation of Grace. The Second Coming has happened in Revelation 19:11-21, which ends the Seven Year Tribulation and will be followed by The Millennial Reign (Rev. 20). The new heaven and new earth happen after the Millennial Reign (Rev. 21:1 - Rev. 22:5), which speaks of the eternal future for those who remain in Christ. Revelation 22:6-21 concludes this book by giving certain instructions and warnings for all man.

6. END-TIMES

There are those who read certain terms in the Bible and equate them with other terms. I was always brought up believing the end-times referred to the last seven years of this dispensation.

Foundations For Building A Biblical Time-line

When people use this term, they are referring mostly to that seven year period. I was astonished when I first read Hebrews chapter 1.

> God, who at sundry times and in divers manners spake in time past unto the fathers by the prophets, Hath <u>in these last days</u> spoken unto us by his Son, whom he hath appointed heir of all things, by whom also he made the worlds (Heb. 1:1-2).

Knowing Jesus was being referred to in the 1st century, it was clear that the end-times, or last days, had more meanings than the last seven years of this age. Simply explained, you can't look at every earthquake in prophecy or every blood red moon and assume it's speaking of the same one. We need to get all scriptures on a subject together in order to harmonize them. This has been done by Finis Dake from his Annotated Reference Bible. I highly recommend this invaluable study tool!

The true meaning for "last days" is as follows: latter times - last years ending this age before the Millennium (1 Tim. 4:1), latter years - Armageddon and the end of this age (Ezek. 38:8, 16), latter days - the future Tribulation (Num. 24:14; Dt. 4:30; 31:29; Jer. 23:20; 30:24; 48:47; 49:39; Dan. 2:28; 10:14), latter day - Millennium (Job 19:25), latter days - Millennium (Hos. 3:5), last days - end of this age preceding the Millennium (Dan. 8:19; 2 Tim. 3:1; Jas. 5:3; 2 Pet. 3:3; Jude 1:18), last day - the rapture, at least seven years before the Millennium and Second Coming (Jn. 6:39-40, 44, 54; 11:24), last days - the Tribulation period or last seven years of this age (Acts 2:16-21), last days - First Coming (Heb. 1:1-2), last times - First Coming (1 Pet. 1:20), last time - apostolic times and the whole Church Age (1 Jn. 2:18, last time - Second Coming (1 Pet. 1:5), last days - Millennium (Gen. 49:1; Isa. 2:1; Mic. 4:1), and last day - end of the Millennium (Jn. 12:48; cp. with Rev. 20:7-15).

You may be scratching your head at why I am giving some of this information, but stay with me and you'll see. You haven't been painting a fence, you've been karate training. Learning to harmonize

Scripture subjects will make you a black-belt watcher. Book 4 will be able to better settle in your understanding with these foundational knowledge building blocks. For example, if a day is as 1,000 years, and the plan of God for man began about 6,000 years ago, then we know the rapture will not be 10,000 years from now, no, not even 1,000 years from now. Most likely no even more than 100 years from now.

God took His rest on the 7th day. We know there is a 1,000 year reign of Jesus with His saints, while God the Father is in heaven. With this picture, we know the plan of God for man even before He sets His throne on earth to dwell on earth forever, instead of on heaven. It will be about 7,000 years. The end-time expressions are only used for the First Coming onward, to the end of the Millennial Reign. This is a period of about 3,000 years.

By looking at a week, we would know the first of the week is the first 3 days, while the middle of the week is the 4th day. The end of the week is the last 3 days. Knowing historic genealogy from Scripture, we know Adam was made from created dirt about 6,000 years ago and there is another 1,000 years coming soon. If one's understanding is open, then one can clearly see the end-time expressions have clued us in to know the Millennial Reign is coming in a matter of years. Thus, the rapture is any year now, being at least seven years before the beginning of the Millennial Reign. The last 3,000 years are the end times of a 7,000 year period.

7. War Of Gog And Magog

Ezekiel 38 – 39

Three wars are talked about in the watcher world. Three wars are the watchers waiting for. They are the Psalms 83 War, the Destruction of Damascus (Isa. 17:1), and the War of God and Magog

(Ezek. 38 – Ezek. 39). Many theories and much conjecturing has been birthed from hype about these wars or battles. Time-lines have gone a rye. Most who speak of these events have only heard others speak of them. Good studying often is laid aside for good stories full of speculation. If a man of God is teaching it, then it must be true, right? The Thessalonians even examined Paul (Acts 17:11).

Many watch Israel's Middle East conflicts in anticipation for the Ezekiel 38 War, even hypothesizing the rapture may happen at the start of it. There really is no good basis for this, but I do know where it comes from. They place this at the time of "Sudden Destruction," speculating this war may even be the cause of sudden destruction (1 Thess. 5:3). The problem with these ideas is this war takes place at the end of the Tribulation, just like that of the sudden destruction. The following will prove this to be true, that the War of Gog and Magog in Ezekiel 38 – Ezekiel 39 is Armageddon. Ironically, the War of Gog and Magog and sudden destruction will happen at the same time, just not the beginning of the Tribulation as so many have believed.

Since you've picked out this kind of book to learn from, it isn't a stretch of the imagination to think you've watched or read the Left Behind series. If you'll recall, the movie begins with an air invasion upon Israel, ending with the jets being supernaturally shot down. This is a day or so before the rapture, where most are left behind. This battle is inserted into the Left Behind series at that point because of the previously mentioned belief that the War of Gog and Magog will occur right before the Tribulation, during the rapture, or at the very beginning of the Tribulation. This thought process is rooted in the following reference:

> And they that dwell in the cities of Israel shall go forth, and shall set on fire and burn the weapons, both the shields and the bucklers, the bows and the arrows, and the handstaves, and the spears, and they shall burn them with fire <u>seven years</u>: So that they shall take no wood out of the field, neither cut down any out of the forests; for they shall burn the weapons with fire:

and they shall spoil those that spoiled them, and rob those that robbed them, saith the Lord GOD (Ezek. 39:9-10).

I'll take you through some reasons in sequential order proving this battle is the War of Armageddon, but first, I'll address the best reason many have for their placement of this war being at the beginning of the Tribulation. I have honestly never heard anyone else mention my upcoming rebuttal. The reason this war is believed to be at the beginning of the Seven Year Tribulation is obvious after reading the verse above.

A seven year period for burning the weapons of the enemies of Israel has been mentioned. Is every earthquake mentioned in the Bible the same earthquake (1 Kings 19:11-12; Isa. 29:6; Mat. 27:54; 28:2; Acts 4:31; 16:26)? What about narrowing our search to 70th Week of Daniel (Rev. 6:12-17; 8:5; 11:13, 19; 16:17-21)? Of course not, there will be many (Mat. 24:7; Mk. 13:8; Lk. 21:11). There are other seven year periods in Scripture (Gen. 41:26-30, 45-55). Is the time of seven years of famine the same as the seven years of plenty? No. Is the seven years Jacob worked for Rachel the same seven years he had to work for her sister (Gen. 29:18-27)? Not at all. All these separate examples have back to back seven year periods. Let's examine this activity of Israel for seven years, for the same is true for the seven years Israel burns the weapons of their enemies.

What do we know about the activities of Israel for the seven year period of tribulation? In short, they are protected by the Antichrist from all their neighboring enemies, who uses his alliance with Israel to get support to take over the Revised Old Roman Empire. For the first 3 ½ years of the Tribulation, there is great war going on all around them as the Antichrist is on his way to conquer the areas best known today as Turkey, Greece, and Egypt. The Antichrist is head of the Syrian Territory. It'd be best to look at a map of the Old Grecian Territory from Alexander the Great's time.

By the middle of the Tribulation, he conquers these other three kingdoms he has been battling with for 3 ½ years, and then the rest of the ten kings give him authority over their kingdoms (Rev. 13; 17). For the next 3 ½ years, he desires to annihilate Israel. Some remnant Jews remain in Israel when the rest run for safety (Rev. 12:14). The headquarters of the Antichrist moves to Jerusalem for the last 3 ½ years (11:7-8). Now, does it make any sense at all that Israel will be burning their enemy's weapons for all those years while they are being persecuted and exterminated worse than any other time in history?

During this time, 66% of the Jews will be killed (Zech. 13:8-9). Does it make sense that any nation will be burning weapons during a time when they are so outnumbered and being hunted for destruction? Or, does it make sense that the weapons will be burned for fuel during a time of peace on earth where there is no longer a threat of being overtaken by those who hate you? The battle of Armageddon is the only war predicted by the prophets that could possibly be referred to in these chapters (Ezek. 38:17). Before the days of Ezekiel, Armageddon is mentioned many times by the prophets of God (Isa. 1:25-31; 3:25-26; 13:1-16; 24:21; 63:1-6; Jer. 25:30-33; 30:11, 20-24; Joel 2-3; Oba. 1:15-21; Mic. 1:3-4; 2:12-13; 5:5-15; etc.). Is Ezekiel the only one who does not mention this great war on Israel from the largest military force mankind has ever seen? Is Ezekiel the only one to mention a battle at the beginning of Daniel's 70th Week?

The defeat of Gog and his armies (Ezek. 38:18-23; 39:1-6, 17-20) is identical with the statements about Armageddon (Joel 3; Zech. 14; Rev. 19:11-21). Gog is a person, for personal pronouns are used of him (Ezek. 38:2-4; 6:11, 13-17, 21-22; 39:1-7) and he is leader of the great army that will fight at Armageddon (Ezek. 38:4-9, 11-23; 39:1-7). He will fall in battle like others (Ezek. 39:4-5). Many prophets prophesied many things of him (Ezek. 38:17), for Gog is none other than the "Antichrist" of 1 John 2; the "little horn" of Daniel 7 and 8; "the prince that shall come" of Daniel 9; "the king of the north" (Dan. 11); the "man of sin," "the son of perdition," and "that wicked" of 2 Thessalonians 2; the "king of Babylon" of Isaiah 13 - Isaiah 14; "the Assyrian" of Micah 5; and "the beast" of Revelation 13.

God will not magnify and sanctify Himself and set His glory among the heathen (as stated in Ezekiel 38:23; 39:21-24) until He comes at the Second Coming of Christ at Armageddon (Zech. 14:1-21; Mt. 24:29-31; Rev. 19:11-21). Gog will not bring the many armies of the nations into Palestine to be destroyed until the time of the Second Coming of Christ, at Armageddon, as referred to in Ezekiel 38:18-23; 39:1-7; and proved in Zechariah 14:1-5; Revelation 16:13-16; 19:11-21. The great earthquake of Ezekiel 38:20 will not take place until the seventh vial and the Second Coming (Zech. 14:1-5; Rev. 16:17-21; 19:11-21). God's presence will not destroy Gog and his army until the Second Coming, at Armageddon (Ezek. 38:20; 39:2-7; Zech. 14:1-5; Rev. 19:11-21).

The great supper for the fowls and beasts will only be at Armageddon (Ezek. 38:17-23; 39:4, 17-20 with Mt. 24:27-28; Lk. 17:34-37; Isa. 34:1-8; Joel 3:13-14; Rev. 14:20; 19:17-21). The presence of God (Ezek. 38:18-21; 39:1-6,17-24) will not be until Armageddon (Isa. 63:1-6; Zech. 14:1-5; Rev. 19:11-21). The supernatural destruction of Gog and his armies (Ezek. 38:21-23) will not be until Armageddon (Isa. 63:1-6; Joel 2-3; Zech. 14; Rev. 19:11-21). Gog and his army cannot be destroyed in a war in Palestine before the Second Coming at Armageddon to fulfill Ezekiel 38:18-23; 39:1-7, 17-20, and then be destroyed again at Armageddon to fulfill Isaiah 63; Joel 2-3; Zechariah 14. It is at the Second Coming of Christ that God's glory will be set among the heathen and Israel will be completely gathered and blessed (Ezek. 39:21-29; Zech. 14; Mt. 24:29-31; Rom. 11:24-29; Rev. 19:11-21).

It's time for Christians to study and stop hearing other people talk about what the Bible does and does not say. As far as the Psalms

83 War, there isn't one verse of prophecy in that chapter. It reads like it can be from any time during the Time of the Gentiles, for these nations have habitually hated Israel through time. The Isaiah 17:1 war has another theory. And that is that it was fulfilled by Assyria (2 Ki. 16:9-18; Isa. 17:1-11).

Isaiah 17:12-14 is the only part of Isaiah 17 that has a future fulfillment. It pictures the gathering of many nations against Israel (Isa. 17:12-13). It will be when God will rebuke them and fight for Israel (Isa. 17:13). This couldn't be the time of judgment on Israel, spoken of in previous verses, for this is God's judgment on the nations gathered against Israel (Ezek. 38 - Ezek. 39; Joel 3; Zech. 14; Rev. 19). The day Christ comes to earth during Armageddon is the only time in the future when the night will be as bright as day to give enough time to destroy the great armies gathered against Jerusalem and the Jews. The whole night will be like it was in Joshua's long day (Josh. 10:13-14). Zechariah plainly predicts that it will become light at evening (Zech. 14:1-8). Here, it reveals how long this light will last, which is a full night, for by morning the fleeing armies will be destroyed. Such will be the judgment, or "portion of them that spoil us (Israel)" (Isa. 17:14).

No great war against Israel with a supernatural outcome needs to be searched for other than that of the last day battle against the armies of Antichrist and the nations that are demonically influenced to join him in order to destroy Israel and fight against Christ and His armies (Rev. 16:13-16). The reason, in my opinion, for the persistence in looking for a war, or battle with Israel before the Tribulation, is because the rapture would be at the door with our head's poking through. The motivation would then be good, however, we must stick with harmonizing Scripture to get an accurate picture. We can put together the pieces of Bible prophecy and get whatever picture we desired if we want to, but I'd rather have the unblurred photo. I want a clear picture, even if it seems to show a picture of our blessed hope being many years away, though I don't believe it is years away.

8. Two Witnesses

This will just go and show you how that groundbreaking information can come to you when you spend time in the Word. Studying all about the two witnesses one day in summer of 2010 gave me understanding beyond what I could have done naturally. Too many times we blow off subjects in the Bible because we don't see the benefit, and after all, we've heard that story or Scripture before. What I'll reveal to you concerning the timing of the ministry of the two witnesses was given to me by the Holy Spirit as I prayed for another piece of the end-time puzzle. I simply wanted a clearer picture.

The following from Zechariah 4:11-14 and Revelation 11:3-13 is all the specific information directly associated with the story of these two witnesses. By harmonizing other points of Scripture, we can learn so much more. So please read on with great anticipation as we study to show ourselves approved (2 Tim. 2:15). You've never heard what I'm about to teach in these pages.

> 3 And I will give power unto my two witnesses, and they shall prophesy a thousand two hundred and threescore days, clothed in sackcloth. 4 These are the two olive trees, and the two candlesticks standing before the God of the earth. 5 And if any man will hurt them, fire proceedeth out of their mouth, and devoureth their enemies: and if any man will hurt them, he must in this manner be killed. 6 These have power to shut heaven, that it rain not in the days of their prophecy: and have power over waters to turn them to blood, and to smite the earth with all plagues, as often as they will. 7 And when they shall have finished their testimony, the beast that ascendeth out of the bottomless pit shall make war against them, and shall overcome them, and kill them. 8 And their dead bodies shall lie in the street of the great city, which spiritually is called Sodom and Egypt, where also our Lord was crucified. 9 And they of the people and kindreds and tongues and nations shall see their dead bodies three days and an half, and shall not suffer

Foundations For Building A Biblical Time-line

their dead bodies to be put in graves. 10 And they that dwell upon the earth shall rejoice over them, and make merry, and shall send gifts one to another; because these two prophets tormented them that dwelt on the earth. 11 And after three days and an half the Spirit of life from God entered into them, and they stood upon their feet; and great fear fell upon them which saw them. 12 And they heard a great voice from heaven saying unto them, Come up hither. And they ascended up to heaven in a cloud; and their enemies beheld them. 13 And the same hour was there a great earthquake, and the tenth part of the city fell, and in the earthquake were slain of men seven thousand: and the remnant were affrighted, and gave glory to the God of heaven (Rev. 11:3-13).

11 Then answered I, and said unto him, What are these two olive trees upon the right side of the candlestick and upon the left side thereof? 12 And I answered again, and said unto him, What be these two olive branches which through the two golden pipes empty the golden oil out of themselves? 13 And he answered me and said, Knowest thou not what these be? And I said, No, my lord. 14 Then said he, These are the two anointed ones, that stand by the Lord of the whole earth (Zech. 4:11-14).

As you learned from book 1, the resurrection of the two witnesses ends the first resurrection that began with the resurrection of Christ (Mat. 27:52-53; 1 Cor. 15:20, 23; Eph. 4:8-10; Rev. 11:7-11). The two witnesses are none other than Enoch and Elijah. They have never tasted death, nor have these two been resurrected, yet they have both been in the presence of God day and night for thousands of years each (Zech. 4:11-14). The identity of these two witnesses for Christ is not as important as the timing of their ministry, though we will brush up on the subject of the two witnesses for knowledge sake.

Enoch lived before the world-wide flood of Noah. He was seventh from Adam and walked with God in the same sense that

Adam walked with God in the garden. He had a son when he was sixty five years old, named Methuselah. He then walked with God for three hundred years until he was caught up in his natural body to be with the Lord until his mission on earth to be one of Christ's two witnesses at the end of our dispensation (Gen. 2:19; 3:8; 5:21-24). He has currently been in heaven for more than five thousand years. He was translated 992 years after the recreation of the earth in Adam's day.

The second witness is Elijah. This is in little dispute among those who agree that these two witnesses are men, and not not covenants, dispensations, angels, or anything else. Malachi foretells Elijah's return before the Day of the Lord, which is the Millennial Reign. (The Second Coming until the last day of the Millennial Reign - 2 Pt. 3; Rev. 19:11 – Rev. 21:27).

An interesting fact is that these two witnesses will fight against the enemies of Israel and kill them in the ways that their enemies seek to kill them (Rev. 11:5). Enoch is the great grandfather of Noah, who all get their DNA from. Essentially and literally, Enoch will be fighting against and killing his own flesh and blood... his great, great (many times over) grand children.

> Behold, I will send you Elijah the prophet before the coming of the great and dreadful day of the LORD: And he shall turn the heart of the fathers to the children, and the heart of the children to their fathers, lest I come and smite the earth with a curse (Mal. 4:5-6).

Before the Day of the Lord, Elijah will physically come back. Even religious Jews accept this and look for him every Passover. They set a place at the table for him and leave their door open. If they accepted the full revelation of Scripture, then they'd be setting two places at their tables.

Elijah and Enoch are the only two men to never taste death from prior generations. They will be allowed to be killed at the end of their ministry, which is for 1,260 days, or 3 ½ years. After they are killed, their bodies will lay in the streets for 3 ½ days before God brings their souls back to those bodies and raises them to their immortal condition forever. After that, a great voice from heaven will say, "Come up hither!" They will then ascend up to heaven in their immortal bodies this time (Rev. 11:7-12), which is unlike the first time they ascended to heaven (Gen. 5:21-24; 2 Ki. 2).

In the summer of 2010, I had been studying intensely, looking for any clues from the history the Bible has foretold before it has actually happened. I was studying the timing of the two witnesses, looking for that 3 ½ portion of the Tribulation they would be active in. The majority believe it will be in the first half. I was examining both halves of the Tribulation from teachers from both parties. I'll explain many reasons for concluding their ministry is in the last half, and then show you the unfolding of the implications that lead to some ground breaking information! Even the way God set up His calendar confirms how precise this treasure of discovered knowledge is.

Evidence that the 2 Witnesses' ministry is the second half of the Tribulation

This section of nine paragraphs is from the Dake Annotated Reference Bible. I mean, if this is what I was studying when I found the clearest absolute truth concerning which half of the Tribulation the two witnesses would fulfill, then why reinvent the wheel for you? It is from this simple knowledge from harmonizing Scripture that I received my revelation in the next section that will blow the lid off time-line confusion.

They will prophesy 1,260 days or during the same period of time that the Antichrist reigns supreme, the Holy City is trodden down of the Gentiles, and the woman flees into the wilderness for protection (Rev. 11:2-3; 12:6, 14; 13:5). That they will prophesy during the last three and one half years, instead of the first 3 ½, seems clear from the following: All passages of forty-two months, 1,260 days, and 3 ½ years, in both Daniel and Revelation, always refer to the last half of Daniel's Seventieth Week (Dan. 7:25; 12:7, 11-12).

The fact that the two witnesses are not mentioned until the middle of the Week or after the seals and the first six trumpets, proves that they do not prophesy during the fulfillment of these things in the first 3 ½ years. If they were to prophesy during the first 3 ½ years, the prophecy concerning them would surely be placed before the events of this period so that we should naturally understand that they were to prophesy during that time instead of during the last 3 ½ years. Why should their ministry be revealed in connection with the middle of the Week if it is to end at that time?

We naturally understand that the 1,260 days or forty-two months of Revelation 11:3 are the same as the forty-two months of Revelation 11:2, for both periods are in the same prophecy. There is no break between these verses as to two periods of time. Since the city is not trodden underfoot by the Gentiles until the last half of the Week, the two witnesses must prophesy during that time instead of the first half of the Week.

The angel of Revelation 10 will come down from heaven after the sixth trumpet in the middle of the Week and just before the seventh. It is this angel who states, "I will give power to my two witnesses." This implies futurity from the time when the angel comes down. To place the fulfillment of Revelation 11:3-13 back during all the seals and trumpets is to take it out of the place given and intended of God.

The main argument of those who teach that the two witnesses prophesy during the first 3 ½ years is that the beast, when he comes out of the abyss in the middle of the Week will immediately destroy them. There is no statement that the beast comes out of the abyss in the middle of the Week and where can it be found that he destroys the witnesses immediately after he arises? Verse 7 does not teach that. It simply states that the beast which comes out of the abyss will destroy them at the end of their testimony, but as far as proving the above, it does not. On the contrary, it is clear that the beast will come out of the abyss sometime before the 70th Week and cause the rise of the Antichrist out of the ten kingdoms, who, in turn will make the seven years covenant with Israel.

This is further proven from the fact that the two witnesses will withstand Antichrist from the middle of the Week onward for the purpose of protecting the Israeli's who do not flee into the wilderness. There will be no reason for protecting them during the first 3 ½ years, for Antichrist will do that himself. Therefore, there will not be such a great need for the ministry of the two witnesses in the first 3 ½ years. However, during the last 3 ½ years, the Antichrist will oppose Israel, hence the need for the protection of the two witnesses at that time.

What will be the purpose of their prophecy and working of miracles unless Israel is to be persecuted during their ministry by Antichrist? The fact that they cannot be killed by the beast until they have finished their testimony proves that the beast, when he comes out of the abyss, does not immediately destroy them, and further shows the antagonism between the beast and the two witnesses during the 1,260 days.

God has no intention of withstanding the beast until he breaks his covenant with Israel and begins to destroy them. Therefore, the ministry of the witnesses would be without purpose during the first 3 ½ years. Their ministry will be fitting only for the terrible days of the Great Tribulation caused by Antichrist in the last 3 ½ years. God is retaining these two men in heaven for this particular purpose.

If there were a statement to the effect that the two witnesses had prophesied 3 ½ years previous to the time the passage was given to John, then the position of it here would be clear, but there is no such statement. Unless it is clear in the parenthetical passage that it is not to be fulfilled in the place it is given, then we can rest assured that it is given in its proper order. Malachi 4:5-6 proves that the time of their ministry is before the great and notable day of the Lord, which will begin at the Coming of Christ. This, then, places their ministry during the last 3 ½ years.

2 Witnesses Ministry And 1264 Days

With that foundation laid, I'll bring you into one of the greatest pieces of the end-time time table God's ever revealed to me. Understanding the way the fall feasts will be fulfilled gives you the time of the Seven Year Tribulation. The extent of the seven year period is from the seasons of fall to fall. The rapture will happen on the feast of trumpets, while the Second Coming will take place on the feast of atonement. The days between those days is always greater than 2,520 days (1,260 + 1,260). This is why many try to make one of the halves 1,290 days, even though the text of Daniel 12 makes it obviously clear there will be an extra 30 days after the end of Daniel's 70th Week (Dan. 7:25; 12:7, 11), and an additional 45 days on top of that (Dan. 12:12).

This is why it is so important to have a good understanding of eschatology. If you know their ministry on earth will be the last half of Daniel's 70th Week, then you will also conclude that it will begin in spring, since the Tribulation will begin and end in the fall based on fulfilling the fall feasts of the Lord (Lev. 23). We know the last half of the 70th Week is 1,260 days. So in finding more knowledge of the timing of the end-times, we will subtract 1260 days (3 ½ years) from the Second Coming of Christ, which we concluded will be on Yom Kippur (The Feast of The Great Day of Atonement) and we will land in the spring time.

Foundations For Building A Biblical Time-line

For illustration purposes, we will be using 2016 – 2023 as a learning tool. Now, if we use 2023 for the Second Coming (a 2016 rapture), then we will find out when the day of atonement is, which lands on September 26, 2023. Then, subtract 1,260 days and you get April 14, 2020. This is how most people would do this. As you see, the beginning of the two witnesses ministry will begin in spring.

But their ministry is 1,260 days, and then they are killed and dead in the street for 3 ½ days before they are resurrected and raptured. They are raptured before the Second Coming, because all saints from Abel until the two witnesses will have part in the Marriage Supper of the Lamb, and come back to earth at the Second Coming with Jesus. They certainly will not be raised from the dead 3 ½ days after the Second Coming. And if they were, would they be raised up in the clouds to enter heaven while heaven was emptied out? No, it is clear the Second Coming has not happened since frightened enemies were still on the earth to see them raptured (Rev. 11:12-13).

This means that the two witnesses have to start their ministry as Christ's witnesses and the defenders of Israel at least 1,264 days before the Second Coming on the Feast of Atonement (1,260 + 3 ½ days). With much research on several different 7 year periods, I saw many 7 year periods with exactly 1,264 days between Passover in spring, and the day of atonement in the fall. Others were 1,265 days and 1,266 days.

Sticking with our instructional example of 2016 – 2023, we get April 8, 2020 when we subtract 1,266 days from the Feast of Atonement in 2023 (Sept. 26). This lands us on Passover, the first of the 7 feasts of the Lord and His appointed times (Gen. 1:14; Lev. 23; Col. 2:16-17).

I began thinking, "What would be the most significant day for Antichrist to stop the Jewish sacrifices that will soon resume, and declare himself God?" It is Passover! What is significant about this is that religious Jews expect Elijah to come back to earth on Passover in order to prepare the way for the Lord (Mal. 4:4-5). Even more significant for my conclusion was that I didn't find out religious Jews expected Elijah on Passover until after I concluded the same from simple study time of implications from newly learned facts.

That may have been confusing, but understand that there must be AT LEAST 1,264 DAYS in between the beginning of the two witnesses' ministry and the Second Coming, because they absolutely have an exact ministry on earth of 1,260 days (Rev. 11:2-3), THEN they are killed and lay in the street dead for 3 ½ days until they are resurrected and brought to heaven, BEFORE the Second Coming (Rev. 11). Now if they begin their ministry on Passover, as orthodox Jews expect, then we count to see if there are at least 1,264 days between that Passover and the day of atonement (When we expect the Second Coming in order to fulfill this feast).

Just as the rapture is never said to be the start of Daniel's 70th Week, the Second Coming is never said to be on the 1,260th day of the Great Tribulation. There are short gaps of time at the beginning and the end of Daniel's 70th Week from the rapture and the Second Coming.

In looking for the significance of the 1,264 days in between the Passover's and the Day of Atonement's in the next few years, I found that it is not rare at all, and there are other time-spans that would fit if this was all we had to go on. The bold-face text is what fits perfectly, though it is possible there could be more days in between the death of the two witnesses and the Second Coming than just 4 days. So, all is feasible. Fortunately, we have much more evidence. All we needed was at least 1,264 days. The irony is that this is common and further proves God's creative and mathematical precision with His lunar calendar given to Israel.

Feast of trumpets rapture to Passover is 3 ½ years. Passover to feast of atonement is 3 ½ years. There must be at least 1,264 days before the day of atonement for the two witnesses to fulfill their ministry and then be killed, then raised in 3 ½ days. As you can see in these eight sequential 3 ½ year periods, there seems to be something to this 1,264 days period that must be between the two witnesses' ministry and the Second Coming.

Passover (April 4, 2015) to Day of Atonement (September 19, 2018) = **1,264 days**

Passover (April 22, 2016) to Day of Atonement (October 8, 2019) = **1,264 days**

Passover (April 11, 2017) to Day of Atonement (September 28, 2020) = 1,266 days

Passover (March 31, 2018) to Day of Atonement (September 16, 2021) = 1,265 days

Passover (April 20, 2019) to Day of Atonement (October 7, 2022) = 1,266 days

Passover (April 8, 2020) to Day of Atonement (September 26, 2023) = 1,266 days

Passover (March 28, 2021) to Day of Atonement (October 12, 2024) = 1,294 days

Passover (April 16, 2022) to Day of Atonement (October 2, 2025) = **1,264** days

The Two Witnesses and Passover

> I will send you Elijah the prophet before the coming of the great and dreadful day of the LORD (Malachi 4:5).

This is part of the last prophecy in the Old Testament. It concerns the return of Elijah the prophet to the earth, from heaven, shortly before the coming of the great and dreadful Day of the Lord (Mal. 4:5-6). Jews have always expected him to return from heaven. It is not an incarnation, but a literal return from heaven in the same body he had thousands of years ago. John the Baptist said from his own mouth that he was not Elijah (Jn. 1:21), so we are not speaking figuratively, referring to the spirit of Elijah.

Those days will bring one of the greatest spiritual awakenings in the history of mankind. The hearts of fathers and sons, all children and parents, will be turned toward one another. Families will be united in Christ. The Holy Spirit will be poured out upon all flesh and even all of Israel will be saved as a result of the ministry of Elijah and Enoch as Malachi 4:5-6; Revelation 11:3-10; Acts 2:16-21; Romans 11:25-29; Isaiah 66:7-8; and other scriptures will be literally fulfilled.

It's incredibly fascinating that religious Jews and rabbis wait for Elijah the prophet on Passover. They actually leave the door open because they leave a place at the table for him with a poured glass of wine waiting in his place. This coincides perfectly with the timing of the mid-tribulation time frame when they will be beginning their 1,260 day ministry. I'm not for certain why the Jews believe Elijah comes back on Passover, but I'm still awestruck that I learned about this fact after I had already found that they should be beginning their ministry at Passover, coinciding with the beginning of the Great Tribulation (last 3 ½ years of Daniel's 70th Week, which is Jacob's Trouble). This is the day when the peace treaty is broken, as the Antichrist takes over Jerusalem, stops their daily sacrifices, and declares himself God.

The ministry of the two witnesses will be exactly 1,260 days, 42 months, or 3 ½ years (Rev. 11:2; 12:6, 14; 13:5; Dan. 7:25; 9:27; 12:7, 11-12). If the Holy Spirit testified to the exact amount of days, then man has no authority to make it anything else, unless figurative, symbolic, or typical language has been used. We see none of that for the time line of days according to the book of Daniel and Revelation.

The reason I make this clear is because it is pertinent to the precision of the time table.

We know for sure that the ministry of the 144,000 is during the first 42 months (Rev. 7:1-8; 9:4; 12:4-5; 14:1-5), but an exact day count was never given. If we had a 2016 rapture, then September 20, 2023 is exactly 1,260 days after the middle of the Tribulation (April 8, 2020 / Passover). This is important, because we know the ministry of these two lasts for 1,260 days, yet they die at least 3 ½ days before the Second Coming (Rev. 11:1-13).

Using a 2016 rapture as our example, this is how we know the Second Coming would have fallen on September 26, 2023. Not only does it fit, but it also falls on Yom Kippur (the Feast of Atonement). Just like the rapture doesn't have to fall on the first day of the Tribulation, so also, neither does the Second Coming have to fall on the same day as the end of the 2,520th day of the Tribulation… (2,520 days equals all the days of the Daniel's 70th Week. 7 x 360, or 1,260 + 1,260).

The Second Coming is the event Jesus was referring to as no one knowing the day or the hour, for this is the entire focus of the questions from His disciples that Jesus is answering in response to these questions (Mat. 24:3). The disciples did not even know of the rapture when asking about the time of the end of this age and when Jesus was coming back.

This evidence must conclude that the time frame for the ministry of the two witnesses of 1,260 days, and then death for 3 ½ days, and resurrection, fits perfectly between the time of Passover and the Second Coming. This is true for any 7 year period. It has been widely accepted that the Second Coming falls exactly 1,260 days after the Antichrist breaks the treaty with Israel in the middle of the Tribulation. This can't be the case, and biblically has no authority. Human reasoning without learning all the facts and implications is unwise. It's simply not an absolute.

9. Sun-Clothed Woman

1 And there appeared a great wonder in heaven; a woman clothed with the sun, and the moon under her feet, and upon her head a crown of twelve stars: 2 And she being with child cried, travailing in birth, and pained to be delivered. 3 And there appeared another wonder in heaven; and behold a great red dragon, having seven heads and ten horns, and seven crowns upon his heads. 4 And his tail drew the third part of the stars of heaven, and did cast them to the earth: and the dragon stood before the woman which was ready to be delivered, for to devour her child as soon as it was born. 5 And she brought forth a man child, who was to rule all nations with a rod of iron: and her child was caught up unto God, and to his throne. 6 And the woman fled into the wilderness, where she hath a place prepared of God, that they should feed her there a thousand two hundred and threescore days (Rev. 12:1-6).

This is an important six verses to wrap our watching minds around since many are expecting it's fulfillment in September, 2017. This is a picture of something being shown symbolically in space that is actually happening on earth at the same time. This is astronomy. God created the stars and put them in their proper place, knowing the end from the beginning. Now that's precision!

Let's look at two popular interpretations that need correcting up front. This is not in any way referring to Mary giving birth to Jesus, Who was immediately caught up to be with God before His throne. That is said by most to be a concise gospel message of the earthly ministry of Jesus. As we have learned from books 1 - 3, everything after Revelation 4:1 is future. Revelation 1:19 says the third division of the Book of Revelation is after the things that are (Rev. 2 – Rev. 3), which is after the church has been raptured (Rev. 4:1). There's not one piece of history in all of Revelation 4:1 – Revelation 22:21. Further proof of this can be identified by reading the rest of Revelation 12.

12 Therefore rejoice, ye heavens, and ye that dwell in them. Woe to the inhabiters of the earth and of the sea! for the devil is come down unto you, having great wrath, because he knoweth that he hath but a short time. 13 And when the dragon saw that he was cast unto the earth, he persecuted <u>the woman</u> which brought forth the man child. 14 And to <u>the woman</u> were given two wings of a great eagle, that she might fly into the wilderness, into her place, where she is nourished for <u>a time, and times, and half a time</u>, from the face of the serpent. 15 And the serpent cast out of his mouth water as a flood after <u>the woman</u>, that he might cause her to be carried away of the flood. 16 And the earth helped <u>the woman</u>, and the earth opened her mouth, and swallowed up the flood which the dragon cast out of his mouth. 17 And the dragon was wroth with <u>the woman</u>, and <u>went to make war with the remnant of her seed, which keep the commandments of God, and have the testimony of Jesus Christ</u> (Rev. 12:12-17).

The woman spoken of here is the same woman spoken of a few verses prior. Is this speaking of Mary as well? Did Satan wage war in heaven at the rapture of Jesus? Was he then cast to the earth where he knew he only had 3 ½ years left (vs. 12, 14)? Did Mary take flight to the wilderness for 3 ½ years after Jesus was raptured in order to be safe from Satan? After that, did Satan go after her other children since God gave her a way of escape? We have to say no to all of the above.

The second point that many are missing, is that this constellation will literally be seen from heaven at the fulfillment of Revelation 6. The 2017 viewing will be seen on earth. As I write this in September, 2016, more than two years have gone by where people are talking about this happening on September 23, 2017. This sign in heaven occurs on the feast of trumpets, 2017. It has been claimed that this is the first time the sign has appeared in 7,000 years. I know I remember watchers speaking of this same sign in the heavens occurring in September, 2013. I'm not going to research the validity of the rarity of that claim, because it is irrelevant. Let me explain.

In truth, the sign is seen in heaven (Rev. 12:1), not on earth. It doesn't say the sign was in the second heavens, and we saw it on earth. John was taken to heaven to see the things (i.e. events), which must shortly come to pass (Rev. 1:1). The events are the subject matter of the Book of Revelation: Events of the whole church age (Rev. 1 - Rev. 3), events in heaven (Rev. 4 - Rev. 5), events of the future tribulation of Daniel's 70th week (Rev. 6 - Rev. 19), events of the Millennium (Rev. 20), and the events of the eternal new heavens and the new earth (Rev. 21 - Rev. 22). The symbol of the constelation paired with other heavenly bodies is seen in heaven, but the thing symbolized is on earth (Rev. 12:6, 13, 15-16).

As you see, the events in Revelation 12 are taking place during Daniel's 70th Week. To further prove the sight of the sign in heaven is seen from the view of heaven, let us examine some things going on in the text. Revelation 12 begins us with the fact that, "And there appeared a great wonder in heaven..." In Revelation 1:10, we see that John was in the Spirit and saw Jesus in the midst of the candlesticks, or churches (Rev. 1:11-20). In Revelation 4:1-2, we see that John was taken to heaven to be shown the things which must be hereafter (after the Church Age) (Rev. 4:1 - Rev. 22:7).

John was in heaven for the scenes shown to him. Revelation 12:5 says the man-child was taken to the throne of God, which is where John was at the time of his view of the heavenly conjunction and constellation. The throne is the center of the activities of the book. It is mentioned forty times in Revelation (Rev. 1:4; 3:21; 4:2-6, 9-10; 5:1, 6-7, 11, 13; 6:16; 7:9-11, 15, 17; 8:3; 12:5; 14:3, 5; 16:17; 19:4-5; 20:4, 11; 21:5; 22:1, 3).

Heaven is an unknown distance directly north from the earth (Job 26:7; Ps. 75:6; Isa. 14:13). I'm sure the stars were set up in their specific places and given their specific dimensions for our view of them. Perhaps for signs and appointed times (Gen. 1:14). So, are the stars' placements the same for heaven? I can't say for sure, but probably not. However, it appears the Revelation 12 constellation is seen with the same likeness (Rev. 12:1-6). God id more than capable to set that up without flaw.

In the beginning (sometime in the dateless past), God made THE heaven and THE earth (Gen. 1:1). Like all of the created heavenly bodies, heaven is round and is a planet (Gen. 1:1; Job 38:4-7), so there is a star-view from heaven. The angels were on heaven when they watched God create the earth (Job 38:4-7). Heaven is not a spiritual place with no material substance as we picture. If people without their bodies can be clothed, exist in spirit form and be confined to material places such as hades (Lk. 16:19-31; Rev. 20:11-15) and the altar in heaven (Rev. 6:9-11); and if other spirit beings can be confined to tartarus (2 Pet. 2:4; Jude 1:6-7) and the abyss (Rev. 9:1-21; 20:1-3), and if natural man can exist there for thousands of years (Zech. 4:11-14), then we must realize that heaven is a real place with real dimensions. God is orderly and His creation on earth reflects what is in heaven (Rom. 1:20).

Hell is in the lower parts of the earth, which is the place for spirits of unjust and filthy people (Rev. 22:11) who feel physical pain and anguish (Isa. 66:22-24; Mat. 8:12; 13:42; 24:51; Lk. 13:28; 16:19-31). Hell is located in the lower parts of the earth, not on the surface of the earth as the grave (Mt. 12:40; Eph. 4:8-10; Ps. 16:10; 63:9; Job 11:8; Dt. 32:22; Isa. 14:9 66:22-24; Prov. 9:18; 15:24; Ezek. 31:14-18; 32:18-24). Hell is contrasted with the highest heaven as being the lowest and deepest part of the earth.

There is yet another constellation that has gone ignored by a lot of watchers, though not all. Many forget about the dragon constellation that is another sign from heaven happening at the same time (Rev. 12:3-4). Isaiah says, "By his spirit he hath garnished the heavens; his hand hath formed the crooked serpent." This is most likely the constellation of the serpent, called Draco. The best information I could find said the Draco constellation appears in the fall and winter seasons, like that of the woman. Again, this will be seen in heaven while the actual event is happening on earth. There may be watchers in heaven who are anticipating the resurrection of the righteous just as much as us.

It could still be a sign for us on earth, but we have no biblical authority to match the date with the sign as we will see it. If it is as rare as some say it is, then it could certainly be a signal for those on earth that the actual event is coming soon. The main reason the rarity of these constellation conjunctions is irrelevant is because of their timing. They seem to be appearing in the fall. The events of Revelation 12 and 13 are smack dab in the middle of the Tribulation. This will occur in the spring, not the fall.

So, if the woman is not Mary, then who is the woman? Israel is often spoken of as a woman married to God under the terms of the old covenant (Isa. 54:1-6; Jer. 3:1-14; Hos. 2:14-23). "For thy Maker is thine husband; the Lord of hosts is his name; and thy Redeemer the Holy One of Israel; The God of the whole earth shall he be called. For the Lord hath called thee as a woman forsaken and grieved in spirit, and a wife of youth, when thou wast refused, saith thy God" (Isa. 54:5-6).

The church is more often referred to in masculine language, as the body of Christ. At the time of the middle of the Tribulation, the church has been in heaven for 3 ½ years (Rev. 4:1). The great whore is feminine (Rev. 17), but this is the false church of Catholicism, Islam, or something new to that time. Satan is not trying to destroy this religious system, so she is not the sun-clothed woman. The woman must symbolize national Israel. The sun, moon, and 12 stars symbolize Israel, as proved in Genesis 37:9-11. National Israel is the only people in Scripture spoken of as going through travail in the last days (Rev. 12:2-5; Mt. 24:8; Mk. 13:8; Isa. 66:7-8; Jer. 30:6-9; Mic. 5:3; Zech. 12:10 - Zech. 13:1).

The persecution, flight, and protection of the woman in the wilderness prove her to be Israel (Rev. 12:6, 13-16), because the prophets Isaiah, Ezekiel, Daniel, Hosea, and Jesus foretold of these events. Isaiah predicts the flight of Israel into Moab and Edom, and mentions Sela, the ancient capital of Edom as their headquarters during tribulation, and predicts the protection of Israel until the tribulation has past (Isa. 16:1-5; 26:20-21; 42:11-13). Jesus' descent at the Second Coming is foretold from the direction of Edom, where the Israelites are to be protected (Isa. 63:1-5), which is what Jesus was referring to in Matthew 24:27.

Psalms prophesies that God will reserve Edom from the Antichrist and refer to the leading of Israel into the strong city (Ps. 60:6-12; 108:8-13). Ezekiel (Ezek. 20:33-44) speaks of Israel being gathered back from the nations in the last days and of her going into the wilderness where God will plead with her as He did when she came out of Egypt. The two witnesses of Revelation 11 will be the "Moses and Aaron" of those days. Daniel (Dan. 11:36) reveals the conquest of many countries, including Palestine, but predicts that Edom, Moab, and Ammon will escape him (the Antichrist). This is the place reserved of God for Israel to be protected in the wilderness 3 ½ years (Rev. 12:6, 14).

Hosea (Hos. 2:14-23) speaks of the wilderness where Israel will flee from the Antichrist. Matthew (Mt. 24:15-22) predicts the Antichrist breaking his 7 year covenant with Israel (Dan. 9:27), the setting up of the abomination of desolation in the temple at Jerusalem, and the flight of Israel from Judea into the mountains or wilderness during the Great Tribulation. Revelation (Rev. 12:6, 13-16) makes the final prediction of Israel going into the wilderness to be protected 3 ½ years from the Antichrist. The woman is without doubt Israel, and her flight will be in spring.

10. 144,000

Now, who is the man-child if all events from Revelation 4:1 – Revelation 21:7 are yet in the future, meaning the man-child is not Jesus? The man-child symbolizes the 144,000 Jews who are the first-fruits to God from Israel (Rev. 14:4). They are said to be the first-fruits because they are the first Jews to be saved after the rapture of all saved Jews after the Church Age ends. The woman is Israel, so her offspring has to also be Jewish. The man-child is not a group of Gentiles or the church, and there are no other classes of people in this context through Scripture (1 Cor. 10:32). The only specific fellowship of Jews mentioned in Revelation is the 144,000.

And it was commanded the locusts from hell to not hurt the grass of the earth, neither any green thing, neither any tree; but only those men which have not the seal of God in their foreheads (Rev. 9:4), which are the 144,000 Jews (Rev. 7:1-8; 14:1-5). Special direction is given here to the 5th and 6th trumpet judgment angels not to hurt them, the first judgment angels having been commanded not to blow their trumpets until they were sealed (Rev. 7:1-3).

Thus, they are being protected from all these plagues. This proves they are all alive at the time of these judgments, or all of them could not be protected. The next time we see them they are in heaven before God, yet no word has been spoken of their death (Rev. 14:1-5). The 144,000 are the same ones referred to in Revelation 9:4, because Revelation 14:1 says they have the name of God written on their foreheads, which is the seal of God (Rev. 9:4).

No one could possibly represent the man-child other than the 144,000, a company of saints that are saved after the rapture of the church and all Old Testament saints. These are the Jews who Daniel spoke of as being delivered from the Great Tribulation (Jacob's Trouble). "But those who are delivered are redeemed, for they are in the Lamb's Book of Life" (Dan. 12:1). We see the full revelation of how they were delivered by Revelation 12:5. They are caught up, or raptured, and this is how they are next seen before the throne of God in heaven (Rev. 14:1-5).

Isaiah gives us another great passage telling us that Israel will bring forth a man-child before she is delivered at the end of the 70th Week.

> 7 <u>Before she travailed, she brought forth; before her pain came, she was delivered of a man child</u>. 8 Who hath heard such a thing? who hath seen such things? Shall the earth be made to bring forth in one day? or shall a nation be born at once? for as soon as Zion travailed, <u>she brought forth her children</u>. 9 Shall I bring to the birth, and not cause to bring forth? saith the LORD: shall I cause to bring forth, and shut the womb? saith thy God (Isaiah 66:7-9).

This passage reads, Before she (Israel) travailed for her own deliverance at the end of the 70th Week, she was delivered of a man-child, which is plural as seen by "her children" (Isa. 66:7; Zech. 12:10-14). We know that Israel has 144,000 with the new birth after the rapture (Rev. 7:1-8; 14:1-5), therefore they are in the Book of Life (Dan. 12:1), so it is without dispute who the man-child is who will be caught up to heaven (Rev. 12:5; 14:1-5).

11. Babylon

There are two Babylons in Revelation we need to understand. Believe it or not, even Babylon research can help you be a better watcher. If it's being revealed to us by God the Father, Who gave it to Jesus, Who gave it to an angel, to give it to His servant John, to give to the seven churches in Asia, to pass down to Christians forever, then we need to understand everything we are told (Rev. 1:1). One Babylon is a literal city built where ancient Babylon was (Rev. 18). The second Babylon is a religious system that is called a whore by God (Rev. 17). There are so many amazing facts to the future two Babylons, especially when compared to Old Testament prophecies. Isaiah 13:6, 9-14, 19-22; 14:1-27; Jeremiah 50:4-20; 51:5-10 refer to a latter-day fulfillment of Babylon and Israel in "the Day of the Lord." I'll keep it fairly short by giving sixteen contrast between the two Babylons from the Dake Annotated Reference Bible, followed by seven similarities.

Sixteen contrasts between the two Babylons: Mystery Babylon of Revelation 17 is symbolic; literal Babylon of Rev. 16:17-21; 18:1-24 is not. One is a mystery (Rev. 17:7); the other is not (Rev. 16:19; 18:1-24). Everything in Revelation 17 is explained; all is so clear that nothing needs to be explained in Revelation 16:19; 18:1-24. John wondered at one (Rev. 17:6), but not at the other (Rev. 18:1-24). One rides the beast (Rev. 17:3-7); the other does not (Rev. 18:1-24). One angel promises to tell John all about mystery Babylon (Rev. 17:7); several speak of literal Babylon (Rev. 18:1-20). One is called "the woman," the "great whore," etc.; the other is not.

Names are written on one (Rev. 17:5); this is not true of the other. Mystery Babylon was something new to John (Rev. 17:1-7); literal Babylon was not. One is not mentioned by the prophets; the other, literal Babylon, is mentioned many times. One makes herself rich by duping people (Rev. 17:4); literal Babylon makes others rich (Rev. 18:3,9-19). One is destroyed by man (Rev. 17:12-17); the other by God (Rev. 18:5-20). People rejoice over the destruction of one (Rev. 17:16-17); they lament the destruction of the other, literal Babylon (Rev. 18:9-19). God puts it into the hearts of people to destroy one (Rev. 17:15-17); not the other. People could not destroy mystery Babylon in one hour, as is true of literal Babylon (Rev. 18:8, 10, 17). Thirty articles of commerce are mentioned in literal Babylon (Rev. 18:11-14); none are mentioned in Mystery Babylon.

Seven Similarities of the Two Babylons: Both commit fornication with kings and nations (Rev. 17:2; 18:3-14). Both shed blood of saints (Rev. 17:6; 18:24). Both have cups of sin (Rev. 17:4; 18:6). Both are a city (Rev. 17:18; 18:10-21). Both are made desolate (Rev. 17:16; 18:19). Both are called Babylon the great (Rev. 17:5

with Rev 14:8; 16:19; 18:2). Both are clothed in scarlet and purple and decked with precious stones (Rev. 17:4; 18:16).

12. THE DAY OF THE LORD

Many watchers have a burning passion for looking for the Lord's Coming, both in the air for the saints, and to the earth with the saints. However, their lack of a good grasp on end-time terminology brings confusion and bad conclusions to their studies. Prominent teachers of the Word of God equate the Day of the Lord with Daniel's 70th Week, or the Seven Year Tribulation. In a nutshell, the day of the Lord is the Millennium, from the Second Coming to the rebellion of Satan at the end of that period (Rev. 19:11-20:10). The Day of the Lord cannot come until the Lord comes to reign (Isa. 2:12; 13:6, 9; 34:8; 61:2; 63:1-6; Jer. 46:10; Ezek. 30:3; Dan. 2:44-45; 7:13-14; Amos 5:18; Joel 2; Oba. 1:15; Zeph. 1:8, 18; 2:2-3; Zech. 14; Mal. 4; Mt. 24:29-31; 25:31-46; 1 Thess. 5:2; 2 Thess. 1:7-10; 2:1-12; Jude 1:14; Rev. 19:11-21; 20:1-10).

By the term "Day of the Lord," Scriptures mean the day that Christ literally comes to reign on earth with His redeemed, immortal saints and faithful angels (Zech. 14:1-9; Rev. 19:11-16). A day is as 1,000 years to God, and 1,000 years is as a day. If I wanted to go into crazy detail with this subject, then it wouldn't take much effort. However, I'm just giving a good foundation on these subjects, but don't stop your learning with what I'm giving you. Definitely don't limit your learning with these subjects from this chapter. I'm just giving some sound knowledge on some subjects that have unknowingly tripped up some watchers in a hardcore way in their journey of watching.

I don't like writing out a page of Scripture unless it is sorely a necessity for us to get a full handle on the subject. Don't read me wrong. The most important writings are the scriptures. They are what transforms our mind and our lives (Rom. 12:1-2). It's simply human behavior for most to skim Scripture in a book like this. Here's what I'm going to guide you to do. Read this next passage from 2 Peter chapter 3 and I'll underline what I'm pointing you to that will be discussed afterward. Out of all the references to the Day of the Lord above, this best shows that this day is the entirety of the Millennial Reign, as well as pointing to why we watch.

> 3 Knowing this first, that <u>there shall come in the last days scoffers</u>, walking after their own lusts, 4 And saying, <u>Where is the promise of his coming?</u> for since the fathers fell asleep, all things continue as they were from the beginning of the creation. 5 For this <u>they willingly are ignorant</u> of, that by the word of God the heavens were of old, and the earth standing out of the water and in the water: 6 Whereby the world that then was, being overflowed with water, perished: 7 But the heavens and the earth, which are now, by the same word are kept in store, <u>reserved unto fire against the day of judgment</u> and perdition of ungodly men. 8 But, beloved, <u>be not ignorant of this one thing</u>, that <u>one day is with the Lord as a thousand years, and a thousand years as one day</u>. 9 The Lord is not slack concerning <u>his promise</u>, as some men count slackness; but is longsuffering to us-ward, not willing that any should perish, but that all should come to repentance. 10 But <u>the day of the Lord will come as a thief in the night</u>; in the which <u>the heavens shall pass away with a great noise, and the elements shall melt with fervent heat, the earth also and the works that are therein shall be burned up</u>. 11 Seeing then that all these things shall be dissolved, <u>what manner of persons ought ye to be in all holy conversation and godliness</u>, 12 <u>Looking for and hasting unto the coming of the day of God</u>, wherein <u>the heavens being on fire</u> shall be dissolved, and <u>the elements shall melt with fervent heat</u>? 13 Nevertheless we, <u>according to his promise</u>, <u>look for</u> new heavens and a new earth, wherein dwelleth righteousness. 14 Wherefore, beloved, <u>seeing that ye look for such things</u>, be diligent that ye may <u>be found of him in peace, without spot, and blameless</u> (2 Pet. 3:3-14).

Foundations For Building A Biblical Time-line

These twelve verses give us a quick glimpse of at least 1,007 years of time. You'll notice a reference in verse 3 to the last days. There are fourteen end-time expressions like this, but this one is referring to the end of this age preceding the Millennium (Dan. 8:19; 2 Tim. 3:1; Jas. 5:3; 2 Pet. 3:3; Jude 1:18). This mocking from people concerning Jesus' coming has been going on for a number of decades, so we are in these last days of 2 Peter 3. Have peace and be encouraged, for verses 4 and 9 reassure us that His coming is a promise, a sure thing! Have no fear for you who are diligently seeking Him and keeping yourself without sin, and pure (vs. 14; 1 Jn. 3:1-4).

Verse 7 is now speaking of the promise that the earth and the atmospheric heavens will be renovated by the fire of 2 Peter 3:10-13. This will be at the time of the Great White Throne Judgment at the end of the Millennium (2 Pet. 3:7, 10-13; Rom. 8:18-25; Heb. 1:10-12; 12:25-28; Rev. 20:11-15). I once had a friend who believed the earth would be renovated by fire at the Second Coming due to this passage. Understand my friend, we are told not to be willfully ignorant of many things here.

Know that 1 day is as 1,000 years, and the truth from Scripture, when harmonized, will tell you when the great fire storm will devour the earth. It will be on the most well know day of all man, which is the Day of Judgment for the wicked (Rev. 20:11-15). This is apparent with the verses in Revelation at the beginning of Revelation 20 (vs. 1-7). Why tell us that one day is as 1,000 years if it didn't mean the Day of the Lord will last for 1,000 years? Is this not what Revelation 20:1-7 tell us?

The Day of the Lord will come as a thief in the night. Besides the reference in Revelation 3:3 that uses this same expression to speak of judgment on the local church of Sardis, it always refers the Second Coming of Christ (Mt. 24:43; 1 Thess. 5:2-4; 2 Pet. 3:10; Rev. 16:15). Many mockers will be caught off guard (vs. 3-4, 9). I thank God for you who are watching. There are few. If you are busy watching, then you are too busy to be caught off guard. You will be looking diligently and living blameless lives (vs. 14).

Verses 11-14 exhort us to live a life of holiness in view of the Day of the Lord, as well as for eternity. Verse 12 introduces a new term for us that is seldom heard from the teachers of the churches today. The Day of God is coming as well, when God rules supremely again over all His creation without one person rebelling against Him (1 Cor. 15:24-28; Eph. 1:10; Rev. 21:1 - Rev. 22:5; Isa. 65:17; 66:22-24; 2 Pet. 3:13). The day of God is a period from the end of the last rebellion of Satan at the end of the Millennial Reign, until forever and ever. "The heavens being of fire shall be dissolved, and the elements shall melt with fervent heat" will be at the end of the day of the Lord and the beginning of the day of God (2 Pet. 3:7,10-13; 1 Cor. 15:24-28; Rev. 20:7-15). Revelation 20 clearly shows the length of the Day of the Lord (Rev. 20:1-7), followed by the Great White Throne Judgment (Judgment Day; Rev. 20:7-15). Judgment Day is when the heavens and the earth are renovated by fire.

I'm not sure if you believe your time as a watcher ends when the rapture happens, but it most certainly does continue on. Verses 12, 13, and 14 each exhort us to look for these promises (Isa. 65:17; 66:22-24). The watcher will look for the new heaven and the new earth with the anticipation and passion we have now. We are now looking for Jesus to return so the Day of the Lord may begin.

In His day, we will be looking for the Day of God, when all rebellion and all death will finally be swallowed up in victory, and the finality of all salvation phases will be concluded, which even takes into account the restoration of the creation itself (1 Cor. 15:24-28; Rom. 8:18-25). Even in the Millennial Reign, Scripture will remain and we will know the year of Judgment Day based on the 1,000 year time-frame. Shall we continue to believe we are to stick our heads in the sand?

This Day of the Lord is the time that Paul said would come after the hinderer of lawlessness is removed from the earth, and after the reign of the Antichrist. In 2 Thessalonians 2:1-12, Paul made it clear that two things must precede the Day of the Lord, which is a great falling away and the man of sin being revealed. This emphatically associates the Day of the Lord with the Coming of the Lord to destroy Antichrist. Therefore, this day cannot take in the Seven Year Tribulation and the dominion of the Antichrist. It begins with the destruction of Antichrist at the Second Coming at least seven years after the rapture of the church (Zech. 14:1-5).

> Then cometh the end, when he shall have delivered up the kingdom to God, even the Father; when he shall have put down all rule and all authority and power. For he must reign (for the one thousand years of Rev 20:1-10), till he hath put all enemies under his feet. The last enemy that shall be destroyed is death. For he hath put all things under his feet. But when he saith, all things are put under him, it is manifest that he is excepted, which did put all things under him. And when all things shall be subdued unto him, then shall the Son also himself be subject unto him that put all things under him, that God may be all in all (1 Cor 15:24-28).

At that time when all opposition and rebellion are put down and death is destroyed, the heavens and the earth will be purified by fire and the new heavens and the new earth will begin (Isa. 65:17; 66:22-24; 2 Pet. 3:10-13; Heb. 1:10-12; 12:25-28; Rom. 8:14-25; Rev. 21:1 - Rev 22:5). Then, the Day of God will be here (2 Pet. 3:10-13). The kingdoms of this world will then truly become the kingdoms of God the Father, Christ, the Holy Spirit, and all the faithful saints (Rev. 11:15). The original purpose of man was not abolished at the fall of Adam, merely postponed.

Chapter 11

PUTTING TOGETHER THE BIBLICAL TIME-LINE

After all the foundation has been laid from all key doctrinal information, this is what a time-line can look like. I'm going to use 2016 – 2023 as my seven year period. This is only an example. I'll explain the mind-set for some of these dates after the time-line has been laid out. I want to make sure we're tracking on the same page at the same time.

I. 2016 – 2023 Timeline

This year has two different possibilities for the first month, and as such, both are presented. Each year's beginning should be confirmed by report of the barley crop in Israel. The feast of trumpets is the first day of the Jewish year. Coincidentally, this is the first day of tribulation for Israel in the soon coming Seven Year Tribulation, right after the second phase in the first resurrection happens (1 Thess. 3:13; 4:13-18; 1 Cor. 15:51-54). The 70th Week will begin a few days or weeks later.

A. *September 3 - 4, 2016 or **October 3 - 4, 2016

The rapture of the church on Feast of Trumpets at the last trump.

This is what the saints will be doing for 7 years on the planet heaven:

Putting Together The Biblical Time-line

a. Presentation before God (Eph. 5:27; Col. 3:4; 1Thess. 3:13)

b. Saints declared blameless (1Thess. 3:13; 5:23)

c. Settlement in mansions (Jn. 14:1-3; Heb. 11:10-16; 13:14; Rev. 3:12)

d. Judgment of saints (Rom. 14:10; 2 Cor. 3:11-15; 5:10-11)

e. Regular worship (Rev. 19:1-9; Lk. 22:16)

f. Routine of living (Lk. 22:29-30; Jn. 14:1-3; Rev. 1:6; 2 Cor. 2:9)

g. Marriage of the Lamb (Rev. 19:1-9)

h. Preparation for the Second Coming, the battle of Armageddon, and the establishment of an eternal government on earth (Rev. 19:11-21; 20:1-10; Zech. 14)

About *22 days or **52 days from the beginning of the 7 Year Tribulation

No children will be left behind. This will settle once and for all the question of what the age of accountability is.

B. About *22 Days or **52 Days

Time for the great deception of visible UFO's and aliens (demonic origins) (Gen. 6:1-4; Eph. 6:10-20; Col. 1:16; 2 Thess. 2:7-12)

The beginning of the great revival due to the Rapture (Acts 2:16-21; Joel 2:28-29; Rev. 6:9-11; 7:1-17; 15:2-4)

The Beast rises from the Abyss in order to cause the rise of the Antichrist out of the 10 kingdoms

The Antichrist to be demonically thrust into position to sign the 7 year peace treaty with Israel (Dan. 9:27; couple with Dan. 7:21-25; 8:9-14, 22-25; 11:36-45; Mat. 24:15-24; 1 Thess. 5:1-5; 2 Thess. 2:3-4; Rev. 13:1-18)

C. October 26, 2016

The beginning of the 7 Year Tribulation

Antichrist signs the 7 year peace treaty with Israel (Dan. 9:27)

From this point on the earth will experience the plagues and judgments of God, possibly by the use of Planet X (also called Nibiru) (Rev. 8 – Rev. 9). It will pass by the earth which will cause much of the destruction due to the gravitational pull and pole shift of the earth

This is a summary of the events to occur during the first 3 ½ years:

a. The 1st seal: rise of Antichrist (Rev. 6:1)

b. The 2nd seal: war (Rev. 6:3-4)

c. The 3rd seal: famine (Rev. 6:5-6)

d. The 4th seal: death and hell (Rev. 6:7-8)

e. The 5th seal: first martyrs (Rev. 6:9-11)

f. The 6th seal: wrath of God (Rev. 6:12-17)

g. The 144,000 Jews sealed (Rev. 7:1-8)

h. The Tribulation martyrs worship (Rev. 7:9-17)

i. The 7th seal: silence in heaven (Rev. 8:1)

j. The 7 angels given 7 trumpets (Rev. 8:2)

k. Priestly angel ministers (Rev. 8:3-5)

l. The 7 angels prepare to sound (Rev. 8:6)

m. The 1st trumpet: hail, fire, blood (Rev. 8:7)

n. The 2nd trumpet: sea to blood (Rev. 8:8-9)

o. The 3rd trumpet: waters poisoned (Rev. 8:10-11)

Putting Together The Biblical Time-line

p. The 4th trumpet: planets darkened (Rev. 8:12)

q. Angel announces 3 woes (Rev. 8:13)

r. The 5th trumpet: the first woe - loosing of demons to torment people (Rev. 9:1-12)

s. The 6th trumpet: the second woe - loosing of 200,000,000 demons to slay 1/3 of mankind (Rev. 9:13-21)

D. October 26, 2016 – April 8, 2020

The temple will be rebuilt in late 2016 – early 2017 in Jerusalem

The fulfillment of Revelation 6:12 that brings a mega earthquake during what appears to be a blood red moon, though the last eclipse of the special and rare tetrad ended September 28, 2015. Revelation 6:12 appears to be very close to the beginning of the Tribulation. Perhaps Planet X or one of its moons will cause this. There are 3 total lunar eclipses (causing a blood red moon) from October, 2016 – April, 2020. The next is in January, 2018, giving 15 months for the acts of war (Rev. 6:2-4), causing the famine (Rev. 6:5-6), which causes pestilences (Rev. 6:7-8; Ezek. 14:21; Mat. 24:6-7), which causes much death (Rev. 6:7-8), which causes hell to become more full (Rev. 6:7-8). Then, the blood moon will happen (Rev. 6:12-17).

Planet X will pass and cause Revelation 8 to unfold. This will be before the invasion of the army listed next that will fulfill Revelation 9.

The invasion of the demonic army of 200 million will occur before the middle of the Tribulation (Rev.9:14-20). This appears to be closer to 2018 – 2020.

E. April 8, 2020

Passover begins

The beginning of the Great Tribulation

3 ½ years after the rapture & 3 ½ years before the Second Coming

The rapture of the 144,000 within days before the beginning of the Great Tribulation (Rev.12:5; 14:1-5)

The Antichrist breaks covenant with Israel and takes over Jerusalem with his armies as his new headquarters

The Antichrist stops the sacrifices in the new temple in Jerusalem

The Antichrist declares himself to be God

Israel flees to the wilderness

Final war in heaven when Satan is kicked out forever, but cast to earth

Beginning of the ministry of the 2 Witnesses for the next 1260 days

Here is a summary of the events taking place in the last 3 ½ years:

a. Temple and city defiled (Rev. 11:1-2)

b. The 2 witnesses appear on earth (Rev. 11:3-12)

c. Great earthquake in Jerusalem (end of last 3 ½ years) (Rev. 11:13)

d. The 7th trumpet: announcements (Rev. 11:15-18)

e. Heavenly temple opened (Rev. 11:19)

f. Sun-clothed woman travails (Rev. 12:1-2)

g. Dragon attacks the man-child (Rev. 12:3-4)

h. Man-child caught up to heaven before the last 3 ½ years (Rev. 12:5)

i. The woman flees for 3 ½ years (Rev. 12:6)

j. War in heaven (Rev. 12:7-12)

k. Satan attacks the woman (Rev. 12:13-16)

l. Satan attacks the remnant (Rev. 12:17)

m. Beast out of sea; Antichrist given power over nations (Rev. 13:1-10,18)

n. Beast out of earth: false prophet begins beast worship (Rev. 13:11-17)

o. The 144,000 Jews, the man-child, presented to God (Rev. 14:1-5)

p. Everlasting gospel preached by an angel (Rev. 14:6-7)

q. Fall of Babylon announced by angel (Rev. 14:8)

r. Doom of beast worshipers announced by an angel (Rev. 14:9-12)

s. Blessing to martyrs announced (Rev. 14:13)

t. Harvest: Armageddon (end of the last 3 ½ years) (Rev. 14:14-16)

u. Vintage: Armageddon (Rev. 14:17-20)

v. The 7 vial judgments prepared (Rev. 15:1, 6-7)

w. Tribulation martyrs worship (Rev. 15:2-4)

x. Heavenly tabernacle opened (Rev. 15:5 - Rev. 16:1)

y. The 1st vial: sores on people (Rev. 16:2)

z. The 2nd vial: sea to blood (Rev. 16:3)

aa. The 3rd vial: rivers to blood (Rev. 16:4-7)

bb. The 4th vial: great heat (Rev. 16:8-9)

cc. The 5th vial: darkness (Rev. 16:10-11)

dd. The 6th vial: Euphrates dried up (Rev. 16:12)

ee. The 3 unclean spirits: mobilization of nations to Armageddon (Rev. 16:13-16)

ff. The 7th vial: great earthquake - literal Babylon and other cities destroyed (Rev. 16:17-21; 18:1-24) gg. Kings of earth commit fornication with the great whore (Rev. 17:1-5)

hh. The great whore martyrs saints (Rev. 17:6-7)

ii. The 8th kingdom formed (Rev. 17:8-13)

jj. War on the Lamb (Rev. 17:14)

kk. War on the great whore (Rev. 17:15-18)

ll. Marriage of the Lamb (Rev. 19:1-10)

mm. The Second Coming of Christ (Rev. 19:11-16)

nn. Angel invitation to birds (Rev. 19:17-18)

oo. Battle of Armageddon (Rev. 19:19-21)

pp. Binding of Satan (Rev. 20:1-3)

qq. The first resurrection completed: Millennial Reign of Christ begins (Rev. 20:4-6)

F. June 2, 2023

The end of the 2,300 evenings and mornings of the ceased sacrifices

Jerusalem is recaptured by Israel while Antichrist and his armies are taking control of Russia and Germany and other nations.

G. September 20, 2023

The end of the 1,260th day of the Great Tribulation

2 Witnesses are killed

People of the earth rejoice and make merry for 3 ½ days.

H. September 26, 2023

The 2 Witnesses are resurrected and raptured (Sept. 24) to complete the first resurrection that Jesus was first in, the resurrected and raptured Old Testament saints and Church Age believers were second in, the 144,000 were third in, and the tribulations saints were forth in, within days before the 2 Witnesses

The Second Coming of Christ and all saints of all times and all holy angels in order to retake the earth in order to re-establish it in holiness during the Millennium in order for God to set His throne on earth and live with man forever

Yom Kippur (the Day of Atonement)

Israel restored in holiness by repentance and faith in the Son of God, Jesus the Messiah, Who they visibly will see (Not ironically on the 40th and last day of the 40 days of Teshuvah and the days of Awe).

I. October 1-7, 2023

Sukkot (the Feast of Tabernacles)

The first gathering of representatives to Jerusalem to worship the King, the Lord of hosts, and to keep the feast of tabernacles yearly (Zech. 14:16)

J. October 20, 2023

The end of the 1,290th day (Dan. 12:11)

K. December 4, 2023

The end of the 1,335th day (Dan. 12:12)

L. September 26, 2023 – December 4, 2023

The battle of Armageddon (Joel 3; Zech. 14; Rev. 19:11-21)

Burial of the dead begun (Ezek. 39:8-22)

Great earthquake and splitting of the Mount of Olives (Zech. 14:1-5)

Rounding up of the prisoners of the armies of Antichrist and disposition of them (Ezek. 39:2; Joel 2:1-11)

Rounding up and casting of Satan and every demon and fallen angel into the abyss (Isaiah 24:21-22; Rev. 20:1-3)

Gathering of Israel by the angels (Isa. 11:10-12; Mat. 24:31)

Gathering of the nations to judgment (Mat. 25:31-46)

Separation of the tares and wheat (Mat. 13:39-50)

Cleansing Jerusalem and beginning its rebuilding for the eternal kingdom (Ezek. 48)

Rounding up of all beast worshipers and all who have the mark of the beast to be sent to hell (Rev. 14:9-11)

Erection of the millennial temple (Ezek. 40-46; Zech. 6:12-13)

Sending out the resurrected saints as the new earth rulers to take over every inhabited part of the earth (Dan. 7:18, 27; 1 Cor. 6:2; Rev. 5:10; 11:15; 22:4-5)

Sending out missionaries from Jerusalem to evangelize the nations (Isa. 2:2-4; 11:9; 52:7; Zech. 8:23)

Establishing government offices in every part of the earth and publishing the new laws of the kingdom of heaven on earth (Isa. 2:2-4)

Division of the promised land into 12 strips and the settlement of the 12 tribes in their portions (Ezek. 48)

Settling of the nations in their own portions of the earth (Deut. 32:8; Acts 17:26)

Opening of the earth and starting of the Millennial river (Ezek. 47)

All necessary work in making the deserts blossom as a rose, waters to spring forth in the deserts, changing the animals, regulating the solar system as it was before the fall, and many other events that will continue throughout the Millennium and new earth forever

Chapter 12

WHEN IS THE RAPTURE?

Though we can't know for sure the exact year, we have learned this event will be on a specific day in an unknown year, most likely in our own life time. If the rapture is not in a month from now on the feast of trumpets in 2016, then I'll be intently watching for 2017 and 2018. 2017 is 40 years after Israeli victory and reunification of the City of Jerusalem. Israel had to recapture Jerusalem for latter day prophecy to be fulfilled. It is clear that Israel has control over Jerusalem and sets up their third temple in the 7 Year Tribulation. The 7th prophetic tetrad since Christ happened in 1967 – 1968. The Israel event occurred during this tetrad.

2018 is 70 years after Israel became a nation on May 14, 1948. Jeremiah 25:9-12; 29:10 (Dan. 9:3) speaks of the 70 years of Israeli captivity Jews will endure for not keeping the the last 70 Shemitah years, which is the seventh year. This means there were 490 years of disobedience to God (70 x last year of a 7 year period = 490). Daniel's prayer in the beginning of Daniel 9 was at the end of the 70 year captivity of Israel. Daniel was asking what would happen to his people. His answer was ironically similar to Israel's 490 years of disobedience.

There would be 490 more years where God is focused upon Israel. The 1st division is 7 weeks, 49 years for the rebuilding of Jerusalem (Dan. 9:25). The 2nd division is 62 weeks, 434 years from the completion of the city at the end of the 49 years to the time the Messiah is cut off, or crucified for men (Isa. 53; Dan. 9:25-26). The 3rd division is one week, 7 years, the last 7 years of this age, ending with the Second Coming of Christ to fulfill the six events of Daniel 9:24.

David said in Psalms 90:10, "The days of our years are threescore years and ten; and if by reason of strength they be fourscore years, yet is their strength labour and sorrow; for it is soon cut off, and we fly away." It is because of this that many believe a generation may be 70 years, which brings us to Jesus' words in Matthew 24.

Now learn a parable of the fig tree; When his branch is yet tender, and putteth forth leaves, ye know that summer is nigh: So likewise ye, when ye shall see all these things, know that it is near, even at the doors. Verily I say unto you, This generation shall not pass, till all these things be fulfilled (Mat. 24:32-34).

We get heavy into this theory and teaching in Book 4, *Signs of His Coming*, but now, I'll just use this to say why 2018 is a high watch year. The 6th prophetic tetrad since Christ happened in 1949 – 1950. The Israel event occurred before this tetrad in 1948. As you can see, the Israel event of 1948 happened before the 1949 – 1950 sixth prophetic tetrad since Christ. The Israel event of 1967 happened during the 1967 – 1968 seventh tetrad since Christ. The Israel event has not happened before or during the 2014 – 2015 eighth tetrad since Christ, but there is precedence from pattern to believe this event could happen after the prophetic tetrad.

As I write this, it is four weeks before the feast of trumpets, 2016. I want to be an open book to show the mind of a watcher. 2016 could be the year, but this book won't be published until days before, so you who reads this will know if 2016 was the year or not. If you are reading this after the rapture, then you will be in a great position to fully understand what is coming and when. As for before the rapture, I am only looking at the evidence revealed to me. I will also point to things many watchers were looking at for 2015. Reviewing the past can always teach us to better prepare for the future. What can we glean from the past to make us better watchers?

It is with great anticipation that I watch every feast of trumpets every year since 2006. Some years have been very hopeful when comparing Bible prophecy with current events. In no way will I tell anyone to expect the rapture to absolutely happen in a specific year, but I do alert very high watch years when things are lining up. 2015 was one of those years. The following information will be brief, as I am going to give a more bottom line explanation of why the fall of 2015 looked to be the most promising watch year of my life. You'll need the following chart to better help you see what I'm saying in the rest of this chapter.

Shavuot = A seven year period from September of year 7 on Elul 29, the feast of trumpets, until the same day of the next 7th year. Example: September 29, 2008 – September 13, 2015

Shemitah = The 7th year of a Shavuot from September of year 6 and ends September of year 7 on Elul 29, the feast of trumpets. Example: September 2014 – September 13, 2015

Jubilee = The 50th year, or the year following the 7th Shemitah of the 7th Shavuot. It is like a super Shemitah; a year of restoration. Example: September 2015 - September 2016

	Year 1 Jubilee	Year 2	Year 3	Year 4	Year 5	Year 6	Year 7 Shemitah
Shavuot 7	1911	1912	1913	1914	1915	1916	**1917**
Shavuot 1	**1918**	1919	1920	1921	1922	1923	**1924**
Shavuot 2	1925	1926	1927	1928	1929	1930	**1931**
Shavuot 3	1932	1933	1934	1935	1936	1937	**1938**
Shavuot 4	1939	1940	1941	1942	1943	1944	**1945**
Shavuot 5	1946	1947	1948	1949	1950	1951	**1952**
Shavuot 6	1953	1954	1955	1956	1957	1958	**1959**
Shavuot 7	1960	1961	1962	1963	1964	1965	**1966**
Shavuot 1	**1967**	1968	1969	1970	1971	1972	**1973**
Shavuot 2	1974	1975	1976	1977	1978	1979	**1980**
Shavuot 3	1981	1982	1983	1984	1985	1986	**1987**
Shavuot 4	1988	1989	1990	1991	1992	1993	**1994**
Shavuot 5	1995	1996	1997	1998	1999	2000	**2001**
Shavuot 6	2002	2003	2004	2005	2006	2007	**2008**
Shavuot 7	2009	2010	2011	2012	2013	2014	**2015**
Shavuot 1	**2016**	2017	2018	2019	2020	2021	**2022**

As you have read so far, the feast of trumpets will be fulfilled by the rapture, just as Passover was fulfilled by the death of the Lamb of God. From the pages of book 4, *Signs of His Coming*, you'll see from every possible angle that this is the generation the rapture event will happen, as well as the 7 Year Tribulation. With this knowledge alone, the natural progression is to look for the year.

From the pattern of the Shemitah, it looked like 2015 would be that seventh year, which would begin another seven year cycle. Daniel's 70th Week is a seven year cycle. To refresh you, "70th week of Daniel" is a phrase that describes the last seven years before the Lord's return, a sabbatical cycle. The phrase from Daniel 9:24, "seventy weeks" literally means "seventy sevens" (Hebrew: for "week" is *shabuwa*` (HSN-<H7620>), seven). It is not only believed by orthodox rabbinical Jews that the last week (7 years) of Daniel 9:27 will be a complete sabbatical cycle, but common sense would say the same.

The Jubilee is a God ordained "Sabbath" that occurs once every 49 years. The theme of this special Sabbath was liberation for God's people and their land. Like the seven day week, the Jubilee is also a shadow of things to come. It is believed that the Messiah will return in a Jubilee year to grant liberty to mankind. The original jubilee cycle has been lost to antiquity, but some rabbinical sources point to 1966-1967 as being the most recent jubilee year, because that is when the Six Day War happened and Jerusalem was reclaimed by Israel as its capital city once again.

If it is true, then 2015-2016 will be the next Jubilee. 2015-2016 would be September 2015 to the October of 2016, not January to January. This Jewish New Year for 2015 begins on September 14-16 on the feast of trumpets. That is how God's calendar works. It will end on October 3-4 on the next feast of trumpets.

All this points to is a sabbatical cycle (a 7 year cycle), so that we may anticipate better when this may be. This would be a major piece of information to have in the watch for the coming of the Lord, both for the saints in the air and with the saints to the earth. Knowing this is the last generation, it would be of significance to know the 7 year cycles. Many expect the Lord to come on a Jubilee year, but 2015 would only point to the sabbatical cycle. The Second Coming would be in the fall of 2022 if 2015 had been the beginning of the 70th Week of Daniel. Again, the exact year of the Jubilee is lost to us at the moment. It is widely believed that 2001, 2008, 2015, 2022, 2029, etc. are the beginning of sabbatical cycles, though this is not agreed upon throughout the watching community.

When Is The Rapture?

Interesting enough those four very rare blood moon tetrads did occur during the later part of the apparent sabbatical cycle. Those blood moon tetrads were so very rare, and the last eclipse occurred over Jerusalem like a bulls eye, making it even more rare and very Biblically prophetic had the rapture happened two weeks earlier on the feast of trumpets. Also note those blood moon tetrads occurred on the Lord's feast days, found in Leviticus 23, which is what makes a tetrad a biblical tetrad according to 21st century terminology.

These particular very rare blood moon tetrads occurred on Passover, April 15, 2014; on the Feast of Tabernacles, October 8, 2014; on Passover, April 4, 2015; and on The Feast of Tabernacles, September 28, 2015. The rabbis teach that blood moons (total lunar eclipses) are a sign used by God for the judgment of the nation of Israel. The rabbis also teach that solar eclipses over Jerusalem are a sign for the judgments of the nations of the world.

Now, I want to share again about the solar eclipses which all occurred on the 1st of Av for three consecutive years. This is very rare indeed to say the least. The first one occurred on August 1, 2008 which is the 1st of Av according to the biblical calendar. The next one was on July 22, 2009, again on the 1st of Av. The last one was on July 11, 2010, again occurring on the 1st of Av on the Jewish lunar calendar that God gave them to keep. These are rare events and occurred on the same day on the Jewish calendar makes it even more of a rare occurrence.

Av 1 sits in the middle of Tammuz 17 to Av 9. The rabbis like to call these three weeks "The dark time," or "Between the straits." Moses had found the people worshiping the golden calf on Jewish calendar day of the 17th of Tammuz. Also from Av 1st – Av 9th there are to be no comforts to be enjoyed. No bathing, no clean clothes, no shoes, and they must read from the Book of Lamentations during those days. However, there will come a time when God will change that and turn that into days of joy and feast as we read this in Zechariah.

Thus saith the LORD of hosts; The fast of the fourth month (Tammuz 17), and the fast of the fifth, (Av 9) and the fast of the seventh, and the fast of the tenth, shall be to the house of Judah joy and gladness, and cheerful feasts; therefore love the truth and peace (Zechariah 8:19).

Major events occurring in the "dark days" between Tammuz 17 to Av 9 is vast, and beyond coincidence. The last day of this three week period is Av 9th, and is when Nebuchadnezzar destroyed the Temple. 600 years later, Rome destroyed the temple on 9th of Av. All the Jews were kicked out of England in 1290 on the 9th of Av, as well as Spain in 1492. World War I started on the 9th of Av. Hitler's proclamation to kill the Jews came on the 9th of Av. The Gaza strip was evacuated at sundown on the 9th of Av. This is the same day Israel rejected the land 3,500 years ago. There are days and times being signaled to us if we are awake and watching.

Back to the Sabbatical cycles, rabbis teach that events occurring during the start of a Sabbatical cycle set the tone for the rest of that particular cycle. The events of 9/11 set the tone for the previous Sabbatical cycle (2001 - 2008). The first day of the 2008 – 2015 cycle began with a major drop with the Dow Jones stock trades of 777.68 points. This happened on the feast of trumpets, which is the first day of the Jewish calendar and the day they credit the creation of the world.

These are the consecutive total solar eclipses occurring on the same day of the Jewish calendar: Av 1 (August 1, 2008); Av 1 (July 22, 2009); and Av 1 (July 11, 2010). Here is the second reason why I believed 2015 should be the most highly anticipated year during the feast of trumpets to be watching for the Lord to come FOR the saints. The Sabbatical cycle of 2008 – 2015 is book-ended by eclipses. It begins and ends with rare eclipses... rare because they most certainly point to something, as they all fall on significant and important days for Israel and the Jewish people.

When Is The Rapture?

This should make Christians stand up and take notice since the purpose of the 7 Year Tribulation brings God's focus completely back to Israel. Sadly, the vast majority of the church is sleep walking through life. If the church only understood Israel in prophecy, then they would understand why Israel is to be the focus for determining what time the prophetical clock is at. If the church has very little concept of this, then how far are those who have not the profession of a Christian (1 Pt. 4:17-19)?

Remember from book 1, the purpose of the 70th Week of Daniel is to purify Israel and bring the nation back to a place where God can fulfill the everlasting covenants made with the fathers of Israel (Isa. 2:6; 3:26; 16:1-5; 24:1-23; 26:20, 21; Ezek. 20:33, 34; 22:17-22; Rom. 11:25-29). To purify Israel of all rebels (Ezek. 20:33, 34; 22:17-22; Zech. 13:8, 9; Mal. 3:3, 4). To plead with and bring Israel into the bond of the new covenant (Ezek. 20:33, 34; 36:24-28; Jer. 30:3-11; Zech. 12:10 – Zech. 13:9; Mal. 4:3, 4). To judge Israel for their rejection of the Messiah and make them willing to accept Him when He comes the second time to the earth (Ezek. 20:22, 34; Zech. 12:10 – Zech. 13:9; 14:1-15; Mt. 24:15-31). To judge the nations for their persecution of Israel (Isa. 16:3-5; Joel 3; Rev. 6:1 – Rev. 19:21). To bring Israel to complete repentance (Zech. 12:10 – Zech. 13:9; Rom. 11:26-29; Mt. 23:39). To fulfill the prophecies of Daniel 9:24-27; Revelation 6:1 - Revelation 19:21; Matthew 24:15, 29, etc. To cause Israel to flee into the wilderness of Edom and Moab (modern Jordan) where they will turn to God for help (Isa. 16:1-5; Ezek. 20:33-35; Dan. 11:40 – Dan. 12:7; Hos. 2:14-17; Mt. 24:15-31; Rev. 12).

The third main reason I saw 2015 as a major watch year was because the tetrad (four blood red moons) ends on the feast of tabernacles, a couple weeks after the feast of trumpets, 2015. However, there is still a marker with the feast of trumpets. It even had an eclipse during that day. This eclipse is a partial solar eclipse. I find this significant!

From many studies of the significant events that have happened surrounding the Jewish people, we have been slightly perplexed as to when the major event would happen. The main event usually happens the year before the prophetic tetrad begins, or during its 1 ½ year cycle. This is why feast of trumpets, 2013 was anticipated at a slightly higher degree. 2014 was not be ruled out, as it was the second most anticipated year due to it being in the tetrad cycle, though it held none of the other significant attributes that 2015 held.

SHEMITAH

2015 stuck out like a soar thumb for three main reasons: The 2014 – 2015 tetrad; The Shemitah year of September 2014 – September 2015; The Year of Jubilee from September 2015 – September 2016. A tetrad is a series of 4 total lunar eclipses that fall back to back over a two year period in spring, fall, spring, and fall again. They are rare. There have been 62 over the last 2,000 years. 2014 – 2015 was the last one, being the most spectacular of them all.

What makes this more rare is when they fall on biblical feast days, such as the first feast of Passover, and then the last feast of tabernacles (Lev. 23). We call tetrads that fall on these biblical feast days, biblical tetrads, or a prophetic tetrad. Out of the 62 rare events in the last 2,000 years we call a tetrad, there have only been 8 biblical tetrads. All have been surrounded by significant events involving the people that God gave these feasts too, the Jewish people.

There have only been 7 biblical tetrads since Christ, not including the one we were just in (2014 - 2015). All have meant something appointed for Israel. For example, the last 3 were in 1493 - 1494, which is the Spanish Inquisition and the Jews were kicked out of Spain. Then almost 500 years later in 1949 - 1950, around the time of Israel becoming a state again after a couple thousand years. The last one was in 1967 - 1968, which is when Jerusalem was

When Is The Rapture?

recaptured as Israel's capital city. Out of them all, the 2014 - 2015 biblical tetrad is the most perfect, because of the eclipse's symmetry of equal days from each other and the last moon being a super blood-red moon seen over Jerusalem. You can see this chart from this link: http://bloodmoonscoming.com/?page_id=127

Because of this tetrad, I've been looking for the rapture year with great anticipation since 2008. I've thought it most likely to be in 2008, 2010, 2011, 2012, and 2015. I never suspected 2015 would come and go without a rapture, but it only means that the appointed time was not before 2015. God is not slack concerning His promises (2 Pt. 3). 2015 came and went, and we have to be aware of one thing... the event signified by these biblical tetrads has always happened before the last blood moon. But this is only the eighth, and there are no Scriptures to tell us if this is always the way it will be.

The next biblical tetrad will not occur for another 600 years in 2582 – 2583. We would be wise to acknowledge that our Lord is trying to grab our attention that something BIG is about to happen. This is why I am currently looking at 2016, feast of trumpets, as the appointed time for the Church Age to end. If not 2016, then we are close. The astronomical signs are crazy in the heavens. The feast of trumpets, 2017 has the sign of Revelation 12 as seen from heaven, so this could be a sign to us on earth that the sign in heaven will be seen soon. The Revelation 12 constellations are seen from heaven's view and would not occur at the same time as earth's view. This goes and shows that there might just be watchers in heaven awaiting their resurrection if the appointed day has not been made clear to them.

There is talk of two huge asteroids coming toward earth, but both have less than a 2% chance of hitting. The first asteroid is expected in the year 2029, in April. If we are looking for Revelation 8's asteroids, then they will be in the beginning of the Tribulation. If the 7 year period is 2001 – 2008; 2008 – 2015; 2015 – 2022; 2022 – 2029; then April of 2029 is not the time the asteroids of Revelation 8 will strike. The rapture would be in the fall of 2029. If this is one of the asteroids of Revelation 8, then 2022 – 2029 is not the correct 7 year period.

The other asteroid coming close to earth is in August, 2032. If 2022 – 2029 is a correct Shavuot, and the 2032 asteroid is one of the two large asteroids from Revelation 8, then Revelation 8 – Revelation 9 will be fulfilled in the last eight months of the first half of the Tribulation (Fall, 2029 – April, 2033). August, 2032 is 8 months from April, 2032. A portion of Revelation 8 – Revelation 9 lasts 5 months (Rev. 9:5), and the rest of the trumpets could have happened quickly. Therefore, 2029 – 2036 fits the evidence in front of us, not that I want to be here for 13 more years.

This has been an example of what a watcher should be looking for. Does it grieve me to think I'll have to wait until I'm in my 50's to be raptured? Of course, but we must watch without biased expectations. I remember being on a pre-tribulation watcher forum in 2010. How many times did I read a person saying they couldn't imagine we would be here much longer with how fast things were heating up in Israel? Yet, here we are. I believe the rapture will happen quicker than that, but we must not let emotions get in the way.

Another thing we should be prepared for is the rapture not happening until 2022 at the earliest. If the seven year periods truly have been made known to us, then that would be the beginning of the next seven year period. I still remain hopeful for every year, but these are things we cannot anxiously consider in the midst of these seventh year periods, then turn a blind eye if that year has come and gone.

So, the subject of the tetrad begs the question, "Does the Bible say anything about a tetrad?" The answer is no, not by name. But the Bible does say in the very first chapter (Gen. 1:14-19) that the sun, moon, and stars were created for signs and seasons, or 'appointed times' (Gen.1:14). We will refresh since this subject is still so foreign to many. The Hebrew word translated 'seasons' in Genesis 1:14 is 'moed'. mo`ed, mo-ade'; or (feminine) mow`adah, mo-aw-daw'; (2 Chron. 8:13), from <H3259> (ya`ad); properly an appointment, i.e. a fixed time or season; specifically a festival; conventionally a year; by implication, an assembly (as convened for a definite purpose); technically the congregation; by extension, the place of meeting; also a signal (as appointed beforehand) :- appointed (sign, time), (place of, solemn) assembly, congregation, (set, solemn) feast, (appointed, due) season, solemn (-ity), synagogue, (set) time (appointed). — Strong's Talking Greek & Hebrew Dictionary

If you remember the feast days as charted out in a previous chapter, then you'll better understand by the Hebrew word 'moed,' which was translated 'seasons' in Genesis 1:14, is the same word translated 'feasts' in Leviticus 23. To re-cap, the Hebrew word 'moed' has been translated 'season' and 'feast.' As seen by the definitions above, the word does mean those, but even more so. It means appointed times. Is this a stretch for the context? Not at all. It's clear by reviewing the history of the death, burial, and resurrection of Christ that these 'moed' or 'feasts' are appointed times to be fulfilled. The forth feast was fulfilled by the Holy Spirit being sent by Jesus (Jn. 14:16; Acts 2:1-4).

<u>Fulfilled</u> (1) **Feast of the Passover** (Lev. 23:4-5) - *Jesus' death*

<u>Fulfilled</u> (2) **Feast of unleaven bread** (Lev. 23:6-8) - *Jesus' burial*

<u>Fulfilled</u> (3) **Feast of first fruits** (Lev. 23:9-14) - *Jesus' resurrection*

<u>Fulfilled</u> (4) **Feast of Pentecost** (Lev. 23:15-22) - *Outpouring of the Holy Spirit*

<u>Will be fulfilled</u> (5) **Feast of trumpets** (Lev. 23:23-25) - *Rapture of the saints*

<u>Will be fulfilled</u> (6) **Feast of Atonement** (Lev. 23:26-32) - *The Second Coming*

<u>Will be fulfilled</u> (7) **Feast of tabernacles** (Lev. 23:33-44) - *Beginning of the Millennial Reign*

As seen again, these feasts are appointed times. You could have just as easily and correctly said the appointed time of Passover when it was being fulfilled. And with Genesis 1:14, you could just as easily say, "And God said, Let there be lights in the firmament of the heaven to divide the day from the night; and let them be for signs, and for seasons (APPOINTED TIMES), and for days, and years:"

Another quick reference is Jesus in the Gospel of Luke telling His disciples, in reference to these events of Daniel's 70th Week, "And there shall be signs in the sun, and in the moon, and in the stars; and upon the earth distress of nations, with perplexity; the sea and the waves roaring; Men's hearts failing them for fear, and for looking after those things which are coming on the earth: for the powers of heaven shall be shaken" (Lk. 21:25-26). It is a fact that God will use and has used eclipses to give us signs of His appointed times and has ordered their paths to fall on His feast days, or His appointed times, to signal us to when His appointed times for solemn assemblies will be, such as the rapture.

Because of something called the Shemitah (Lev. 25:1-6; Deut. 15:1-2), logic would say the rapture will be at the beginning of the Shavuot (7 year period). The rapture takes place first, before the 7 Year Tribulation begins. The 7 Year Tribulation is a 7 year period that will be a few days longer on each side of Daniel's 70th Week. The 70th Week has it's boundaries in the biblical Shavuot (Dan. 9:24-27). This is because the 7 Year Tribulation is essentially the 70th Week of Daniel (Daniel 7:25; 9:24-27; 12:9, 12-13; Rev. 11:2-3; 12:6, 14; 13:5). But how do we known 2015 – 2022 is a Shavuot? Again, a Shavuot is a 7 year period ordained by God.

Referring back to the Shemitah (Lev. 25:1-6; Deut. 15:1-2): The bottom line of this word means every seventh year is a sabbatical year, or a year of rest. It was a command given only to Israel, the seventh year shall be a Sabbath of rest for the land (Lev. 25:1-6). If this was obeyed, there would be great blessing. If this was disobeyed then a curse would be on the land and the people. In recent times, this can be seen on the land of the United States in the form of financial collapses every 7 years, during a Shemitah year and generally falling on the last day of the Shemitah year, which happens to be the feast of trumpets, or Elul 29 according to the Hebrew calendar.

By this, we can see the 7 year periods God recognizes. Daniel's 70th Week will be during a 7 year period like this, known as a Shavuot, which is a 7 year period (Dan. 9:24-27). By the lack of a homeland for the Jewish people, as well as these people being displaced across the planet, the times God gave to Israel have been lost, but God has been informing us of His times by judging the US every 7 years according to our godlessness. This is at least what appears to be signaled as we watch for signs of His appointed times.

Finding out when financial disaster will happen means nothing to me, but finding out when the Shemitah is will tell us when the Shavuot's seven year time-frame will be. The fact that the rareness of the tetrad is taking place at the Shavuot should open your eyes. Finding out when the Jubilee year is should keep your eyes open and fixed to the sky (Lk. 21:28). Much of this is speculative as we keep an open mind operative with our opened eyes, testing everything according to the authenticity of God's inspired and inerrant Word.

I'll give some facts pointing to the seven year cycle being September 2015 – September 2022. Stock market collapses occurred in the years of 1973, 1980, 1987, 2001, 2008, being seven year intervals. On the other side of the financial market is the bond market. 1994 gave us the Great Bond Market Massacre of '94. The top 3 greatest crashes in US history are as follows: 3) Fall, 1937 – Fall, 1938 was the greatest crash. 2) Fall, 2007 – Fall, 2008 was the greatest recession. 1) Fall, 1930 – Fall, 1931 was the Great Depression.

Financial analysis have been perplexed for years by the phenomenon of financial crashes occurring in autumn, specifically September and October. The mystery was solved when a pastor named, Jonathan Cahn put the pieces together and realized God was warning us with the biblical Shemitah. The 5 greatest point crashes in U.S. history all take place in 7 year increments on or within days of Elul 29, or the feast of trumpets. This day is the feast of the new moon, the first crescent moon after its transition (1 Chr. 23:31; 2 Chr. 2:4; 8:13; 31:3; Ezra 3:5; Neh. 10:33; Isa. 1:13-14; Hos. 2:11; Col. 2:14-17).

Israel uses a lunar calendar, meaning the feast of trumpets, or Elul 29, takes place on a different day on our Gregorian calendar in the months of September or October. The greatest stock market point loss up until that time was on September 17, 2001. This day fell right on Elul 29, or the feast of trumpets. A greater crash came 7 years later on September 29, 2008. This was also on Elul 29 of the Hebrew calendar, the feast of trumpets. In 2015, Elul 29 and the feast of trumpets fell on September 13, 2015. Nothing spectacular happened, but as a watcher who understands we are in the final days, I reason, analyze, and research why this day came and went. I'll get to that in a moment.

The crash in 1973, which was a Shemitah year, followed the Supreme Court ruling that allowed citizens under our law to kill their unborn. This was Roe vs Wade. In the summer of 2015, our highest court in the U.S. made law that same sex marriage was okay, despite what God has ordained. Will our lands continue to prosper much longer? …. Not a chance! Two weeks before the last blood red moon of the 2014-15 tetrad, there was a partial solar eclipse of the feast of trumpets. The last time this happened it was Black Monday.

The U.S. replaced London in 1917, becoming the commerce center of the nations. This was a Shemitah year. The twin towers, a symbol of U.S. financial dominance, were conceived in 1945, a Shemitah year. Their construction began in 1966 and were completed in 1973, both Shemitah years. They fell at the end of a Shemitah year on September 11, 2001, showing the United States financial demise. Six days later was the now infamous Elul 29, the feast of trumpets; and on that day was the greatest stock market point loss up to that time.

Babylon the Great will replace what the U.S.A. has been by becoming the commerce center of the Seven Year Tribulation. What we read from Revelation 16:17-21 and 18:1-24 is that this great commerce city will be destroyed within days before the Second Coming. It seems likely that judgment will come to Babylon the Great, a literal city rebuilt out of the ashes of the original Babylon, at the end of another Shemitah year. I believe that the shift of global financial power will be completely gone from the U.S. with the shifting and shaking of mountains and islands from the greatest earthquake up to that time, as seen from Revelation 6:12-17.

What will happen to North America if the San Andreas and New Madrid fault lines go off from that soon future earthquake, or the big one at the beginning of the 70th Week? The U.S. will be crippled. Google "Future U.S. Navy map" to see possible outcome of an earth shaking earthquake as described in the beginning of the future Tribulation (Rev. 6:12-17). It's clear from Daniel 2; 7; 8; 11; Revelation 13; and 17 that the other side of the planet still exists, yet 1/3 of our planet is in great peril. America's side of the planet makes up 1/3 of the land mass of earth. Why is America not referred to in any way in future prophecy? Just speculating, the U.S. Might not exist soon.

> And I beheld when he had opened the sixth seal, and, lo, there was a great earthquake; and the sun became black as sackcloth of hair, and the moon became as blood; And the stars of heaven fell unto the earth, even as a fig tree casteth her untimely figs, when she is shaken of a mighty wind. And the heaven departed as a scroll when it is rolled together; and every mountain and island were moved out of their places (Rev. 6:12-14).

Jubilee Years (a year of restoration)

The year at the end of seven cycles of shmita (Sabbatical years), and according to Biblical regulations had a special impact on the ownership and management of land in the land of Israel; there is some debate whether it was the 49th year (the last year of seven sabbatical cycles, referred to as the Sabbath's Sabbath), or whether it was the following (50th) year. Jubilee refers largely with land, property, and property rights. According to Leviticus, slaves and prisoners would be freed, debts would be forgiven, and the mercies of God would be particularly manifest.

> And thou shalt number seven sabbaths of years unto thee, seven times seven years; and the space of the seven sabbaths of years shall be unto thee forty and nine years. Then shalt thou cause the trumpet of the jubile to sound on the tenth day of the seventh month, in the day of atonement shall ye make the trumpet sound throughout all your land. And ye shall hallow the fiftieth year, and proclaim liberty throughout all the land unto all the inhabitants thereof: it shall be a jubile unto you; and ye shall return every man unto his possession, and ye shall return every man unto his family. A jubile shall that fiftieth year be unto you: ye shall not sow, neither reap that which groweth of itself in it, nor gather the grapes in it of thy vine undressed. For it is the jubile; it shall be holy unto you: ye shall eat the increase thereof out of the field. In the year of this jubile ye shall return every man unto his possession (Lev. 25:8-13).

As stated above, there is debate on what ushers in a Jubilee year. Is it the 49th or 50th year? Do we start the Shavuot cycles (a period of 7 years) after the 50th year, or Year of Jubilee? Do we only have a series of 7 year cycles so that the Jubilee year actually overlaps the 1st year of the next Shavuot cycle? The answer according to rabbi and New York Times Best seller author, Jonathan Cahn, is that a Jubilee year always follows the Shemitah of the 7th Shavout and overlaps the first year of the next Shavuot period. The chart I made for the beginning of this chapter will help.

It seems we can know the Shemitah based on the patterns God has been giving us for 100 years. Is it possible to know when the 7th Shemitah is so we can know when the Year of Jubilee is? September 1916 – September 1917 was a Shemitah year. The year after that has proof given to be a Jubilee year. In November 1917, the "Balfour Declaration" was incorporated into both the Sèvres peace treaty with the Ottoman Empire, and the Mandate for Palestine.

In short, the Balfour Declaration confirmed support from the British government for the establishment in Palestine of a "national home" for the Jewish people. This was a restoration of hope and a home for the Jewish people. Israel officially became a state in 1948, right before a biblical tetrad of four back to back total lunar eclipses, being four blood moons on the first and last feast of the Lord from Leviticus 23 for two consecutive years. (Passover 1949, Tabernacles 1949, Passover 1950, Tabernacles 1950).

If September 1917 – September 1918 was a Jubilee year, then the next Jubilee year should be directly after the Shemitah year of the 7th Shavuot after 1918. So we count 49 years and find that September 1966 – September 1967 is the next Jubilee. What happened in that parameter? The holy city of Jerusalem was recaptured by Israel in June of 1967. This was prophesied to happen, because we know in Daniel's 70th Week, or the 7 Year Tribulation, that Israel has a temple again in Jerusalem and are even making sacrifices up until the midpoint of the 7 years (Dan. 8:13-14; 9:24-27; 12:13; Mat. 24:15; 2 Thess. 2:4, 7-8).

The capital of Israel was restored! This was a Jubilee year. Lets not forget that this was accompanied with a biblical tetrad (Passover 1967, Tabernacles 1967, Passover 1968, Tabernacles 1968).

The next Jubilee year would have fallen in the year of September 2015 – September 2016. Prophetically, the temple is the next thing that will be restored to the Jewish people. Prophetically, this will happen during the first year of Daniel's 70th Week, or the 7 Year Tribulation. As I write this, it is four weeks until this assumed year of Jubilee ends. My hope is that feast of trumpets, 2016 will bring the rapture at the last moment of the Jubilee year. Perhaps, since this is considered a super Shemitah, the rapture will occur this year. This event will emphatically bring a financial collapse. This would make the official Shavuot of Daniel's 70th Week be from 2016 – 2023.

This doesn't fit the pattern we've seen from the last century, but we've never had a global rapture before, now have we? We hope, we pray, and we live as if that day could be at any time (Lk. 21:36; 1 Thess. 4:13 – 1 Thess. 5:23). Financial experts and YouTube videos are warning of a September 27, 2016 financial collapse. You reading this will know if that happened, but these are things a watcher will watch for. The timing of fall, days before Elul 29, or the feast of trumpets, makes this an eye-catching piece of news.

The Jewish Temple Institute has just announced that they could be ready to begin sacrifices within a week if the political climate is right. They have nominated a high priest. It would only take a week to construct a temporary structure suitable to sacrifice to God in their holy place. Millions vanishing would create such a political shift in the Middle East as to pave the way to allow them to take control of the temple mount by way of being protected by the Antichrist and his 7 year treaty. These are things a watcher will look for and analyze.

Chapter 13

HOW TO BE READY

Is Jesus coming soon to gather the spotless church in the event called the rapture? As you have read thus far in the Millions Vanished series, you can clearly see this is not a true question. That Jesus is coming soon for the righteous and ending this phase in His plan for man is an absolute statement of fact. The only question that matters at this moment in time is, "Are you ready?"

This isn't a complicated question at all. What I mean is are you spiritually ready? Have you confessed to God that you are a sinner and need Jesus to take away your sin. Seven years of food supplies and a bunker is secondary. If I could have a 3,000 square foot bunker, I sure would. I do in fact have a year of food storage for my family in case great catastrophes occur between now and the rapture. This is wisdom, but many are those doomsday preppers who are preparing in an effort to extend their physical life with absolutely no preparation for their eternal existence.

Where there is no Jesus, there is no life (Jn. 14:6; 1 Jn. 5:20; 2 Jn. 9). If you live in a bunker with sin held against you, because you have not put your faith in Jesus and repented from all past sin, then you are spiritually dead. If you physically die in that bunker, then you will be eternally away from the source of life, who is Jesus. The eternal existence of the condemned is called eternal death, not because you cease to exist, but because you eternally exist while forever being separated from the Life source. The only place God created for those who rebel against Him is hell. If you physically die from any means causing physical death, though you be in Christ, then you always live. Now, are you ready?

The conditions for being raptured are the same for going to heaven when you die. You must be "IN CHRIST." If you were left behind, you can still be part of the Tribulation Revival (Rev. 6:8-11; 7:9-17; 13:7, 15-18; 15:2-4; 17:6; 20:4; Mat. 24:9-13, 22; Dan. 7:21-27; 8:24; 9:27; 12:7), instead of being part of the apostasy (2 Thess. 2:1-3, 8-12; Rev. 6:12-17; 9:20-21; 16:8-11).

1. Basic Salvation Knowledge

I need to share some basics and I'd like you to humor me for a moment and read five short paragraphs of some basic salvation knowledge. Sometimes it's hard to hear the implications of what someone says when they teach something we already know. Zoning out is the result. Day dreams kill the time while the teacher is speaking to the people that only heard about Jesus last week. When we believe we already know, then we will not be able to learn what we didn't know we didn't know. I ask for your complete attention and then we can find out how the ones left behind can be ready. We will even find out if suicide is a faster road to get to heaven and escape the things coming on the face of the earth.

Man is a created being, made in the likeness and image of God; however, through the transgression of one man, Adam, sin entered into the world. Death did not come by personal sin, as it did in the case of Adam. Death passed upon all people because of Adam's sin (Gen. 2:17). Wherefore, as by one man sin entered into the world, and death by sin; and so death passed upon all men, for that all have sinned (Rom. 3:23; 5:12-21).

Therefore, all men are born under sin and in the need of a Savior. The unbelieving and sinners shall have their part in the lake of fire, which is the second death that endures forever in a very conscious state (Rev. 21:8)... You MUST believe that Jesus is the Son of God AND follow Him (Jn. 3:16, 36; 5:24, 29; Rev. 14:12; 22:14-15). No sinner escapes the spiritual death penalty unless he repents to be forgiven by God (Mk. 16:15; Lk. 13:1-5; 1 Jn. 1:9). Death was the penalty for original sin under grace as it always was under law (Rom. 1:29 – Rom. 2:11; 6:14-23; 8:12-13; Gal. 4:19-21).

When a person sins, he immediately incurs the penalty of the broken law, and sincere repentance and forgiveness are necessary to avoid the penalty. There is no forgiveness without repentance and putting the sin away by faith in the blood of Jesus. Every time one commits a death penalty sin it will have the same effect on him. This is why Ezekiel was told to warn the wicked to meet the conditions of grace, or they would be lost in eternal hell (Ezek. 3:17-21; 18:1-32; 33:1-20).

Many believe our salvation is based only upon the person of the Lord Jesus Christ, in that everything about Christianity lives and dies on the person, not the teachings, morals, or example of Christ. Everyone who makes a Christian profession ought to walk as Christ did (1 Jn. 2:3-6; 3:1-10; 4:17; 1 Pt. 2:21). You can't be "in sin" and "in Christ" at the same time, and there is no sin on the narrow road (Mat. 7:13-23; Lk. 13:24-27).

Only a follower (doer) of the Word has assurance of salvation, since only those who endure until the end will be saved (Jas. 1:22-25; 1 Cor. 6:9-11; Mat. 10:22). To be eternally saved, one must keep His commandments (Mat. 19:17), not merely start keeping them, but continue. "He that saith, I know Him, and keepth not His commandments, is a liar and the truth is not in him (1 Jn. 2:4-5)."

2. Can The Left Behind Still Be Saved?

The constant question of whether or not a person can be saved during the 7 Year Tribulation has been a topic of confusion based primarily on the confusion of who is taken out of the way before the Antichrist is revealed (2 Thess. 2:1-8). It is obvious that there are going to be Christians during the Tribulation based solely on the amount of martyrs from this time period who were killed for the Word of God and for the testimony which they held; those who will wash their robes, and make them white in the blood of the Lamb (Rev. 6:8-11; 7:9-17; 13:7, 15-18; 15:2-4; 17:6; 20:4; Mat. 24:9-13, 22; Dan. 7:21-27; 8:24; 9:27; 12:7). "Here is the patience of the saints: here are they that keep the commandments of God, and the faith of Jesus (Rev. 14:12)." The church will be gone, but saints are those who follow Christ, therefore, Christians.

The 144,000 Jews will be saved and they are every bit as much human being as you are (Rev. 7:1-8; 9:4; 14:1-5). It would also be otherwise pointless and worthless for God to send an angel to preach the everlasting gospel to them that dwell on the earth, and to every nation, and kindred, and tongue, and people, Saying with a loud voice, Fear God, and give glory to him; for the hour of his judgment is come: and worship him that made heaven, and earth, and the sea, and the fountains of waters (Rev. 14:6-7).

You can't be saved without the Holy Spirit and He will never be taken from the world, for Jesus promised that He would abide with us forever (Jn. 14:16). In Acts 2:16-21; Zechariah 12:10 – Zechariah 13:1; Matthew 24:14; Revelation 7:14; 19:10 and other scriptures we have much proof that the Holy Spirit will still be here throughout the Tribulation and the reign of Antichrist. Therefore, He could not be the hinderer of lawlessness that will be taken out of the way.

But this is that which was spoken by the prophet Joel; And it shall come to pass in the last days, saith God, I will pour out of my Spirit upon all flesh: and your sons and your daughters shall prophesy, and your young men shall see visions, and your old men shall dream dreams: And on my servants and on my handmaidens I will pour out in those days of my Spirit; and they shall prophesy: And I will shew wonders in heaven above, and signs in the earth beneath; blood, and fire, and vapour of smoke: The sun hall be turned into darkness, and the moon into blood,before the great and notable day of the Lord come: And it shall come to pass, that whosoever shall call on the name of the Lord shall be saved (Acts 2:16-21).

And ye shall be hated of all men for my name's sake: but he that endureth to the end shall be saved (Mat.10:22).

"The end" from that verse simply means the end of your life. Even if you repent now and die in one second, then you have endured until the end and will be found faithful. Let the words of Paul be echoed from your own heart if you are to be martyred, or killed in a soon coming judgment upon the earth in a mega natural disaster:

For I am now ready to be offered, and the time of my departure is at hand. I have fought a good fight, I have finished my course, I have kept the faith: Henceforth there is laid up for me a crown of righteousness, which the Lord, the righteous judge, shall give me at that day: and not to me only, but unto all them also that love his appearing (2 Tim. 2:6-8).

Jesus' Parable of How to be Justified

Two men went up into the temple to pray; the one a Pharisee, and the other a publican. The Pharisee stood and prayed thus with himself, God, I thank thee, that I am not as other men are, extortioners, unjust, adulterers, or even as this publican. I fast twice in the week, I give tithes of all that I possess. And the publican, standing afar off, would not lift up so much as his eyes unto heaven, but smote upon his breast, saying, God be merciful to me a sinner. I tell you, this man went down to his house justified rather than the other: for every one that exalteth himself shall be abased; and he that humbleth himself shall be exalted (Lk.18:10-14).

3. SUICIDE

Is this a choice that will take you into the presence of God? This study is a preemptive strike against the suicidal spirit and the deceptive lie that suicide will take you out of pain and into the presence of God as a way of escape. Suicide is self murder (1 Cor. 3:16-17; 10:25-29; 1 Jn. 3:14-15), it is obvious sin and the conscience tells you it's wrong (Jn. 8:9; Heb. 9:9; 10:2, 22; 13:18; Acts 23:1; 24:16; 1 Tim. 3:9; 2 Tim. 1:3; 1 Cor. 8:7, 12-13; Titus 1:15; Rom. 2:12-15; 9:1; 2 Cor. 1:12; 1 Tim. 1:5, 19; 4:2; 1 Pet. 2:19; 3:16, 21; Mat. 27:3).

Anything you know to be wrong is sin when you do it (Jas. 1:13-16; 4:17). Sin, contrary to popular teaching, always condemns one's soul (Gen. 2:17; Ex. 32:32-33; Lev. 18:24-30; 26:13-39; Num. 25:1-8; Deut. 4:23-31; Josh. 7:10-12; Judges 2:1-23; 1 Kings 14:22; 2 Kings 17:1-17; 2 Chr. 36; Isa. 5:24-25; Jer. 2:5-37; Lam. 1:8-9; Ezek. 13:1-23; Heb. 12:28-29; Ps. 69:28; Rev. 3:5; Mat. 7:21; 1 Jn. 4:8, 12, 16, 21; Gal. 1:6-8; Mk. 11:25-26; 1 Cor. 3:16-17; Lk. 8:13; Jn. 6:66; 2 Cor. 5:17; Rom. 11:16; Acts 1:20, 25; Col. 2:8-19; Jude 12-13; 2 Tim. 3:8; Titus 1:16; Phil. 3:7-14; 1 Thess. 3:8; Jas. 5:19-20; & 2 Pet. 1:4-10). Is all suicide sin? YES!

Suicide is not picking up your cross and following Jesus until the end to endure life and be saved by remaining in Christ... Abiding, continuing, enduring (Mat. 10:22, 38-39; Jn. 15:1-6; 2 Jn. 9). "Whosoever will come after me, let him deny himself, and take up his cross, and follow me." The gospel benefits are solely on the basis of personal choice and meeting certain conditions (Jn. 3:16; 1 Tim. 2:4; 2 Pet. 3:9; Rev. 22:17). The main condition is following Jesus

How To Be Ready

habitually, regardless of the price, even to death (Mk. 8:35), not just when it is easy, convenient, and popular (Lk. 9:62; Heb. 10:38-39). Would Jesus ever lead you to kill yourself?

This is the last of four things one must do to be saved after being born again: Continue being willing to follow Jesus (Mk. 8:34; Jn. 7:17; 12:26); Deny himself daily; renounce all self-dependence, self-interests, and self-pursuits which are contrary to God (Mk. 8:34; Rom. 6:16-23; 8:1-13; Gal. 5:19-24; Col. 3:1-10); Take up the cross daily (Mk. 8:34; Lk. 9:23; Rom. 6:11-13; 8:12-13; Col. 1:23; 2:6-7; 3:5-10); and Follow Christ daily, not for a while (Jn. 10:26-28).

Those, even with the Holy Spirit, will be destroyed by God when they destroy themselves (Lk. 12:5; 1 Cor. 3:16-17). "Know ye not that ye are the temple of God, and that the Spirit of God dwelleth in you? If any man DEFILE the temple of God, him shall God DESTROY; for the temple of God is holy, which temple ye are" (1 Cor. 3:16-17). Believers are the temple of God for the indwelling of the Holy Spirit. [defile] Greek: phtheiro (GSN-<G5351>), to corrupt, spoil, ruin, waste, destroy. Translated "destroy" in this same verse; and "to corrupt" (1 Cor. 15:33; 2 Cor. 7:2; 11:3; Rev. 19:2; Jude 1:10; Eph. 4:22). This (1 Cor. 3:17) is a solemn warning against sexual sin, alcoholic drinks, tobacco, narcotics, etc. which destroy the body. 2 Corinthians 7:1 says, "Having therefore THESE PROMISES, dearly beloved, let us cleanse ourselves from all filthiness of the flesh and spirit, perfecting holiness in the fear of God." (these promises) The promises of 2 Corinthians 6:16-18.

"Let us cleanse ourselves from all filthiness of the flesh and spirit, perfecting holiness in the fear of God" (2 Cor. 7:1). Six conditions of the promises are: Be not unequally yoked with unbelievers (2 Cor. 6:14-16). Come out from among them (2 Cor. 6:17). Be separate from them (2 Cor. 6:17). Touch not the unclean thing (2 Cor. 6:17). Cleanse self of all filthiness of the flesh and spirit (2 Cor. 7:1; Mk. 7:19-21; Rom. 1:18-32; 1 Cor. 6:9-11; Gal. 5:19-21; Col. 3:5-10). Perfect holiness in the fear of God (2 Cor. 7:1; Eph. 1:4; 4:24; Gal.

5:24; Rom. 6:14-23; 8:1-13; Heb. 12:12-15). Choosing death over Life (Jesus is Life), is not perfecting holiness in the fear of God.

Why say this? Let the dead bury the dead. If you want life, follow Jesus. In other words, it's too late for the dead. Let no one be deceived. Suicides do not find peace. Follow Him in the race, or fight from His corner. Be an OVERCOMER! To him that overcometh will Jesus give many blessings. Only the overcomer is promised heaven (Rev. 2:7, 11, 17, 26; 3:5, 12, 21). He that overcometh shall not be hurt of the second death, because they have chosen to remain in Life. Again the promise of eternal life is only for the overcomer (Rev. 2:7, 11).

Here are the many motivators for remaining in Christ (in Life), and not killing yourself as one who has been over come, instead of being one who does over come: The tree of life (Rev. 2:7); The crown of life (Rev. 2:10; Rev. 3:11); Escape the second death or lake of fire (Rev. 2:11; Rev. 20:14); The hidden manna (Rev. 2:17); A white stone and a new name (Rev. 2:17); Part in the rapture (Rev. 2:25; Rev. 3:11; 1 Thes. 4:16; Phil. 3:21; Col. 3:4; 1 Cor. 15:23,51-58); Power over the nations (Rev. 2:26-27); Complete defeat of rebels (Rev. 2:27); The Morning Star (Rev. 2:28); Walk with Christ in white (Rev. 3:4-5); Name eternally in the book of life (Rev. 3:5; Rev. 22:18-19); Confession of name before God (Rev. 3:5); A pillar in God's temple (Rev. 3:12); Eternal abiding with God (Rev. 3:12); God's name upon him (Rev. 3:12); Name of the New Jerusalem upon him (Rev. 3:12); New name of Christ upon him (Rev. 3:12); and Eternal throne and kingdom (Rev. 3:21; Rev. 1:6; Rev. 5:10; Rev. 11:15; Rev. 22:4-5).

All in hell would warn against their own mistakes instead of defending and justifying their actions (Lk. 16:19-31). So why are we more worried about offending the living when the living are the only ones we can help? The dead, whether in hell or heaven, would want the truth to be taught and proclaimed!

How To Be Ready

Be not deceived; God is not mocked: for whatsoever a man soweth, that shall he also reap. For he that soweth to his flesh shall of the flesh reap corruption; but he that soweth to the Spirit shall of the Spirit reap life everlasting (Gal. 6:7-8).

Suicide is not sowing to the Spirit. Choosing death instead of life is never the will of God. God is life. Jesus is life (Jn. 14:6). Jesus is eternal life (1 Jn. 5:20). He gave you life and you have no right or authority to take it. How can you expect to be with Jesus, who both gives and is eternal life, if you take your life? Do you receive life eternal for ending your life by choosing death? No, no you don't.

You don't own your life. "What? know ye not that your body is the temple of the Holy Ghost which is in you, which ye have of God, and ye are not your own? For ye are bought with a price: therefore glorify God in your body, and in your spirit, which are God's" (1 Cor. 6:19-20). You cannot take your life by killing yourself, because it is not yours to take. Can you fornicate because your body is yours? Can you get drunk because your body is yours to do with what you will? Can you think any thoughts you want because it is your brain, or your mind? You know you can do what you will, but there are consequences from God. Your life is not your own (1 Cor. 6:19-20).

Some justify sexual sin by claiming it hurts no one. The following passage of 1 Corinthians 6:16-20 shows that fornication is a sin against yourself, which is damning.

> What? know ye not that he which is joined to an harlot is one body? for two, saith he, shall be one flesh. But he that is joined unto the Lord is one spirit. Flee fornication. Every sin that a man doeth is without the body; but he that committeth fornication sinneth against his own body. What? know ye not that your body is the temple of the Holy Ghost which is in you, which ye have of God, and ye are not your own? For ye are bought with a price: therefore glorify God in your body, and in your spirit, which are God's (1 Cor. 6:16-20).

What then is self murder? Can it be claimed that it is not hurting anyone? No, your body is not your own and it is a sin against yourself. God gave you life. If you take your life that is a gift to be used for God, and then expect a better life in return, then you are being deceived and will be cast into hell. Death you want and death you shall eternally receive. What you sow is what you will reap (Gal. 6:7-8; Rom. 8:12-13; Jas. 1:13-16).

The Apostle Paul said, "It would be better for me to die than that any man make my glory void" (1 Cor. 9:15). There is no intention or connotation of being about taking his own life as one man claimed who wrote to me. As a matter of fact he goes on to say in the next couple of breathes one of the greatest passages one could read concerning endurance till the end, and the result of not enduring until the end.

> Know ye not that they which run in a race run all, but one receiveth the prize? So run, that ye may obtain. And every man that striveth for the mastery is temperate in all things. Now they do it to obtain a corruptible crown; but we an incorruptible. I therefore so run, not as uncertainly; so fight I, not as one that beateth the air: But I keep under my body, and bring it into subjection: lest that by any means, when I have preached to others, I myself should be a castaway (1 Cor. 9:24-27).

If you are in a race and do not finish, then you will be a castaway, a reprobate, rejected.... Forfeiting the prize. Those who endure until the end will be saved (Mat.10:22). The race is set, but not by us. We don't know how long our race is. If anyone started a race and decided to stop at some point, could they say they finished their race? NO, not unless they endure and cross the finish line. God and eternal life are at the finish line. Death awaits for those who drop out or decide to finish their race premature.

> Wherefore seeing we also are compassed about with so great a cloud of witnesses, let us lay aside every weight, and the sin

which doth so easily beset us, and let us run with patience the race that is set before us, Looking unto Jesus the author and finisher of our faith; who for the joy that was set before him endured the cross, despising the shame, and is set down at the right hand of the throne of God. For consider him that endured such contradiction of sinners against himself, lest ye be wearied and faint in your minds. Ye have not yet resisted unto blood, striving against sin. And ye have forgotten the exhortation which speaketh unto you as unto children, My son, despise not thou the chastening of the Lord, nor faint when thou art rebuked of him: For whom the Lord loveth he chasteneth, and scourgeth every son whom he receiveth. If ye endure chastening, God dealeth with you as with sons; for what son is he whom the father chasteneth not? But if ye be without chastisement, whereof all are partakers, then are ye bastards, and not sons (Hebrews 12:1-8).

Paul showed how He followed Jesus (Eph. 5:1) when he penned these words at the end of his life: "I have fought a good fight, I have finished my course, I have kept the faith: Henceforth there is laid up for me a crown of righteousness, which the Lord, the righteous judge, shall give me at that day: and not to me only, but unto all them also that love his appearing" (2 Tim. 4:7-8). Paul finished his course and kept the faith. Could that be said of a suicide? Because of his endurance till the end, Paul will receive a crown of righteousness.

Is it sin or righteous to witness to people who you know will kill you for professing Jesus? What if you move to the Middle East to be a missionary in an ISIS infested land? A mother knows she will die by giving birth, but does not end the child's life anyway. She gives her life for the child to live. A soldier jumps on a grenade to save others, knowing he would be killing himself. Jesus died so those who come to Him will live if they abide and endure.

The "devils advocate" rationale can't even say any of those examples were suicides. None of them wanted to die. They did so out of love to save others. Suicide is not giving your life in order to save others. Suicide has been proven to be sin, but will one unrepented sin cause you to lose your salvation? What if you have a moment to repent and plan your death this way? Will God honor such lip service? Are we to gamble with our eternal salvation when it came at such a high price?

One sin is sufficient to damn a soul. One sin cut the whole race off from God: "By one man sin entered into the world.... by one man's offense death reigned. ... by the offense of one, judgment came upon all men to condemnation.... by one man's disobedience many were made (constituted) sinners" (Rom. 5:12-21; Gen. 2:17; 3:1-19). One sin, whether committed before or after a person is saved, will have the same effect that the one original sin had. "When the righteous turneth away from his righteousness, and committeth iniquity ... All his righteousness that he hath done shall not be mentioned ... in the sin that he hath sinned, in them shall he die ... for his iniquity that he hath done shall he die" (Ezek. 18:24-26). Again "The righteousness of the righteous shall not deliver him in the day of his transgression.... for the iniquity that he hath committed, he shall die because of it (Ezek. 33:12-20).

One sin cursed the whole race (Rom. 5:12-21); Cain (Gen. 4:8-13; 1 Jn. 3:12); Pharaoh and Egypt (Ex. 3:2; Rom. 9:15-23); Nadab and Abihu (Lev. 10:1-7); Achan (Josh. 7); Gehazi (2 Ki. 5:20-27); Judas (Acts 1:25); Ananias and Sapphira (Acts 5:1-11); and many others (1 Tim. 1:19, 20; 2:14; 5:11, 12, 15, 20; 6:10; 2 Tim. 2:18, 26; 4:10; Heb. 4:11; 1 Cor. 10:1-18; Jas. 2:10; etc.). One sin caused Lucifer and one third of the angels to fall (Isa. 14:12-14; Ezek. 28:11-17; Rev. 12:3-4). One sin caused many other angels to be confined to hell (2 Pet. 2:4; Jude 6-7).

Suicide is not the way to escape this! Temptation to end your life due to depression is not a valid excuse on Judgment Day.

Temptation will always be the lot of the child of God, but no sin need be committed and no self-condemnation need be indulged in just because of the presence of temptation (Heb. 2:18; 4:14-16; 1 Cor. 10:12-13; 1 Pet. 1:6-7; 4:12; 5:8-9; Jas. 1:2-12; 4:7). There is freedom in Christ, but this freedom is not a freedom to sin. No, this is a freedom from sin. This freedom means we are now free and able to walk in holiness and the bonds and wages of sin are no longer attached to us. We are free from sin and free to walk how Jesus walked, which was righteously. We are not free to sin with no penalty. Jesus will only come as a thief to those who are sleeping, dead in sin, lukewarm, not sober, not enduring on the narrow path, not continuing in holiness, not abiding in sound doctrine, not remaining in Him, not watching.

4. Qualifications for Partakers in the Rapture

The one and only necessary requirement for men, whether they are dead or alive, is to be "in Christ" (1 Thess. 4:16, 17; 2 Cor. 5:17; 1 Cor. 15:23; Gal. 5:24). "For the Lord himself shall descend from heaven with a shout, with the voice of the archangel, and with the trump of God: and the dead <u>in Christ</u> shall rise first: Then we which are alive *and* remain shall be caught up together with them in the clouds, to meet the Lord in the air: and so shall we ever be with the Lord" (1 Thess. 4:16-17). The major point of contention seems to be the definition of being "in Christ." Most are deceived into thinking their profession alone defines them as being in Christ, regardless of sin that may be in their life. "Therefore <u>if any man *be* in Christ, *he is* a new creature: old things are passed away; behold, all things are become new</u>" (2 Cor. 5:17). That was a true case of allowing Scripture to interpret Scripture.

These qualifications are expressed in a nine-fold way in Scripture. One must: Be "Christ's" (1 Cor. 15:23; Gal. 5:24); Be "in Christ" (1 Thess. 4:16, 17; 2 Cor. 5:17); Be "blessed and holy" (Rev.

20:4-6; Heb. 12:14); "Have done good" (Jn. 5:28, 29); Be in "the way, the truth, and the life" (Jn. 14:1-6); Be "worthy" (Lk. 21:34-36); Be in "the church" or "body of Christ" (Eph. 5:27; 1 Cor. 12:13). The body of Christ and the church are the same (Eph. 1:22, 23; Col. 1:18, 24); Purify "himself, even as he is pure" (l Jn. 1:7; 3:2, 3; 2 Cor. 7:1; Gal. 5:16-26; Heb. 12:14); and Be without spot or wrinkle . . . and without blemish" (Eph. 5:27). The conditions for receiving eternal life at death are also the same it takes to be raptured!

5. Reasons For Being Left Behind

Sin (Rom. 8:12-13; 1 Cor. 6:9-10), unforgiveness (Mat. 6:12-15), producing no fruit (Jn. 15:1-6), hating someone (1 Jn. 3:14-15), denying God (Mat. 10:33), unbelief (Rev. 21:8), and teaching or believing a false doctrine (Jas. 3:1; 2 Tim. 2:15-19; 2 Tim. 3 – 2 Tim. 4; Rev. 22:18-19). There is no sin on the narrow road that goes through the narrow gate into eternal life (Mat. 7:12-27; Lk. 13:24-27; Jn. 5:28-29; Gal. 6:7-8). You can never be in sin and in Christ at the same time. Choose one.

The bottom line is you need to repent and follow Jesus, Who alone is the only way to eternal life. He is eternal life (1 Jn. 5:20). He was killed for our sins, He rose in a glorified body that is immortal and incorruptible, and this is why He will come for those who are spotless, to get the glorious church, which are those who are not living in sin or have any sin accounted to them. For when He appears, so then we who are His children will be like Him; for we shall see him as he is (1 Jn. 3:1-10; Eph. 5:27).

IF YOU DON'T BELIEVE, BECOME A BELIEVER.

IF YOU ARE A BELIEVER, BECOME A FOLLOWER.

IF YOU ARE A FOLLOWER, ABIDE, REMAIN, ENDURE!

CONCLUSION

Despite the Bible's numerous warnings and last day prophecies about what to watch for, many people will be taken off guard when these events culminate (Lk. 21:8-11, 25-36; 1 Thess. 5:2-6; Rev. 6 – Rev. 18). Take heed to yourselves! Do not be blinded by the enemy of your soul so that you cannot see what to watch for, or how to be and stay watchful (Mt. 24:4-5, 11, 24; Lk. 21:8; 1 Cor. 6:9; 15:33; Gal. 6:7; Eph. 5:6; 2 Thess. 2:3).

Jesus will only catch the ones off guard like a thief for those who are sleeping spiritually, dead in sin, lukewarm, not sober, not enduring on the narrow path that's not paved with sin, not continuing in holiness, not abiding in sound doctrine, not remaining in righteousness and truth, not watching. These are the ones who will be caught off guard when the Master comes. In their hearts they have said that their Master has delayed His Coming, so they are not fighting the desires of their flesh. They are not resisting the devil so he will flee. They are not taking their thoughts captive and following the Holy Spirit, because they believe they have time to repent later.

> The lord of that servant shall come in a day when he looketh not for him, and in an hour that he is not aware of, And shall cut him in pieces, and appoint him his portion with the hypocrites: there shall be weeping and gnashing of teeth (Mat. 24:50-51).

People will mock the warning signs of the end of the age saying, "These signs have always been around" (2 Pet. 3:3-4). As all prophecy watchers know, people are willfully blind to all the signs around them at an unprecedented level. It should be no wonder to us. If the cross is foolishness to those who are perishing (1 Cor.1:18), then it stands to reason that the Second Coming of Christ is even more absurd to the lost, which is most the world (Mat. 7:13-14; Lk. 13:23-30). What is disturbing to the watchers is that most professing

Christians also mock the times we live in and even the doctrines that make up the end-times.

You have now been given all the information you need to be a watcher. There is much more to learn and discover, so I challenge you to keep studying these subjects and learn more. Use these studies you've been given on end-time subjects to rightfully divide the Word of Truth. So many time-lines and teachings go very far off course because of a simple error in examining the true meaning of a certain subject. I have much more faith in those of you who have chosen to harmonize all these intriguing subjects God gave us through time, by way of the prophets. You have the keys to make ground breaking discoveries as God allows. You've taken the first steps, now finish the race ahead of you (Heb. 12:1)!

FOR FURTHER CONTACT

The Author: Brian Paul Lakins
Speaking
Questions
Prayer

Website and Contact:
www.MillionsVanished.com
1thes4.16@gmail.com
https://www.facebook.com/millionsvanished/
https://twitter.com/BrianLakins

OTHER BOOKS:
THE MILLIONS VANISHED SERIES
Unveiling Raptures and Resurrections (Part 1)
7 Rapture Views (Part 2)
The Watcher's Guide (Part 3)
Signs of His Coming (Part 4)
Billions Left Behind (Part 5)

THE OBEDIENT CHRISTIAN SERIES
My Road to the Path (Part 1)
Eternal Laws From God and Christian Warnings (Part 2)
Eternal Security's Evidence, Conditional Salvation's Verdict (Part 3)
The Billions Who Lost Salvation From Genesis Through Revelation (Part 4)
Tough Christian Questions, Tough Biblical Answers (Part 5)
The Lost Pillars of Conditional Salvation (Part 6)

ABOUT THE AUTHOR

BRIAN LAKINS was ingrained into the Christian faith as a young child, but the seed that was sown had no root, so the word in him only endured for awhile. When temptation came, there was no fight against his flesh and he was swayed far away from God's path. Had the book of his life been shut in his sins, his portion would have been the lake of fire. In his darkness, the light of God shined on him and he saw the true filth he was wallering in, fell to his knees in horror and repented. After seeking his own ways for many years, the prodigal son returned to Jesus with an authentic passion and a God-given ability to write and speak to Christians and seekers, inspiring them to live holy in an unholy world.

He earned his Biblical Studies degree from Liberty University and is the founder of the *Millions Vanished* movement, which seeks to lead people away from entering the soon coming 7 Year Tribulation and lead the ones who do enter to eternal life by way of this book series, even after we have been taken to heaven. He believes what you leave behind can warn and save the ones left behind with clear biblical warnings and teachings to give the reader faith, hope, and power to live with valor and victory.

Keeping his hand on the pulse of the many modern Christian beliefs, Brian's analytical mind and passion for examining all doctrinal beliefs has molded him to be an expert in addressing relevant topics while anticipating and answering questions derived from all his teachings.

www.ingramcontent.com/pod-product-compliance
Lightning Source LLC
LaVergne TN
LVHW051115080426
835510LV00018B/2048